# HISTORY OF THE KINGS OF BRITAIN

GEOFFREY OF MONMOUTH, also known as Geoffrey Arthur, was born about 1100 A.D., presumably at Monmouth, South Wales, near Caerleon, the supposed site of King Arthur's court. From about 1129 to 1150 Geoffrey was a secular Augustinian canon at St. George's college (in Oxford castle). It was at Oxford that Geoffrey wrote his *History of the Kings of Britain,* about 1138-39. He became Bishop of St. Asaph's in North Wales in 1152, but never actually occupied the diocese. He died in 1155.

Sebastian Evans prepared his translation of the *History* in 1903; it was first published in *Everyman's Library* in 1912.

# HISTORY

## OF THE

# KINGS OF BRITAIN

*By*
**GEOFFREY OF MONMOUTH**

*A Dutton* **dep** *Paperback*

The SEBASTIAN EVANS translation
Revised by Charles W. Dunn

NEW YORK
**E. P. DUTTON & CO., INC.**

SBN 0-525-47014-X

# CONTENTS

*(Refer to first index for page numbers
of individual chapters within each book)*

# INTRODUCTION

I. *The Beginnings of Arthurian Story.*—Arthurian romance is known to us in its best and purest form through the lays and romances that were produced in France during the twelfth and thirteenth centuries. It is a body of pre-eminently imaginative literature, and although it reflects the chivalric life of France at the time in which it was composed, it deals essentially with a world of unreality and mystery, of prowess, beauty, love, and enchantment, where valorous heroes achieve impossible adventures, and messengers from fairyland appear easily and naturally on marvellous errands. A brilliant part of our literary heritage from France, it does not, however, like the *chansons de geste*, the great Carolingian epics, represent French national legend. It is a composite whole, which embodies Oriental stories, bits of classical myth, and above all Celtic tradition—those "idle and pleasant tales of Britain," as they were called by a twelfth-century French poet, Jean Bodel, who justly gave to the Arthurian material the designation that has ever since clung to it, "the matter of Britain." [1] In this material the central name, but not the most prominent figure, is that of Arthur, King of Britain; for Arthur himself in the romances is little more than a *roi fainéant*, who remains in the background, while the true glory of adventure belongs to the knights whose proudest boast it is that they are attached to his court. Never could his name have become so potent, if he had not in earlier tradition been accredited with more valiant deeds than he accomplishes in romance.

It is not in the romances alone, however, that Arthurian story is recorded, and such light as we have upon Arthur's early fame is shed from literature of a different class. The mediæval chronicles are a valuable source for our knowledge of the legend, which although it has but a slender historical

[1] *Chanson des Saisnes* (ed. Michel, Paris, 1839), vs. 6 ff.

basis, rests upon established fact. Nothing apparently could be much further removed from the field of romance than what we are too prone to regard as the arid waste of the chronicles of the middle ages. They are almost wholly monastic compositions, and from the sixth to the sixteenth centuries formed an important part of the productions that emanated from the cloisters of Europe in both Latin and the vernacular. Originally, with some few exceptions, little more than bare annals setting down the events of a given year, they came to assume a more elaborate form, to give greater space to detail, and in their most flourishing period, which extends from the twelfth to the fifteenth century, to show some individuality on the part of the writers. But these were credulous and uncritical centuries, and in general the chronicles accepted and repeated what they found in the works of their predecessors, discriminating little between fact and fiction. Some two hundred of them record Arthurian material,[1] and although they supply us with an interesting branch of Arthurian literature, with the exception of those written by Geoffrey of Monmouth, Wace, and Layamon, they cannot be said to make truly important additions to our knowledge of the cycle.

Geoffrey of Monmouth has been called again and again the father of Arthurian romance, and it is primarily his position as an Arthurian chronicler that will engage our attention here. To appreciate his work, we must know what material he had before him, and where he had found already painted a picture of

"that Kynge Artour,
Of whom the Bretons speken grete honour."

For the alphabet of Arthurian history we turn to a still earlier chronicle than that of Geoffrey. This is the *Historia Britonum* ("History of the Britons"), a brief Latin treatise, of which the authorship and date still remain highly problematic, in spite of the elaborate critical discussion to which it has been subjected.[2] It is, however, generally attributed in its present form

---

[1] The Arthurian material in the chronicles has been collected and discussed by Dr. R. H. Fletcher in *Studies and Notes in Philology and Literature*, X. (Boston, 1906), a work to which I am indebted for many facts given below without specific acknowledgment.

[2] The monumental work on the subject is *Nennius Vindicatus* (Berlin, 1893) by the late H. Zimmer. See, however, for an important bibliography, Fletcher, *Studies and Notes in Philology and Literature*, X., 8, n. 1.

to Nennius, a native of South Wales, who is believed to have amplified and redacted, about the year 826, a compilation of the seventh or eighth century, consisting of extracts from a *Life of St. Germanus* added to a brief *History of Britain* written in 679, into which still other material had been interpolated before Nennius worked it over into the *Historia Britonum* that always passes under his name. The sections that concern us here give an account of the reign of the wicked British king, Vortigern, under whom the Britons lived in continual fear from the incursions of the Picts and Scots, the Romans, and finally the Saxons, who effected a landing in Britain, and being received as friends by the imprudent Vortigern succeeded in making a settlement. After the death of Vortigern, Nennius continues, the Saxons grew strong and multiplied. "Then Arthur, together with the kings of the Britons, fought against them in those days, but he himself was leader of the battles." Here follow the names of twelve battles: "The eighth was at the fortress Guinnion, when Arthur bore the image of the ever-blessed Virgin Mary on his shoulders, and on that day the pagans were put to flight and the slaughter of them was great by virtue of the Lord Jesus Christ, and by virtue of the Holy Virgin Mary, his Mother. . . . The twelfth battle was at Mount Badon, when Arthur in one day slew nine hundred and sixty men in one onslaught; no one laid him low save he alone, and in all the battles he was victor." [1] In the so-called *mirabilia,* a list of natural phenomena of Britain, appended to the *Historia* by Nennius or some earlier redactor, one of the wonders is said to be a stone in the province of Buelt, on which the hound of Arthur, the warrior, had left the print of his foot, when Arthur was hunting the boar Troynt; and if it were removed from the pile of stones which Arthur had heaped up beneath it, on the next day it would reappear in its place. Another of the wonders is the tomb of Anir in Ercing. Anir was the son of Arthur, the warrior, who killed and buried him there, and his tomb never twice measures the same length. [2]

The section of the *Historia Britonum* in which Arthur is mentioned was almost certainly contained in the work before it reached the hands of Nennius. We may, therefore, safely assume that our earliest record of Arthur belongs approximately to an unknown date prior to the ninth century, when

[1] Chap. 56.
[2] Chap. 73.

Nennius made his redaction; and we may accept it as an historic fact that there lived in Britain at the time of the Saxon invasions in the fifth century[1] a valiant warrior, named Arthur, who held a military position of authority,[2] and who led his countrymen in victorious conflict against their Saxon foes. Even before the ninth century a story-loving age had naturally begun to attach legend to his heroic name. No chronicler is recounting sober history when he tells us, as Nennius does, that a warrior slew exactly nine hundred and sixty foes in a single battle, that he hunted a boar, which we know from other sources was enchanted, that he was the owner of a marvellous dog, and evidently the builder of a tomb of magic properties. It has in fact recently been demonstrated that even the battle of Mount Badon is an importation into the authentic list of Arthur's victories, inasmuch as it was really fought two centuries after his time, and that being a famous battle in the Saxon campaign it was worked into the *Historia Britonum* as one of the glories of Arthur's career.[3]

For a hundred and fifty years after Nennius, the chronicles contribute nothing to our knowledge of Arthur. But in the second half of the tenth century, a Welsh anonymous writer compiled a series of brief Latin records, the *Annales Cambriæ* ("Cambrian Annals")[4] in which, under the year 516, he made the following entry:—"Battle of Badon, in which Arthur carried the cross of our Lord Jesus Christ for three days and three nights on his shoulders, and the Britons were victorious." This

[1] The discussion of the chronology of Arthur by A. W. Wade-Evans in *Y Cymmrodor*, XXII. (1910), 125 ff., has shown that Arthur's victories, hitherto placed in the sixth, probably belong to the fifth century.

[2] The title *dux bellorum* (leader of the battles) that Nennius applies to Arthur is believed to refer to a military office established at the time of the Roman occupation of Britain.

[3] For this theory, see Wade-Evans, as above, pp. 132-135. Gildas, a Welsh writer, who was born in the year of the battle of Mount Badon, in his treatise, *De Excidio de Conquestu Britanniæ* (§ 26), says that at Mount Badon occurred the last slaughter of the barbarians, but he leaves Arthur out of the account. Gildas, however, was writing for the express purpose of denouncing his countrymen for their sins, and he intentionally refrains from softening his harsh invectives by any commendation of British leaders. This, it has hitherto been supposed, was the reason for his silence in regard to Arthur, which, if the above chronology for Arthur be correct, is readily accounted for on other grounds.

[4] Ed. J. Williams ab Ithel (Rolls Series), 1860.

is evidently a parallel tradition to that connected by Nennius with the eighth battle of Arthur, transferred here, in no unusual fashion, from the less important conflict at fortress Guinnion to what had come to be regarded as the great and decisive battle of Arthur's career.[1] There is a further note for the year 537: "Battle of Camlann, in which Arthur and Medraut fell." These battles it has been shown, should be dated respectively in the years 492 and 470.[2]

From these scanty records we pass on through another century and a half, receiving no fresh information from the chroniclers as to the story of our hero. But in the beginning of the twelfth century we find among them a man of a somewhat different type to his forerunners, William of Malmesbury, an influential monk of Malmesbury Abbey, ambitious to produce more than a typical monkish chronicle. In 1125 he wrote his *Gesta Regum Anglorum* ("Exploits of the English Kings"), in which he followed his precursors closely so far as possible, adopting where their versions were inconsistent an eclectic method, presenting their facts with a certain elegance of style, and enlivening his narrative with popular tales and songs. In his account of the Saxon conquest, one paragraph is important for our purpose. Here he tells us that when the strength of the Britons was growing weaker after the death of Vortigern's son, the barbarian foes were hard pressed by Ambrosius, a Roman general, aided by the warlike Arthur. "He is the Arthur about whom the Britons rave in empty words, but who, in truth, is worthy to be the subject, not of deceitful tales and dreams, but of true history; for he was long the prop of his tottering fatherland, and spurred the broken spirits of his countrymen on to war; and finally at the siege of Mount Badon, trusting in

[1] There is a legend, recorded first in a thirteenth-century manuscript of Nennius, that Arthur visited Jerusalem, and there made a copy of the true cross, by which he prayed our Lord that He would grant him victory. He also took with him from Jerusalem an image of the Blessed Virgin. The writer of the *Annales Cambriæ* probably knew this legend, which has come down to us in a source two hundred and fifty years later than he, and confused it purposely or unwittingly, with the story that Nennius gives. The original tradition undoubtedly related that Arthur bore the figure of the Virgin, or of the cross, on his shield; and the statement in Nennius that he bore it on his shoulders, which must be a Welsh tradition, is due to a confusion between the Welsh words for "shield" (*ysgwyd*) and "shoulder" (*ysgwydd*). See Fletcher, *Studies and Notes*, X., 32-34.

[2] See Wade-Evans as above, pp. 126, 131, 132.

the image of the Mother of God, which he had fastened on his armour, he alone routed nine hundred of the enemy with incredible bloodshed." [1]

We are so fortunate as to possess a clue to these empty tales and foolish dreams of the raving Britons. While sober annals and serious chronicles were silent, tradition was awake and gathering irresistibly about the name of the valiant leader of an oppressed people. "Britons loved him greatly," says Layamon, "and oft . . . say many things respecting Arthur . . . that never were transacted in this world's realm." As early as 1090 the stories of Arthur had attained sufficient importance to reach the distant shores of Italy, where they had become so popular that Arthur's name, in forms derived from the French *Artus*, was given to children in baptism;[2] and during the first decade of the twelfth century a scene from Arthurian story, not yet identified, was made the subject of a carving on the archivolt of the north-east portal of the cathedral at Modena.[3] Even more significant of the hold that Arthur had on the affections of his people is the account written about the year 1146, describing a journey that some monks from Laon in Brittany made to England in 1113. The men of Devon pointed out to them among the rocks of their coast "the chair and the oven of that King Arthur renowned in the stories of the Britons;" and when in the church at Bodmin in Cornwall, one of their servants dared question the statement of a certain Cornish man that Arthur still lived, he received a blow for his temerity, and speedily became the centre of a small riot, which was quelled with difficulty in spite of the restraints of the sanctuary.[4] It is clear, then, that before the time of Geoffrey, the legend had assumed real importance, and that by the year 1113 Arthur occupied a place among the heroes of saga, whose return to earth was earnestly believed in by those who cherished their memory. The "hope of Britain" (*l'esperance de Bretaigne*), as

[1] Ed. Stubbs (Rolls Series), 1887-1889, p. 11.

[2] For an interesting and valuable discussion of the early occurrence of Arthurian proper names in Italy, see P. Rajna, *Romania*, XVIII., 161, 355; see especially p. 169.

[3] This relief has been described and discussed by W. Förster, *Zeitschrift für romanische Philologie*, XXII., 243 ff., 527 ff. See also for a reproduction and discussion, Venturi, *Storia dell 'arte Italiana*, III., 161 ff.

[4] For a complete account of this incident, see Zimmer, *Zeitschrift für französische Sprache und Literatur*, XIII., 106 ff.

it is called, was no lightly held tradition. No taunt at a vague expectation would have stirred a quarrel within the sacred precincts of a Cornish church; it was a deeply rooted belief, we may be sure, among the Britons of this time, that death could not forever withhold the brave leader from his vanquished fellow-countrymen, and that Arthur would surely come back to them.

Very scanty information of the Arthur of Welsh tradition before the twelfth century has reached us. Practically our only reliable picture of him is in *Culhwch and Olwen,* one of the tales contained in the *Red Book of Hergest,* a Welsh manuscript belonging to the first half of the fourteenth century, which, under the title *Mabinogion,* has been translated into English with great distinction by Lady Charlotte Guest. While five of these stories are connected with the Arthurian cycle, only two of the five, *Culhwch and Olwen* and the *Dream of Rhonabwy* are uncontaminated by the French and English romances, and show what we may regard as pure Welsh tradition, and even this in the latter is not untinged by Irish influence. Of these two tales the former is the more distinctly primitive in character, and gives the more recognisably early conception of Arthur. The exact date of composition is uncertain, but whatever it be, the present form bears indications of a fairly long growth of legend about an archaic original.

The story represents Arthur as the mighty King of Britain, surrounded by an enormous following of warriors. To his hall none may gain entrance but "the son of a king of a privileged country, or a craftsman bringing his craft;" yet he deems it an honour to be resorted to by those who crave a boon from him, for, as he instructs his followers, "the greater our courtesy, the greater will be our renown, and our fame, and our glory." He is the fortunate owner of many magic belongings, and the lord of chieftains endowed with marvellous attributes. One of his followers, by standing on the highest mountain in the world can make it a plain beneath his feet; another can suck dry the sea on which are three hundred ships—"he was broad-chested;" still another can spread his red, untrimmed beard over the eight and forty rafters of Arthur's hall. With the aid of such gifted champions as these Arthur performs for his young cousin, Culhwch, certain difficult adventures, the achievement of which is the price set upon the hand of the beautiful maiden, Olwen, Culhwch's love. Wild adventures, too, they are, the quest of enchanted objects that lead the adventurer into other-world perils—the capture of the shape-shifting cubs of a she-wolf, the pursuit of a wild man, the great hunt of the ferocious magic boar Trwyth, the search for the blood of a witch. No sooner is one adventure accomplished than the king is ready for the next. "Which of the marvels will it be best for us to seek now?" is his eager question as soon as each exploit is ended. He is essentially a mighty prince, not of historic Britain, but of a fairy world, the undaunted performer, not of the deeds of knight-errantry, but of supernatural adventures. Plainly the primitive traditions that are characteristic of Wales and her early mythology[1] have become connected with the British hero, whose victories in war Nennius recorded.

Of this, then, we may feel assured:—that before the beginning of the twelfth century to the name of the historic Arthur, the successful British leader, there had already become attached much legendary and even mythological material, that his people cherished an exalted memory of his valour, and wistfully looked for his return to earth. Such was the general attitude of the Britons toward Arthur at the time when his story began to occupy the attention of Geoffrey of Monmouth.

II. *Geoffrey of Monmouth.*—To all students of Geoffrey of Monmouth's great work, the *Historia Regum Britanniæ* ("History of the Kings of Britain"), he becomes a vivid personality, yet about his life we have scanty information. Even of the date of his birth we know nothing more definite than that it was sufficiently long before 1129 for him to be able to sign his name in that year as witness to the foundation charter of Osney Abbey. He was a Welshman, and he gave himself the title *Monumetensis* ("of Monmouth"), but whether because Monmouth was his birthplace, or because he was educated at the Benedictine monastery there, we cannot determine. Of his parents we may say only that his father appears to have been named Arthur. Geoffrey was appointed archdeacon of Llandaff probably in 1140, when his uncle Uchtryd, who had been archdeacon, was made bishop. It looks as if his life as an ecclesiastic were not of vital moment to Geoffrey, for he postponed his ordination to the priesthood until a few days before he was

[1] For the theory that Arthur was originally a Celtic divinity, see J. Rhŷs, *Arthurian Legend,* pp. 23, 25-38.

consecrated in 1152, as bishop of the small and impecunious see of St. Asaph, which he had never visited at the time of his death, three years later, at Llandaff.

Whether the priesthood was dear to Geoffrey's heart or not, there is no question that he had long coveted preferment in the church, which came to him so late and in so insignificant a form. A little less than twenty years earlier he had taken steps to win the favour of patrons who might advance him, and though ecclesiastical dignity tarried, he did not fail in acquiring fame. Geoffrey, in fact, was a person well fitted to make life a successful enterprise. He had an eye for the main chance, and knew how to take the tide in his affairs at the flood. He lived at a period when England was responding to the intellectual stimulus that had come to her with the Norman conquest, and when her literary life, which had been lying dormant, had begun to blossom afresh under the influence of the scholars, the chroniclers, and the minstrels brought by the Normans across the Channel. Henry I., whose reign began almost contemporaneously with Geoffrey's life, in the midst of his active administration of the affairs of the realm, did not fail to show his appreciation of letters, and surrounded himself with a gay and song-loving court, where storytellers and poets were welcome guests. The Normans after their half-century's occupation of England were beginning to take a keen interest in the past history of their newly-acquired domain, and to turn with zest to the traditions of early Britain. But the taste of the Norman noble demanded something less mysterious, less fantastic, and less remote from his own world than Celtic myth afforded him, and also something more polished and entertaining than the bare chronicles at his disposal. Latin was still the recognised vehicle for serious literary productions, and ecclesiastics as well as nobles were the patrons of letters. Geoffrey had a peculiarly facile nature, an eager intelligence, and a distinctly inventive turn of mind; he was a student, an accomplished Latin scholar, and the master of a finished Latin style. Quickly he perceived the trend of men's thoughts, and saw an opportunity of winning distinction for himself, while catering to the taste of the time.

About the year 1135, probably with the scheme of a greater work already in mind, he put out a "feeler" in the shape of a brief Latin tract, known as the *Libellus Merlini* ("Little Book of Merlin"), in which he introduced to his readers a mysterious youth, the son of a princess of South Wales and her other-world lover, gifted with prophetic power, and called *Merlinus* (Merlin), the Latinised form of the Welsh name *Myrddin*, already known as that of a famous Welsh bard and prophet of the sixth century. Geoffrey's book purported to be a translation from the "British tongue" into Latin, and contained a series of prophecies relating chiefly to the Saxon wars, delivered to Vortigern by Merlin; to these Geoffrey prefixed as introduction the story of a supernatural boy, Ambrosius, and his experiences with Vortigern, which he had found in Nennius,[1] but which he expanded and transferred bodily from its original hero, Ambrosius, to Merlin, happily avoiding the complication that the different names of the youths might cause by the simple expedient of saying that Merlin "was also called Ambrose." The entire work he dedicated to Alexander, Bishop of Lincoln, in a letter sufficiently eulogistic to be a high bid for the prelates' favour. This *Libellus Merlini* has come down to us only through Geoffrey's *Historia*, into which he incorporated it, letting the prophecies with the dedicatory epistle form his Seventh Book. At the beginning of the Seventh Book he says that he had reached that point in his history (namely, the scene where Merlin begins to prophesy to Vortigern), when, "the subject of public discourse happening to be concerning Merlin," he was persuaded by the urgent entreaties of his friends, and especially of Bishop Alexander, to publish his translation of Merlin's prophecies. This remark Geoffrey, knowing that nothing succeeds like success, doubtless made with the full consciousness that his own already published tract had drawn public discourse to Merlin, a figure about whom we have no direct information that antedates the *Historia*. Moreover, we know that the *Libellus Merlini* met at once with credence and favour,[2] and its reappearance in the *Historia*, as Geoffrey must have foreseen, would only tend to increase the popularity of the latter.

It is practically certain that before Geoffrey published the *Libellus*, he had begun to write the *Historia Regum Britanniæ*, which we know that he had composed (whether in the form

[1] §§ 40 ff.
[2] It was known in Iceland before 1218, in a form independent of the *Historia*. See H. G. Leach, *Modern Philology*, VIII., 607 ff.

that has come down to us or not) as early as 1139.[1] He dedicated this book to one of the most distinguished patrons of
literature of the time, Robert, Earl of Gloucester, who is believed to have rewarded him by advancing him to the arch-
deaconry at Llandaff. In the *Historia* Geoffrey undertook to
relate the history of the Britons from the time of their epony-
mous founder, Brutus, the grandson of Ascanius, to the death
of Cadwallader, the last British king. He divided his material
into twelve books, of which the Arthurian history (*i.e.*, the
events from the landing of Constantine in Britain to the death
of Arthur) occupies five, and of these, Arthur's own reign two.
In the plan and outline of his book, he follows closely the most
famous of his predecessors, Gildas, Bede, and Nennius, making
much more extensive use of Nennius than of the others. He
dissects their material, transposes it, embellishes it, interpolates
and expands it enormously; yet he frequently adopts their very
words and phrases, sometimes merely recasting their sentences
into a more finished form. There is no question that he freely
availed himself of the most reliable sources at his disposal, as
any other chronicler of early British history would naturally
have done. Of a large part of his history, however, these chronicles contain no trace; for Geoffrey, in his wide excursions from
their limits, gathered his material from episodes in the chronicles of his contemporaries, William of Malmesbury, and Henry
of Huntingdon, from ancient Celtic records, the legends of
Celtic saints, Celtic myth, Biblical history, classical and Scandi-
navian story, the universal stock of folk-tales, local British tradition, the Carolingian cycle, familiar facts of general history,
and from events in the life about him; in short, he drew freely
upon all such resources as an unusually well-informed man of
his time would have had at his command. A critical examination of his text makes this indisputable. Yet Geoffrey himself in
his dedicatory epistle to Robert of Gloucester gives an account
of his own proceedings that is altogether irreconcilable with
them. It had often occurred to him, he says, that a history of
the Kings of Britain would form an excellent subject for a
book, and that extraordinarily little had already been written
about them:—

[1] For a discussion of the question as to whether Geoffrey wrote a
later revision of his history, see Fletcher, *Publications of the Modern
Language Association of America*, XVI., 461 ff.

"Now, whilst I was thus thinking upon such matters, Walter, Archdeacon of Oxford, a man learned not only in the art of eloquence, but in the histories of foreign lands, offered me a certain most ancient book in the British language that did set forth the doings of them all in due succession and order from Brute, the first King of the Britons onward to Cadwallader, the son of Cadwallo, all told in stories of exceeding beauty. At his request, therefore, albeit that never have I gathered gay flowers of speech in other men's little gardens, and am content with mine own rustic manner of speech and mine own writing-reeds, have I been at the pains to translate this volume into the Latin tongue. For had I besprinkled my page with high-flown phrases, I should only have engendered a weariness in my readers by compelling them to spend more time over the meaning of the words than upon understanding the drift of my story."

These words are evidently not to be taken *au pied de la lettre,* for no one very ancient British book could have contained all the material which Geoffrey avers that he is translating from "British" into Latin. Some of it he might have drawn from such a book, but it is highly improbable that any combination of subject-matter like that found in his history could have existed in early British literature, or that Geoffrey's polished style can be a rendering of the rude diction in which an ancient British book would have been written. In fact, the book of Archdeacon Walter is now very generally regarded as one of the great ruses of literary history.[1] But although it is certain that Geoffrey does not give a truthful account of his own doings, we may well be slow to criticise him harshly. Every mediæval writer had his direct source to which he adhered pretty slavishly, but which he was especially in the habit of citing as an authority when he wished to depart from it. *Come li livres dist,* "as the book saith," is a common signal that a statement made probably out of the writer's own head is coming. Geoffrey himself does not appear to have regarded the "British book" with tremendous seriousness. If he had felt that he was practising a culpable deception, he would scarcely have dared make a worthy brother archdeacon accessory to the fraud, or to be so unguarded as to say, as he does in one passage,[2] that some of his stories he has heard verbally from Archdeacon

[1] For arguments in favour of the British book, see E. W. B. Nicholson, *Y Cymmrodor,* XIX., 5, note.
[2] Book XI., chap. 1.

Walter. His public was far too uncritical to question sources closely. The resemblances to the well-authenticated chronicles, the adherence to literary convention by the reference to a source, the air of verisimilitude that the narrative had, these qualities were quite sufficient to satisfy most of Geoffrey's readers. To some scholars of his time his subterfuge was transparent. William of Malmesbury and Henry of Huntingdon, whose works had brought grist to his mill, evidently thought it an innocent deception; otherwise assuredly they would have challenged him to produce his wonderful buok, when in the last chapter of his history he threw down the gauntlet before them in the form of a warning:—

"Howbeit, their Kings who from that time[1] have succeeded in Wales I hand over in the matter of writing unto Karadoc of Lancarvan, my contemporary, as I do those of the Saxons unto William of Malmesbury and Henry of Huntingdon, whom I bid be silent as to the Kings of the Britons, seeing that they have not that book in the British speech which Walter, Archdeacon of Oxford, did convey hither out of Brittany, the which being truly issued, in honour of the aforesaid princes, I have on this wise been at the pains of translating into the Latin speech."

William of Newburgh,[2] writing somewhat later in the century did, it is true, pour out the vials of his wrath upon Geoffrey, denouncing him as a reporter of mere fables about Arthur, which he had taken from the Britons and elaborated according to his own devices either from a love of lying, or from a desire to please the Britons. Some people were inclined to make Geoffrey's concoctions the subject of witticisms, and Giraldus Cambrensis,[3] at about the same time that William of Newburgh was giving vent to his displeasure, relates that when evil spirits were tormenting beyond endurance a certain Welshman, Melerius, their familiar, they vanished if the Gospel of St. John were laid on his bosom, but if Geoffrey's *Historia* were substituted for the gospel, the devils settled on it in greater numbers, and found it a congenial resting-place.

We shall probably never know just what written sources beside the chronicles Geoffrey had before him; but we see quite

[1] *I.e.*, the time following the death of Cadwallader.
[2] Ed. Howlitt, *Chronicles of Stephen*, London, 1884, I., 12, 13.
[3] *Itin. Kambriæ*, I., 5, pp. 57-58 (Works of Giraldus Cambrensis, Rolls Series, 1861-91).

enough of his methods to be sure that he was essentially an adroit combiner of existing material, which he made flexible for his own purposes. He had a public and a theme that offered him a chance to do a brilliant piece of work greatly to his liking, which none but a calmly audacious writer could have carried through. He aimed to flatter the Norman conquerors by displaying the greatness of the race that they had subdued, to satisfy their curiosity by transmitting to them ostensibly authentic historic records of that race, to weave his facts together in a narrative embellished by interesting material in reality drawn from countless sources, and to present the whole as sober history in grave and sonorous Latin. The acuteness with which he judged the taste of his contemporaries may be gauged by the success which the *Historia* at once achieved. It immediately won extraordinary popularity in England and on the Continent. An acquaintance with its contents soon became a necessary part of an equipment for polite society, and speedily chroniclers began to treat it as one of the important authorities to be repeated in any serious account of British history.

Although Geoffrey's special claim to distinction in our eyes rests upon the Arthurian sections of his history, it should not be forgotten that there are others of wide importance. In his pages, for instance, are to be found the stories of Cymbeline, King Lear, and Sabrina, "daughter of Locrine," together with many another tale familiar to us all in the works of later English poets, who have used him as their ultimate source. In the figure of Arthur, however, Geoffrey recognised a large opportunity, and he devotes more space to him than to any other single individual. He begins his account of Arthur's career with the romantic story of his birth. He is the son of the great British king Uther Pendragon, who falls madly in love with Igerna, the beautiful young wife of the Duke of Cornwall, wins access to her by the shape-shifting devices of the enchanter Merlin, and thus becomes the father of Arthur. At the age of fifteen years Arthur succeeds to the throne of Britain, and loses no time in entering upon a series of victorious campaigns against the Saxons, Picts, and Scots, Ireland, Iceland, Gothland, and the Orkneys. Twelve years of peace follow; then he proceeds to subdue Norway, Denmark, and Gaul. He returns to Britain to be crowned king; but even before the coronation festival is ended, on receiving a demand for tribute from Rome, he decides to make war upon the Romans themselves, "to demand of them what they had judicially decreed to demand of him." Accordingly he sails to Brittany, and is marching south to Rome, when he learns that his nephew Modred, to whose care he had entrusted the government of Britain in his absence, had usurped the throne and persuaded Arthur's queen, Guanhumara, to marry him. The king immediately returns to Great Britain, and wages war upon Modred. In a furious battle in Cornwall, Modred falls, as do "almost all the commanders and their forces," and Arthur himself, mortally wounded, is carried from the field to the island of Avalon to be healed.

For this remarkable history Geoffrey used the account of Nennius as a mere basis, reducing in fact the number of Arthur's battles against the Saxons; and aided by the tales that had been gathering about Arthur's name on the lips of the British, he proceeded with the zest of a born *raconteur* to create a new Arthur for his Norman readers. In his hands his hero becomes more than a valiant champion of his people; he is an imperial conqueror, a performer of daring exploits, and the splendid king of a Norman court. The Saxon victories of Nennius's *dux bellorum* pale beside the extensive foreign campaigns of Geoffrey's Arthur, who with the true lust for imperialism gloats over the awe that he inspires in other kings, and feeding his soul on their terror forms designs for the conquest of all Europe. War does not supply him with his only opportunity for distinguishing himself; romantic adventures also agreeably checker his career—a duel with the giant Ritho, a fight with the giant of Mont St. Michel for the succour of a captive maiden, a brilliant single combat as champion of Britain with Flollo, the champion of Gaul. A tissue of episode and exploit is woven about him by the clever fingers of Geoffrey, such as that of which professed romancers were wont to make their chosen heroes the centre. This is not all that he does for Arthur. He surrounds him by a court that mirrors the Anglo-Norman life of the twelfth century. Arthur, when he is established on his throne, distributes lands, repairs the damages of war, and conducts himself in general after the fashion of a Norman king of England. Geoffrey's description of Britain at the time of Arthur's coronation, which must have been modelled on a Norman festival, is often cited as a striking example of his introduction of chivalric customs into Arthurian history:—

"For at that time was Britain exalted unto so high a pitch of dignity as that it did surpass all other kingdoms in plenty of riches, in luxury of adornment, and in the courteous wit of them that dwelt therein. Whatsoever knight in the land was of renown for his prowess did wear his clothes and his arms all of one same colour. And the dames, no less witty, would apparel them in like manner in a single colour, nor would they deign have the love of none save he had thrice approved him in the wars. Wherefore at that time did dames wax chaste and knights the nobler for their love."

Never before had the ideals of courtly life been connected with Arthur. They blossomed, it is true, in their richest form in Southern France, and did not take firm root in England until the second half of the twelfth century, when they were transported from the south by Eleanor of Aquitaine, queen of Henry II., and by Provençal poets who stayed in England for longer or shorter periods; but Geoffrey's own words are a proof that they were current there even in his day. Yet we cannot but observe that Arthur in the *Historia* does not embody all the virtues of the chivalric hero *par excellence*. Courtesy, valour, youth, glad energy, liberality—these were all saving graces in the courtly life cultivated in twelfth-century France; and with all these Arthur is endowed. At the time of his accession, when he is fifteen years old, the accepted age for a mediæval hero of adventure to begin his career, he is said to have been a youth of a "courage and generosity beyond compare, whereunto his inborn goodness did lend such grace as that he was beloved of well-nigh all the peoples in the land." After he had established peace in the realm, "he invited unto him all soever of most prowess from far-off kingdoms, and began . . . to hold such courtly fashion in his household as begat rivalry amongst peoples at a distance." He is a shining example of liberality, an essential quality in courtly demeanour. Even highway robbery afforded in the Europe of the middle ages a convenient and profitable means for a man to enrich his followers, if he were of propensities too liberal for his purse, and Arthur, having impoverished himself by bestowing bounties freely, resorted to the sword to slake his thirst for munificence.

"For he that hath within him a bountiful nature along with prowess, albeit that he is lacking for a time, natheless in no wise shall poverty be his bane for ever. Wherefore did Arthur, for that in him did valour keep company with largesse, make resolve to harry the Saxons, to the end that with their treasure he might make rich the retainers that were of his own household. And herein was he nourished of his own lawful right, seeing that of right ought he to hold the sovereignty of the whole island in virtue of his claim hereditary."

But the all-important virtues of *mésure* (moderation, the observance of the golden mean in all the acts of life) and of love, without which, according to the chivalric code, no man could possibly be of "gentle" heart, the Arthur of Geoffrey knows nothing, very possibly because these qualities are incompatible with some traces of barbarism that survive in Geoffrey's conception of him. He is tinged with the chivalric ideals of a Norman court, but he does not perfectly represent the laws of courtly behaviour which were illustrated a little later in French Arthurian romance.

Although the later romances depend only very indirectly upon Geoffrey, there are nevertheless some elements in his story that he permanently introduced into the cycle. He established Arthur's place in the British royal line, and gave him a heroic birth-story. He first drew a clear picture of the enchanter Merlin,[1] one of the most important, and certainly the most mysterious of Arthurian personages, our dim knowledge of whose origin must rest chiefly upon what we can detect behind the words of Geoffrey, the archdisguiser of sources. In Geoffrey's pages, too, we first find the stories of Modred's treachery, and of the abduction of Guinevere, the latter of which there is excellent reason to believe, is a rationalised remnant of an early mythological tale.

We are to turn to the *Historia*, then, feeling that we are to read not a chronicle, but a romance of early British history, the work of a most skilful combiner, who handled his material with interest and ingenuity. What he has done for Arthurian romance is absolutely clear. He raised a national hero, already the centre of legend and myth, to the rank of an imperial monarch, he substituted for an uncouth a polished *entourage*, for early British customs those of Norman England, he established

---

[1] A curious Latin poem, the *Vita Merlini* ("Life of Merlin"), written about 1148, recounting adventures of Merlin not related in the *Historia*, is usually, but not unquestionably, attributed to Geoffrey.

certain permanent elements of Arthurian romance, he clothed myth in the garb of history. Above all he gave a dignified place in literature to popular national story. He determined definitely the form in which Arthurian history appeared in the chronicles, a form that substantially does not vary for many centuries.

LUCY ALLEN PATON

CAMBRIDGE, MASSACHUSETTS
1911

# BIBLIOGRAPHICAL NOTE

Geoffrey of Monmouth wrote in a terse, dramatic style. His Latin prose repeatedly echoes the language of the Vulgate and of the classics, but his tone is often ironic or even facetious and is always lively. Sebastian Evans has captured the spirit of Geoffrey's style admirably in the appropriately Elizabethan flavor of his translation. In editing this revised printing I have therefore tampered as little as possible with his translation, but I have altered it in the light of the Latin texts and variants in Faral's and Griscom's more recent editions of the *Historia*.

I have introduced phrases or sentences omitted by Evans and have substituted readings from the reliable manuscripts previously unavailable in the place of some palpably wrong readings in the now outmoded San Marte text (1854) of Geoffrey on which Evans perforce relied. Using Tatlock's study of Geoffrey as a chief guide, I have tried to give proper names their most reasonable form, though occasionally the multiplicity of manuscript variations has made the choice difficult or even arbitrary; and I have rendered all place and national names by their accepted modern equivalent. Sometimes the use of a modern substitute such as "Normandy" for "Neustria" or "Breton" for "Armorican" may obscure the archaistic effect which Geoffrey intended, but this loss will be more than compensated if the readers are thereby enabled to comprehend his geographical sweep. In order to facilitate cross-reference, the conventional book and chapter numbers have been retained, though it is now clear that Geoffrey himself did not intend to divide his work into the traditional number of twelve books.

The translator's epilogue which appeared in the first edition has been omitted, since the findings of scholarship based on material unavailable in 1903 to Evans have now been brought together conveniently in Tatlock's book and largely supersede this earlier discussion. Miss Paton's introduction (of 1911) has been reprinted as still useful. Her source of information about Geoffrey's early life (p. xiv) has now been shown to be unreliable; any other significant modifications are suggested in the following summary of the more recent scholarship.

Geoffrey of Monmouth, known also as Geoffrey Arthur, belonged to one of the families of Normans who had invaded Wales; his forebears may have been of Breton origin. He himself presumably spoke both Anglo-Norman and Welsh and would have understood Breton. For a time he may have served in the small and recently founded Benedictine priory at Monmouth, in South Wales, some sixteen miles from Caerleon, the reputed locale of King Arthur's court. He moved to Oxford and from about 1129 to 1150 served as a secular Augustinian canon of St. George's college (in Oxford castle) and probably as a teacher. While there he wrote his *History* (*ca.* 1138-39); in it (Book VII) he included the *Prophecies of Merlin* which he had compiled and of which he sent a separate copy to his ecclesiastical lord, Alexander, who was Bishop of Lincoln from 1123 to 1148. He dedicated the entire *History* to King Henry I's natural son Robert, Earl of Gloucester (died 1147), the most powerful opponent of Stephen's claims to the throne; and in it he ingeniously magnified his patron by inventing important roles for the Earl's fictitious British ancestors Eldol (Book VI, Chap. xvi ff.) and Morvid (Book X, Chap. vi). He issued individual presentation copies with special dedications to King Stephen (reigned 1135-54) and to Galeran of Meulan, Earl of Worcester (died 1166) (see p. 265).

The *History* was written to manufacture for the Celtic Britons a plausible history comparable to the reliable and accurate works being compiled in the twelfth century, such as William of Malmesbury's history of the Anglo-Saxons and Anglo-Normans in England. The sources of this pseudo-history are heterogeneous: the early histories of Gildas, Nennius, and Bede; contemporary histories by Malmesbury and Henry of Huntingdon, traditional Welsh and Breton legend, rather than the specific "British book" mentioned by Geoffrey; international folklore; and the author's imagination. Geoffrey's purpose in describing the succession of the ninety-nine kings of Britain, few of whom are historical, is not to exalt the British over the Normans but to supply a hitherto unappreciated tradition for them which would suggest that they were at least worthy predecessors of the Norman conquerors. According to Geoffrey, the British claimed a noble descent from the Romans through their first king, Brutus the great-grandson of Aeneas, and finally gained world-wide dominion under their ninety-first king, Arthur, who would have conquered Rome itself but for the treachery of Modred. Well may their example, Geoffrey implies, encourage the imperialistic ambitions of the powerful new dynasty of Anglo-Norman kings! Hence Geoffrey does not mention that the Welsh were still resisting the Normans in his own day but closes his work at the year 689 with their decline after the death of Cadwallader (who is a mingling of the historical Cadwallo, King of the Britons, who died in 633, and the Anglo-Saxon Cadwallo, King of Wessex, who died in 689).

About 1148 Geoffrey composed a poem in Latin of some 1500 lines in hexameter, *The Life of Merlin,* for Robert of Chesney, a fellow canon of St. George's, Oxford, who in 1148 succeeded Alexander as bishop of Lincoln. In 1152 Geoffrey was made Bishop of St. Asaph's in North Wales, having first been ordained priest in order to qualify for the appointment, but he was unable to settle in the diocese because of the unrest in the area. He apparently remained in England and died in 1155.

The following bibliography includes the more important works, for the most part more recent than Evans' translation, related to Geoffrey of Monmouth. For a fuller bibliography see F. W. Bateson, *Cambridge Bibliography of English Literature,* London & New York, 1941, 1957, I, 133, 285; V, 160.

Arnold, I., ed., *Le Roman de Brut de Wace,* Paris: Société des anciens textes français, 1938-40, 2 vols. (Anglo-Norman adaptation in verse of Geoffrey.)

Chadwick, H. M., *et al., Studies in Early British History*. Cambridge, 1954. (Celtic traditions of Arthur.)

Chambers, Sir E. K., *Arthur of Britain,* London, 1927.

Faral, E., *La légende arthurienne,* Paris: Bibliothèque de l'école des hautes études 255-257, 1911-1929, 3 vols. (Edn. of Geoffrey's *Historia* and *Vita Merlini* and of Nennius; important intro.)

Giles, J. A., *Six Old English Chronicles,* London, 1891. (Outdated but useful trans. of Gildas and Nennius; numbered list of Geoffrey's kings.)

Griscom, A., ed., *Historia Regum Britanniae,* New York, 1929.

Hammer, J., ed., *Historia Regum Britanniae,* Cambridge, Mass., 1951. (A variant version of *Historia;* echoes of classics and Vulgate noted.)

Jones, G., and Jones, T., trans., *The Mabinogion,* London & New York, 1949. (Native Welsh Arthurian tales.)

King, J. E., ed. trans., *Bedae Opera Historica,* London, 1930, 2 vols. (Bede was the pattern for all subsequent English historians.)

Loomis, R. S., *Wales and the Arthurian Legend,* Cardiff, 1956. (Chap. X suggests the prevalence of a Celtic tradition concerning Arthur prior to Geoffrey; see other works by the same author there referred to.)

Madden, Sir F., ed. trans., *Laʒamons Brut,* London, 1847, 3 vols. (Middle English version of Wace's adaptation of Geoffrey.)

Mason, E., *Arthurian Chronicles,* London, 1928. (Trans. of Arthurian section of Wace and Layamon.)

Parry, J. J., ed. trans., *The Vita Merlini,* Univ. of Illinois Studies in Lang. and Lit., X, No. 3, Urbana, 1925.

Tatlock, J. S. P., *The Legendary History of Britain,* Berkeley, 1950. (Underestimates contribution of Celtic tradition but otherwise an indispensable guide.)

CHARLES W. DUNN

New York University
1958

# HISTORY OF THE KINGS OF BRITAIN

# BOOK I

## [1]

OFTENTIMES in turning over in mine own mind the many themes that might be subject-matter of a book, my thoughts would fall upon the plan of writing a history of the Kings of Britain, and in my musings thereupon meseemed it a marvel that, beyond such mention as Gildas and Bede have made of them in their luminous tractate, nought could I find as concerning the kings that had dwelt in Britain before the Incarnation of Christ, nor nought even as concerning Arthur and the many others that did succeed him after the Incarnation, albeit that their deeds be worthy of praise everlasting and be as pleasantly rehearsed from memory by word of mouth in the traditions of many peoples as though they had been written down. Now, whilst I was thus thinking upon such matters, Walter, Archdeacon of Oxford, a man learned not only to the art of eloquence, but in the histories of foreign lands, offered me a certain most ancient book in the British language that did set forth the doings of them all in due succession and order from Brute, the first King of the Britons, onward to Cadwallader, the son of Cadwallo, all told in stories of exceeding beauty. At his request, therefore, albeit that never have I gathered gay flowers of speech in other men's little gardens, and am content with mine own rustic manner of speech and mine own writing-reeds, have I been at the pains to translate this volume into the Latin tongue. For had I besprinkled my page

3

with high-flown phrases, I should only have engendered a weariness in my readers by compelling them to spend more time over the meaning of the words than upon understanding the drift of my story.

Unto this my little work, therefore, do thou, Robert, Earl of Gloucester, show favour in such wise that it may be so corrected by thy guidance and counsel as that it may be held to have sprung, not from the poor little fountain of Geoffrey of Monmouth, but rather from thine own deep sea of knowledge, and to savour of thy salt. Let it be held to be thine own offspring, as thou thyself art offspring of the illustrious Henry, King of the English. Let it be thine, as one that hath been nurtured in the liberal arts by philosophy, and called unto the command of our armies by thine own inborn prowess of knighthood; thine, whom in these our days Britain haileth with heart-felt affection as though in thee she had been vouchsafed a second Henry.

[2]

BRITAIN best of islands, lieth in the Western Ocean betwixt Gaul and Ireland, and containeth eight hundred miles in length and two hundred in breadth. Whatsoever is fitting for the use of mortal men the island doth afford in unfailing plenty. For she aboundeth in metals of every kind; fields hath she, stretching far and wide, and hillsides meet for tillage of the best, whereon, by reason of the fruitfulness of the soil, the divers crops in their season do yield their harvests. Forests also hath she filled with every manner of wild animal, in the glades whereof groweth grass that the cattle may find therein meet change of pasture, and flowers of many colours that do proffer their honey unto the bees that flit ever busily about them. Meadows hath she, set in pleasant places, green at the foot of misty mountains, wherein be sparkling wellsprings clear and bright, flowing forth with a gentle whispering ripple in shining streams that sing sweet lullaby unto them that lie upon their banks. Watered is she, moreover, by lakes and rivers wherein is much fish, and, besides the narrow sea of the Southern coast whereby men make voyage unto Gaul, by three noble rivers, Thames, to wit, Severn and Humber, the which she stretcheth forth as it were three arms whereby she taketh in the traffic from oversea brought hither from every land in her fleets. By twice ten cities, moreover, and twice four, was she graced in days of old, whereof some with shattered walls in desolate places be now fallen into decay, whilst some, still whole, do contain churches of the saints with towers builded wondrous fair on high, wherein companies of religious, both men and women, do their service unto God after the traditions of the Christian faith. Lastly, it is inhabited of five peoples, Normans, to wit, Britons, Saxons, Picts, and Scots. Of these the Britons did first settle them therein from sea to sea before the others, until, by reason of their pride, divine vengeance did overtake them, and they yielded them unto the Picts and Saxons. Remaineth now for me to tell from whence they came and in what wise they did land upon our shores, as by way of foretaste of that which shall hereafter be related more at large.

[3]

AFTER the Trojan War, Æneas, fleeing from the desolation of the city, came with Ascanius by ship unto Italy. There, for that Æneas was worshipfully received by King Latinus, Turnus, King of the Rutulains, did wax envious and made war against him. When they met in battle, Æneas had the upper hand, and after that Turnus was slain, obtained the kingdom of Italy and Lavinia the daughter of Latinus. Later, when his own last day had come, Ascanius, now king in his stead,

founded Alba on Tiber, and begat a son whose name
was Silvius. Silvius, unknown to his father, had fallen
in love with and privily taken to wife a certain niece of
Lavinia, who was now about to become a mother.
When this came to the knowledge of his father Ascanius,
he commanded his wizards to discover whether the damsel should be brought to bed of a boy or a girl. When
they had made sure of the matter by art magic, they
told him that the child would be a boy that should slay
his father and his mother, and after much travel in
many lands, should, albeit an exile, be exalted unto the
highest honours. Nor were the wizards out in their forecast, for when the day came that she should be delivered
of a child, the mother bare a son, but herself died in
his birth. Howbeit, the child was given in charge unto
a nurse, and was named Brute. At last, after thrice five
years had gone by, the lad, bearing his father company
out a-hunting, slew him by striking him unwittingly
with an arrow. For when the verderers drave the deer
in front of them, Brute thinking to take aim at them,
smote his own father under the breast. Upon the death
of his father he was driven out of Italy, his kinsfolk
being wroth with him for having wrought a deed so
dreadful. He went therefore as an exile into Greece,
and there fell in with the descendants of Helenus, the
son of Priam, who at that time were held in bondage
under the power of Pandrasus, King of the Greeks. For
Pyrrhus, the son of Achilles, after the overthrow of
Troy, had led away with him in fetters the foresaid
Helenus and a great number of others besides, whom
he commanded to be held in bondage by way of revenging upon them his father's death. And when Brute understood that they were of the lineage of his former
fellow-citizens, he sojourned amongst them. Howbeit,
in such wise did he achieve renown for his knighthood
and prowess, that he was beloved by kings and princes
above all the other youths of the country. For among
the wise he was as wise as he was valiant among war-

riors, and whatsoever gold or silver or ornaments he won, he gave it all in largess to his comrades in battle. His fame was thus spread abroad among all nations, and the Trojans flocked unto him from all parts, beseeching him that he should be their king and deliver them from the slavery of the Greeks; the which they declared might easily be done, seeing that they had now so multiplied in the land as that without making count of little ones and women they were already reckoned to be seven thousand. There was, moreover, a certain youth of high nobility in Greece, by name Assaracus, who was no less favourable in their cause. For he was born of a Trojan mother, and he had in them the fullest affiance that by their help he would be able to resist the harassing persecution of the Greeks. For his brother laid claim against him in respect of three castles which his father when dying had conferred upon him, but which the brother was now trying to take away from him because Assaracus had been born of a concubine. The brother himself was Greek both by father and mother, and had rallied the king and the rest of the Greeks to the support of his cause. When, therefore, Brute saw how great was the multitude of fighting men, and also how strong were the castles of Assaracus which were open unto him, he granted their request without misgiving.

[4]

WHEN, therefore, he was thus chosen their Duke, he summons together the Trojans from every quarter and garrisons the strongholds of Assaracus. Howbeit, he and Assaracus, with all the host of men and women that were upon their side, occupied the forests and hills. Then Brute sent his letter addressed unto the King in these words: "To Pandrasus, King of the Greeks, Brute, Duke of them that are left of Troy, greeting: Whereas a nation sprung from the illustrious race of Dardanus

deigned not to be treated in thy kingdom otherwise
than as the purity of their nobility did demand, they
have betaken them into the depths of the forests. For
they held it better to live a life after the manner of wild
beasts, to wit on flesh and herbs, with liberty, than to
be cockered with dainties of every kind and remain any
longer under the yoke of bondage unto thee. If this
offendeth the loftiness of thy power, they are rather to
be pardoned than held to blame, for of all that are in
captivity it is the common aim and desire to recover
their former dignity. Be thou, therefore, moved to mercy
towards them, and deign to bestow upon them their lost
liberty, allowing them to inhabit the forest glades that
they have occupied to the end that thus they might flee
beyond the reach of slavery. But if this thou wilt not,
grant them at least that they may depart unto other nations of the world with thy good will."

[5]

WHEN Pandrasus, therefore, had learnt the drift of this
letter, he was beyond measure amazed that they whom
he had held in bondage should so abound in hardihood
as to address any mandates of the kind unto him. He
therefore summoned a council of his nobles, and decreed that an army should be levied in order to hunt
them down. But whilst that he was searching the wilder-
nesses wherein he supposed them to be, and the stronghold of Sparatinum, Brute issued forth with three thousand men, and suddenly attacked him when he was expecting nothing of the kind. For, hearing of his arrival,
he had thrown himself into the said stronghold the
night before, in order that he might make an unlooked-
for onslaught upon them when they were unarmed and
marching without order. The Trojans accordingly
charged down upon them and attacked them stoutly,
doing their best to overwhelm them with slaughter. The

I Seem to recollect an actual
historical Battle among the
Danes + Swedes c. 875

BOOK I                                                    9

Greeks, moreover, suddenly taken aback, are scattered
in all directions, and scamper off, the King at their head,
to get across the river Akalon that runneth anigh. But
in fording the stream they suffer sore jeopardy from the
whirling currents of the flood. Whilst they are thus fleeing abroad, Brute overtaketh them, and smiteth down
them that he overtaketh partly in the waters of the river
and partly on the banks, and, hurrying hither and
thither amongst them, rejoiceth greatly to inflict upon
them a double death. Which when Antigonus the
brother of Pandrasus beheld, he was beyond measure
afflicted, and as soon as he could recall his straggling
comrades to the ranks, returned and charged swiftly
upon the raging Trojans. For he was minded rather to
die fighting than to make a craven flight only to be
drowned in the muddy whirlpits of the river. Marching,
therefore, in a solid battalion, he exhorted his comrades
to resist like men, and hurl back the deadly weapons
with all their might. Yet did it avail him little or nothing. For the Trojans were accoutred with arms while
the others were unarmed. Pressing forward, therefore,
all the more boldly on this account, they inflicted a
grievous slaughter upon them, nor did they cease to
harry them in such fashion until they had slaughtered
well-nigh the whole of them, and had taken captive
Antigonus and his comrade Anacletus.

[6]

Now, when Brute had achieved the victory, he garrisoned the stronghold with six hundred men, and then
sought out the recesses of the forest wherein the Trojan
folk were expecting his protection. But Pandrasus, in
sore tribulation over his own flight and the capture of
his brother, spent the night in getting his scattered
forces together again, and when the morrow morning
dawned marched with his reassembled people to besiege

the stronghold. For he thought that Brute had again set himself therein together with Antigonus, and the other prisoners. When, therefore, he came anigh the walls, he examined the situation of the castle, and distributed his army in companies, and disposed them in divers places around it, telling off some to forbid all egress to them that were enclosed within, some to divert the course of the rivers, and others again with store of battering-rams and other engines to shatter the fabric of the walls. They all obeyed his orders to the best of their endeavour, devising in what manner most cruelly they might annoy the besieged. When the night came on, moreover, they chose the boldest of their number to keep guard over the camp and tents against any stealthy attack of the enemy, while the rest, worn out with fatigue-labour, refreshed them with undisturbed sleep.

[7]

THE besieged, on the other hand, standing on the top of the walls, endeavour with all their strength to beat back the machinations of the enemy by counter-devices, with one mind busying themselves in their own defence, now flinging down missiles, now lighted brimstone torches among them. When the wall was undermined by sappers working under shelter of a "tortoise," they compelled the enemy to retreat by Greek fire and a shower of boiling water. Suffering, howbeit, from scarcity of victual and the daily travail, they sent a messenger unto Brute, beseeching him to hasten to their assistance, for sore were they afeared lest they should be reduced by weakness to desert the fortress. Brute, therefore, anxious to come to their succour, is sore tormented inwardly for that he hath not enough men to adventure on delivering battle in the field. Howbeit, taking crafty counsel, he maketh resolve to attack the enemy's camp by night, and, by deceiving the sentinels, to slay them sleeping. But, for that he knew this could only be done with the assistance and assent of one of the Greeks, he called unto him Anacletus, the comrade of Antigonus, and, unsheathing his sword, spake unto him on this wise:—

"Most noble youth, thine own life and that of Antigonus are already at an end, save thou faithfully agree to execute that which I shall command thee according unto my will. For it is my purpose on this night following to attack the camp of the Greeks in such sort that I may inflict upon them an unexpected slaughter. But I fear me lest their sentinels should discover my secret intent, and that thus the enterprise be brought to nought. Wherefore, seeing that it behoveth us first of all to turn our arms against the watch, I am desirous of deceiving them by means of you, so that I may have safer passage for attacking the others. Do thou, therefore, acting warily as befitteth a matter of such weight, go to the guard at the second hour of the night, and allaying the suspicions of any by words of feigning, say that thou hast carried off Antigonus out of my dungeons unto a combe in the forest, and that he there lieth hidden among the underwood, being unable to get any further on account of the fetters wherewith thou will feign that he is shackled. Then thou shalt guide them to the issue of the forest as if for the purpose of setting him free, and there will I be with a company of armed men ready to slay them."

[8]

ANACLETUS, therefore, scared all the time by the sight of the sword, which during the time these words were spoken had been raised ready to slay him, made promise by oath that he would execute this command on condition that longer life were granted unto Antigonus as well as himself. The covenant was at last confirmed, and at the second hour of the night, which was then just at hand, Anacletus started on his way towards the guard as he had been commanded. And when at last he arrived anigh the camp, the sentinels on every side who keep eye upon all the hidden corners of the places run up and ask him the cause of his coming, and whether he hath come in order to betray the army? Unto whom he, feigning the greatest joy, made answer: "Of a truth I came not here as a traitor to mine own folk, but as one that hath escaped from the prison of the Trojans do I thus flee unto you, beseeching you that ye come with me to our Antigonus, whom I have rescued from the chains of Brute. Him, indeed, hindered by the weight of his shackles, have I but just now enjoined to lie hidden in the underwood by the issue of the forest until I could find some whom I can lead thither to set him free." Whilst that they were still doubting whether he told truth, came up one who had known him aforetime, and after saluting him, told his comrades who he was. They thereupon, hesitating no longer, summoned the rest who were at a distance to come as swiftly as might be, and followed him as far as the wood, wherein, as he had told them before, Antigonus was hiding. While they, accordingly were making their way through the brushwood, Brute, with his armed companies, cometh forth, and charging upon them soon inflicted a most terrible slaughter on the panic-stricken guard. Then he marched on to the leaguer, dividing his comrades into three companies, and commanding that each should approach the camp at a different point, prudently and without noise, but that after they had effected an entrance into the camp, they should refrain from slaughtering any until such time as he, with his own special company, had taken possession of the King's pavilion, when he would blow his own horn as a signal for them.

[9]

HE further instructed them in what manner they were to do everything that was to be done. Forthwith they lightly make their way into the camp, and after fulfilling all that they have been commanded, await the promised signal, which Brute tarried not long to give as soon as he set foot without the pavilion of Pandrasus, which above all others he was burning to attack. When the signal was heard, they unsheath their swords as swiftly as may be, rush into the sleeping-tents of the drowsy enemy, redouble their death-dealing blows, and march in this wise, all pitiless, throughout the camp. The rest waken up at the groans of the dying, and are stricken helpless with dismay at the sight of the butchers, like sheep seized of a sudden by the wolves. For nought of protection did they think to find, seeing that they had not even time enow either to lay hands on their arms or to take to flight. They could but run without arms to and fro amidst armed men as sudden impulse might lead. But all the time they are being cut to pieces by the onslaught of their enemies. He that escaped half-alive, hurrying forth in his eagerness for flight was dashed to the ground among the rocks and trees and brambles, and yielded up his unhappy soul together with his blood. He that was furnished with a shield only, or other covering, dropped down through fear of death among the same rocks, or swiftly fleeing through the darkness of the night, fell, and in falling brake a leg or an arm. He to whom neither of these mischances befel, not knowing whither to fly, was drowned in the rushing of the neighbouring rivers. Scarce one departed unharmed without peril of any mishap. They within the fortress, moreover, when they knew of the arrival of their fellows in arms, issued forth and redoubled the slaughter that was wrought.

## [ 10 ]

Now Brute, when he had obtained possession of the
royal tent, was careful to bind the King and to keep
him safe. For he knew that he could attain the object
at which he aimed more readily by the King's life than
by his death. But the company that were with him
ceased not from the slaughter they made, which in the
part of the camp they held had wrought a clearance
that was nought less than extermination. When the
night had thus been spent and the light of dawn revealed how mighty a loss had been inflicted on the people, Brute, in a very tempest of delight, now that the
carnage was over, gave permission to his comrades to
deal as they pleased with the spoils of the slain. Then
he entereth the fortress with the King, and there await-
eth until he should have distributed the treasure.
When this was all allotted, he again garrisoned the
castle and gave orders for the burial of the dead. He
then again collected his troops and returned rejoicing
in his victory to the forest. The tidings filled the hearts
of his men with no less joy, and the doughty Duke, after
summoning the elders, made inquiry of them what they
thought ought to be demanded of Pandrasus, for, now
that he was placed in their power, he would grant any
petition they might make to the utmost, provided he
were allowed to go free. Some of them at once proposed
one thing, and some another, according to their incli-
nations. Part exhorted him to ask for a portion of the
kingdom for them to dwell therein; part for leave to go
their way elsewhere and for whatever might be of use
to them upon the journey. And seeing that after a long
while they still hesitated, one amongst them, Mempricius by name, rose up and besought silence, when he
spake thus in the hearing of the rest:—

"Wherefore, fathers, do ye hesitate about that which,

in my opinion, is most expedient for your own welfare?
There is but one thing to be asked for, to wit, leave
to depart, if ye desire that yourselves and your children
should have lasting peace. For if it be that ye grant
Pandrasus his life on condition that ye obtain a part
of Greece, and so be minded to sojourn in the midst
of the Danai, never will ye enjoy an enduring peace
so long as the brethren and sons and grandsons of them
upon whom ye inflicted the slaughter of yesterday remain intermingled amongst ye or are your next neighbours without. For so long as they remember the slaying of their kinsfolk they will hold ye always in eternal
hatred, and taking offence at every the merest trifle,
will do their best to wreak vengeance upon ye. Nor will
ye, seeing that your host is the smaller, have strength
to resist the aggressions of so many indwellers of the
land. For if any strife for the mastery should arise, their
numbers will wax daily while your own will wane. Mine
opinion, therefore, is that ye ask of him his eldest
daughter, whom they call Innogen, as a wife for our
Duke, and along with her gold and silver, ships and
corn, and whatsoever else may be needful for our voyage. And if so be that he will grant her, we will then
with his leave go on our way to seek out other lands."


[ 11 ]


WHEN he had made an end of this speech, with more
to the like effect, the whole assembly signified their assent, and counselled that Pandrasus be brought into
their midst, and, save he should be favourable towards
this their petition, should be condemned to a death as
cruel as might be. No tarrying was there. He is brought
thither and set in a chair on high, where he is instructed, moreover, what tortures he will have to suffer
in case he refuse to do according as he is commanded.
Whereupon he made answer on this wise:—

As least the basis of chivalry
As ne geo, perceives?

"Forasmuch as the gods are against me, and have delivered me and my brother Anacletus into your hands, needs must I grant your petition, lest in case ye should meet with a denial we lose the life which ye have the power to give or to take away as ye may choose. For nought hold I better nor dearer than life, nor is it marvel that I should be willing to ransom it at the price of any outward goods and possessions. Wherefore, albeit against my will, I will obey your orders. Some comfort, nevertheless, seem I to have in this, that I shall give my daughter unto a youth of such prowess, whom the nobility that doth now burgeon within him no less than his renown which hath been made known to us, do declare to be a scion of the house of Priam and Anchises. For who but he could have delivered the exiles of Troy, the bondsmen of so many and such mighty princes, from their chains? Who but he could have urged them to successful resistance against the nation of the Greeks? Who but he with so few would have challenged to battle so mighty a host of armed warriors and at the first onset have led away their King in fetters? But sith that a youth so noble and of so mighty prowess hath been able to withstand me, I give him my daughter Innogen. I give him, moreover, gold and silver, ships, corn, wine, and oil, and whatsoever ye shall deem needful for your journey. And if it be that ye turn aside from your present purpose, and be minded to abide with the Greeks, I yield ye the third part of my kingdom, wherein to dwell. But if otherwise, I will fulfil my first promises in deeds, and that ye may have the fuller assurance, with you will I remain as hostage until I shall have done all things whereunto I have pledged me."

The agreement thus confirmed, envoys are directed to gather ships together from all the shores of Greece. These, when they were assembled to the number of three hundred and fourteen, are duly presented and laden with provision of all sorts. The daughter is married to Brute, and each man, according as his rank demanded, was presented with gold and silver. All his promises exactly fulfilled, the King is set free from prison; and at the same time the Trojans depart from his dominions with a prosperous wind. But Innogen, standing on the lofty poop of the ship, falleth swooning again and again into the arms of Brute, and with sobbing and shedding of tears lamenteth to forsake her kinsfolk and her country; nor turneth she her eyes away from the shore, so long as the shore itself is in sight. Brute, the while, soothing her with gentle words, at one time foldeth her in a sweet embrace, or at another kisseth her as sweetly, nor doth he slacken his endeavour to comfort her until, weary with weeping, she falleth at last on sleep.

In the meanwhile, what with these and other matters, they ran on together for two days and a night with a fair current of wind, and drew to land at a certain island called Leogecia, which had been uninhabited ever since it was laid waste by pirates in the days of old. Howbeit, Brute sent three hundred men inland to discover by whom it might be inhabited. Who, finding not a soul, slew such venison of divers kinds as they found in the glades and the forests. They came, moreover, to a certain deserted city, wherein they found a temple of Diana. Now in this temple was an image of the goddess, that gave responses, if haply it were asked of any votary that there did worship. At last they returned to their ships, laden with the venison they had found, and report to their comrades the lie of the land and the situation of the city, bearing the Duke on hand that he make repair unto the temple, and after making offerings of propitiation, inquire of the deity of the place what land she would grant them as a fixed abiding place. By the common consent of all, therefore, Brute took with him Gerion the augur, and twelve of the elders, and sought out the temple, bringing with them everything necessary for making sacrifice. When they arrived they surrounded their brows with garlands, and set up three altars according to immemorial wont, before the holy place, to the three Gods, Jove, to wit, and Mercury as well as to Diana, and made unto each his own special libation. Brute himself, holding in his right hand a vessel full of sacrificial wine and the blood of a white hind before the altar of the goddess, with face upturned towards her image, broke silence in these words:—

"Goddess and forest Queen, the wild boar's terror,
Thou who the maze of heaven or nether mansions
Walkest at will, vouchsafe thy rede to earthward!
Tell me what lands thy will it is we dwell in?
What sure abode? Lo, there to Thee for ever
Temples I vow, and chant of holy maidens!"

After he had nine times repeated this, he walked four times round the altar, poured forth the wine he held upon the hearth of offering, laid him down upon the fell of a hind that he had stretched in front of the altar, and after invoking slumber fell on sleep. For as at that time it was the third hour of the night, wherein are mortals visited by the sweetest sleep. Then it seemed him the goddess stood there before him, and spake unto him on this wise:—

"Brute,—past the realms of Gaul, beneath the sunset
Lieth an Island, girt about by ocean,
Guarded by ocean—erst the haunt of giants,
Desert of late, and meet for this thy people.
Seek it! For there is thine abode for ever.
There by thy sons again shall Troy be builded;
There of thy blood shall Kings be born, hereafter
Sovran in every land the wide world over."

On awakening from such a vision, the Duke remained in doubt whether it were a dream that he had seen, or whether it were the living goddess herself who had thus foretold the land whereunto he should go. At last he called his companions and related unto them from first

to last all that had befallen him in his sleep. They
thereupon were filled with exceeding great joy, and
advise that they should at once turn back to their ships,
and while the wind is still blowing fair, should get
under way as quickly as possible full sail for the West
in search of that land which the goddess had promised.
Nor did they tarry. They rejoin their comrades and
launch out into the deep, and after ploughing the waves
for a run of thirty days, made the coast of Africa, still
not knowing in which direction to steer their ships.
Then came they to the Altars of the Phileni, and the
Lake of the Salt-pans, steering from thence betwixt
Ruscicada and the mountains Azarae, where they en-
countered sore peril from an attack by pirates. Natheless, they won the victory, and went on their way enriched by the spoil and plunder they had taken.

[ 12 ]

FROM thence, passing the mouth of the river Malva,
they arrived in Mauritania, where lack of food and
drink compelled them to disembark, and dividing themselves into companies, they harried the whole region
from end to end. When they had revictualled their
ships, they made sail for the Columns of Hercules,
where they saw many of the monsters of the deep called
Sirens, which surrounded the ships and well-nigh overwhelmed them. Howbeit, they made shift to escape,
and came to the Tyrrhene sea, where they found nigh
the shore four generations born of the exiles from Troy,
who had borne Antenor company in his flight. Their
Duke was called Corineus, a sober-minded man and excellent in counsel, mighty in body, valiance, and hardiness, insomuch as that if it were he had to deal with a
giant in single combat he would straightway overthrow
him as though he were wrestling with a lad. Accordingly, when they knew the ancient stock whereof he was

*little history*

born, they took him into their company, as well as the people whereof he was chieftain, that in after-days were called Cornishmen after the name of their Duke. He it was that in all encounters was of more help to Brute than were any of the others.

Then came they to Aquitaine, and entering into the mouth of the Loire, cast anchor there. Here they abode seven days and explored the lie of the land. Goffarius Pictus then ruled in Aquitaine, and was King of the country, who, hearing the rumour of a foreign folk that had come with a great fleet and had landed within the frontier of his dominions, sent envoys to make inquiry whether they demanded peace or war? While the legates were on their way to the fleet, they met Corineus who had just landed with two hundred men to hunt for venison in the forest. Thereupon they accost him, and ask him by whose leave he hath thus trespassed into the King's forest to slay his deer? And when Corineus made them answer, that in such a matter no leave nor license whatever could be held as needful, one of their number, Imbert by name, rushed forward, and drawing his bow, aimed an arrow at him. Corineus avoided the arrow, and ran in upon Imbert as fast as he might, and with the bow that he carried all-to-brake his head in pieces. Thereupon the rest fled, just making shift to escape his hands, and reported the death of their fellow to Goffarius. The Duke of the Poitevins, taking the matter sorely to heart, forthwith assembled a mighty host to take vengeance upon them for the death of his messenger. Brute, hearing tidings of his coming, set guards over his ships, bidding the women and children remain on board while he himself along with the whole flower of his army marcheth forth to meet the enemy. When the engagement at last began, the fighting is fierce on both sides, and after they had spent a great part of the day in battling, Corineus thought it shame that the Aquitanians should hold their ground so stoutly, and the Trojans not be able to press forward to the victory. So taking heart afresh, he called his own men apart to the right of the battle, and forming them in rank made a rapid charge upon the enemy, and when, with his men in close order, he had broken the front ranks, he never stinted striking down the enemy till he had cut his way right through the battalion, and forced them all to flee. Good luck had supplied the place of a sword he lost with a battle-axe, wherewith he cleft in twain any that came next him from the crown of the head right down to the girdle-stead. Brute marvels; his comrades and even the enemy marvel at the hardihood and valour of the man, who, brandishing his battle-axe among the flying host, added not a little to their terror by shouting, "Whither fly ye, cowards? Whither fly ye, cravens? Turn back, I tell ye, turn, and do battle with Corineus! Shame upon ye! So many thousands as are ye, do ye flee before my single arm? Flee then! and take with ye at least this comfort in your flight, that it is I who am after ye, I who ere now have so oft been wont to drive the Tyrrhene giants in flight before me, and to hurl them to hell by threes and fours at a time!"

[13]

AT these words of his a certain earl named Subardus with three hundred men turned back and charged down upon him. But Corineus, in raising his shield to ward the blow, forgat not the battle-axe he held in his hand. Lifting it overhead, he smote him a buffet upon the top of his helmet that cleft him right through into two halves. After this, he straightway rusheth in amongst the rest, whirling his axe, and a passing furious slaughter he maketh. Hurrying hither and thither, he avoideth receiving a single stroke, but never resteth a moment from smiting down his enemies. Of one he loppeth off hand and arm, of another he cleaveth the

shoulders from the body, of another he striketh off the
head at a single blow, of another he severeth the legs
from the thigh. All dash headlong upon him only; he
dasheth headlong in upon them all. Brute, who behold-
eth all this, glowing with love of the man, hurrieth
forward with a company to succour him. Then ariseth
a mighty shouting betwixt the two peoples—the strokes
are redoubled, and passing bloody is the slaughter on
the one side and the other. But it endureth not long.
The Trojans win the day, and drive King Goffarius and
his Poitevins in flight before them. Goffarius, escaping
by the skin of his teeth, betook him into the parts of
Gaul to have succour of his kinsfolk and acquaintance.
At that time twelve kings there were in Gaul, each of
equal rank, under whose dominion the whole country
was ruled. They all received him kindly, and with one
accord did pledge them to drive out from the frontiers
of Aquitaine this foreign folk that had arrived there.

## [14]

BRUTE, overjoyed at the said victory, enricheth his
comrades with the spoils of the slain, and after again
forming the ranks in companies, he leadeth his host inland with the intention of sacking the whole country
and loading his ships with the countless treasure. Accordingly, he burneth the cities in all directions, fire
after fire, and ransacketh their hidden hoards; even the
fields were laid waste, and citizen and countryman alike
are subjected to a piteous slaughter, his aim being to
exterminate the unhappy race to the last man. But after
that he had thus visited with bloodshed well-nigh the
whole of Aquitaine, he came into the place where now
standeth the city of Tours, which, as Homer beareth
witness, he afterwards himself builded. Finding, after
diligent survey that the place was convenient as a refuge, he there decided to pitch his camp, so that if need

were he could betake him thereinto. For sore misgiving
had he by reason of the arrival of Goffarius, who had
marched into the neighbourhood along with the Kings
and Princes of Gaul and a mighty host of armed warriors to do battle against him. When his camp was fully
finished, he awaited Goffarius for two days therein, con-
fident alike in his own prudence and in the hardihood
of the young men whereof he was the chieftain.

[ 15 ]

Now, when Goffarius heard of the Trojans being
there, he advanced by forced marches day and night
until he came well within sight of Brute's camp. Gazing
grimly thereon, yet somewhat smiling withal, he burst
forth into these words: "Alas! what grievous destiny is
here? Have these ignoble exiles pitched their camp
within dominions of mine? To arms, ye warriors, to
arms! and charge through their serried ranks! Right
soon may we take captive this herd of half-men like
sheep and hold them in bondage throughout our
realm." Forthwith, all they that he had brought with
him leapt to arms, and marched upon their enemies
ranked in twelve battalions. But not after any woman
wise did Brute range his men and march to meet them.
Prudently instructing his troops as to what they were
to do, how to advance, and in what order to hold their
ground, he gives the word to charge. At the first onset,
the Trojans for a time had the upper hand, and fearful
was the slaughter they made of the enemy, for nigh two
thousand of them fell, and the rest were so daunted
at the sight that they all but turned to flee. But where
the numbers of men are the greater, there the more
often doth victory abide. In this case, therefore, the
Gauls, albeit that at first they were beaten back, yet
being thrice so many as their enemies, made shift to
form themselves again in rank and charged in again

on every side against the Trojans, whom they compelled
after much bloodshed to take refuge in the camp. Having thus obtained the victory, they beleaguered them
within the camp, never thinking but that before they
departed thence the besieged would either offer their
necks to the fetters, or suffer a cruel and lingering
death from the pangs of hunger. In the meanwhile, on
the night following, Corineus entered into counsel with
Brute, and agreed with him that he would issue forth
of the camp that same night by certain secret byways,
and would lie hidden in the neighbouring forest until
daybreak. And when Brute, issuing forth just before
dawn, should be engaged in battle with the enemy, he
himself with his company should attack them in the
rear, and charging in upon them put them to the sword.
Brute applauded this device of Corineus, who, cau-
tiously issuing forth as he had proposed with three
thousand men, betook him to the depths of the forest.
Accordingly, when the morrow morning began to break,
Brute ordained his men in companies, and opening the
gates of the camp, marched forth to battle. The Gauls
straightway set themselves to oppose him, and disposing their troops in battle array came to close quarters
with him. Many thousands of men are at once cut down
on both sides, and many are the wounds given and received, for not a man spareth his adversary. It chanced
that a certain Trojan was there present named Turo-
nus, a nephew of Brute's, than whom was none more
valiant and hardy save only Corineus himself. He with
his single sword slew no less than six hundred men.
Unhappily he was slain before his time by a sudden
onslaught of the Gauls; and the foresaid city of Tours
acquired the name thereof by reason of his being there
buried. And while the troops on both sides were in the
very thickest of the battle, Corineus came upon them
of a sudden and charged the enemy at the double in
the rear. Straightway the others, pressing forward from
the front, renew the attack more hotly and strain them

to the utmost to complete the slaughter. The Gauls
were aghast with dismay even at the very shout of the
Cornishmen as they charged in on the rear, and thinking that they were more in number than they were,
fled, hot foot, from the field. The Trojans are on their
heels, hewing them down in pursuit, nor cease they to
follow them up until the victory is their own. Brute,
nevertheless, albeit he were right glad at heart to have
achieved so signal a triumph, was sore grieved by anxiety on one account, for he saw that, whilst his own
numbers were minished daily, those of the Gauls were
daily multiplied. Wherefore, seeing it was doubtful
whether he could any longer hold out against them,
he chose rather to retire to his ships while the greater
part of his army was still whole and the glory of the
victory still fresh, and to set sail in quest of the island
which the divine monition had prophesied should be
his own. Nor was there any tarriance. With the assent
of his men, he returned to his fleet, and after loading
his ships with all the treasures and luxuries he had
acquired, he re-embarked, and with a prosperous wind
sought out the promised island, where he landed at last
in safety at Totnes.

*Imply democracy of Nobility:
The Vote of t. taken.*

[16]

At that time the name of the island was Albion, and
of none was it inhabited save only of a few giants.
Natheless the pleasant aspect of the land, with the
abundance of fish in the rivers and deer in the choice
forests thereof did fill Brute and his companions with
no small desire that they should dwell therein. Wherefore, after exploring certain districts of the land, they
drove the giants they found to take refuge in the caverns of the mountains, and divided the country among
them by lot according as the Duke made grant thereof.
They began to till the fields, and to build them houses

in such sort that after a brief space ye might have thought it had been inhabited from time immemorial. Then, at last, Brute calleth the island Britain, and his companions Britons, after his own name, for he was minded that his memory should be perpetuated in the derivation of the name. Whence afterward the country speech, which was aforetime called Trojan or crooked Greek, was called British. But Corineus called that share of the kingdom which had fallen unto him by lot Cornwall, after the manner of his own name, and the people Cornishmen, therein following the Duke's example. For albeit that he might have had the choice of a province before all the others that had come thither, yet was he minded rather to have that share of the land which is now called Cornwall, whether from being, as it is, the *cornu* or horn of Britain, or from a corruption of the said name Corineus. For nought gave him greater pleasure than to wrestle with the giants, of whom was greater plenty there than in any of the provinces that had been shared amongst his comrades. Among others was a certain hateful one by name Goemagog, twelve cubits in height, who was of such lustihood that when he had once uprooted it, he would wield an oak tree as lightly as it were a wand of hazel. On a certain day when Brute was holding high festival to the gods in the port whereat he had first landed, this one, along with a score of other giants, fell upon him and did passing cruel slaughter on the British. Howbeit, at the last, the Britons collecting together from all quarters prevailed against them and slew them all, save Goemagog only. Him Brute had commanded to be kept alive, as he was minded to see a wrestling bout betwixt him and Corineus, who was beyond measure keen to match himself against such monsters. So Corineus, overjoyed at the prospect, girt himself for the encounter, and flinging away his arms, challenged him to a bout at wrestling. At the start, on the one side stands Corineus, on the other the giant, each hugging

the other tight in the shackles of his arms, both making
the very air quake with their breathless gasping. It was
not long before Goemagog, grasping Corineus with all
his force, brake him three of his ribs, two on the right
side and one on the left. Roused thereby to fury, Corineus gathered up all his strength, heaved him up on
his shoulders and ran with his burden as fast as he
could for the weight to the seashore nighest at hand.
Mounting up to the top of a high cliff, and disengaging
himself, he hurled the deadly monster he had carried
on his shoulder into the sea, where, falling on the sharp
rocks, he was mangled all to pieces and dyed the waves
with his blood, so that ever thereafter that place from
the flinging down of the giant hath been known as
"Goemagog's Leap," and is called by that name unto
this present day.

[ 17 ]

AFTER that he had seen his kingdom, Brute was minded
to build him a chief city, and following out his intention, he went round the whole circuit of the land in
search of a fitting site. When he came to the river
Thames, he walked along the banks till he found the
very spot best fitted to his purpose. He therefore
founded his city there and called it New Troy, and by
this name was it known for many ages thereafter, until
at last, by corruption of the word, it came to be called
Trinovantum (London). But afterward, Lud, the
brother of Cassibelaunus, who fought with Julius
Cæsar, possessed him of the helm of the kingdom, and
surrounded the city with right noble walls, as well as
with towers builded with marvellous art, commanding
that it should be called Kaerlud, that is, the City of
Lud, after his own name. Whence afterward a contention arose betwixt him and his brother Nennius, who
took it ill that he should be minded to do away the

name of Troy in his own country. But since Gildas, the historian, hath treated of this contention at sufficient length, I have chosen the rather to pass it over, lest that which so great a writer hath already set forth in so eloquent a style, I should only seem to besmirch in mine own homelier manner of speech.

### [ 18 ]

ACCORDINGLY, when the aforesaid Duke founded the said city, he granted it as of right unto the citizens that should dwell therein, and gave them a law under which they should be peacefully entreated.

(At that time Eli the priest reigned in Judæa, and the Ark of the Covenant was taken by the Philistines. The sons of Hector reigned in Troy, having driven out the descendants of Antenor. In Italy reigned Silvius Æneas, the son of Æneas and uncle of Brute, he being the third of the Latin kings.)

# BOOK II

## [1]

Now Brutus knew Innogen his wife and she bare unto him three sons of high renown, whose names were Locrine, Albanact and Camber. When their father departed this life in the twenty-fourth year after his arrival, they buried him within the city that he had builded, and divided the realm of Britain amongst themselves, each succeeding him in his share therein. Locrine, that was eldest born, had the midland part of the island, which in later days was called Loegria (England), after his name. Next, Camber had that part which lieth beyond the river Severn, and is now called Wales, which afterward was for a long time called Cambria, after his name; whence unto this day do the folk of the country call them Cymry in the British tongue. But Albanact, the youngest, had the country which in these days in our tongue is called Scotland, and give it the name of Albany, after his own. And after that these had of a long time reigned in peace and concord, Humber, the King of the Huns, landed in Scotland, and engaging in battle with Albanact, slew him, and compelled the country folk to flee unto Locrine.

## [2]

Locrine, accordingly, when he heard the rumour, besought his brother Camber to accompany him, called out the whole youth of the country, and went to meet the King of the Huns in the neighbourhood of the river

Humber. When the armies met, he compelled Humber to flee, but when he had fled as far as the river, it chanced that he was drowned therein, and thus left his name to the stream. Locrine, therefore, after he had won the victory, distributed the spoil among his comrades, keeping nothing for himself save the gold and silver that he found in the enemy's ships. He also kept for himself three damsels of marvellous beauty, whereof one was the daughter of a certain King of Germany, whom the foresaid Humber had seized along with the two other damsels when he laid waste her father's country. Her name was Estrildis, and so fair was she that scarce might any be found to compare with her for beauty, for no polished ivory, nor newly-fallen snow, nor no lilies could surpass the whiteness of her flesh. Taken with love of her, Locrine would fain that she should share his bed, and that the marriage-torch should be lighted to celebrate their wedding. But when Corineus found out what he was minded to do he was wroth beyond measure, for that Locrine had pledged himself to marry Corineus' own daughter.

[3]

He came accordingly unto the King, and brandishing his battle-axe in his right hand, spake unto him on this wise: "Be these the wages, Locrine, that thou wouldst pay me for the wounds I have suffered in they father's service when he was warring against unknown peoples, that you disdain my daughter and stoop to yoke you with a barbarian woman? If this indeed be so, thou dost it on peril of my vengeance, so long as any strength is left in this right hand, which hath quenched the delight of life in so many giants on the Tyrrhene shores." Shouting these words aloud again and yet again, he brandished the axe as if about to strike him, when the friends of both flung themselves betwixt. And after that

Corineus were somewhat appeased, they compelled Locrine to perform that which he had pledged him to do.


[4]


LOCRINE accordingly married Corineus' daughter, Gwendolen by name; yet, natheless did he not forget the love
he bare unto Estrildis. Wherefore, in the city of London, did he make fashion a chamber underground
wherein he enclosed her, and caused her be right honourably served of the attendants of his household, for
that he was minded to keep his love of her secret. For
he was sore troubled by reason of his dread of Corineus,
so that he durst not hold her openly, but, as hath been
said already, kept her in hiding, and seven whole years
did haunt her in secret, so that none knew thereof save
only they that were the closest of his familiars. For, so
often as he was minded to go unto her, he would feign
that he made hidden sacrifice unto his gods, whereby
he did lightly move others to believe the same, albeit
in truth it were no such thing. In the meantime,
Estrildis did become great with child, and brought
forth a daughter of marvellous beauty, whom she called
Habren. Gwendolen also became pregnant and bare a
son unto whom was given the name of Maddan. This
son was delivered into the charge of his grandfather
Corineus, and had of him his teachings and nurture.

[5]

*According to the laws
of Chivalry.*

YEARS later, after Corineus was dead, Locrine deserted
Gwendolen and raised Estrildis to be Queen. Gwendolen thereupon, being beyond measure indignant, went
into Cornwall, and gathering together all the youth of
that kingdom, began to harass Locrine by leading forays into his land. At last, after both had mustered their

armies, a battle was fought on the river Stour, and Locrine, smitten by an arrow, lost his life and all the joys thereof. Whereupon Gwendolen laid hold on the helm of state, maddened by the same revengeful fury as her father, insomuch as that she bade Estrildis and Habren her daughter be flung into the river that is now called Severn, issuing an edict throughout all Britain that the river should be called by the damsel's name. For she was minded that it should bear her name forever, for that it was her own husband that begat her; whereby it cometh to pass that even unto this day the river in the British tongue is called Habren, which by corruption in other speech is called Severn.

[6]

GWENDOLEN reigned fifteen years after the slaying of Locrine, who had reigned ten years. And when she saw that her son Maddan had grown to man's estate, she conferred upon him the sceptre of the realm, contenting herself with the province of Cornwall, wherein she passed the rest of her life. At that time Samuel the prophet reigned in Judæa, and Silvius Æneas was still living. And Homer was held to be a famous teller of histories and poet. Whilst Madden held the sceptre, his wife bare unto him two sons, Mempricius and Malim. And he maintained his kingdom in peace diligently for forty years. But after his death arose discord betwixt the two brethren as concerning the kingdom, for that each of them was eager to possess the whole island. Mempricius accordingly, desirous of achieving his own ends, entered into conference with Malim as if for the purpose of establishing concord betwixt them. But kindled, as it were, by the firebrand of treason, he slew him in the presence of them that had come to take counsel in the matter, and having thus obtained the government of the whole island, exercised so sore a tyranny

over the people that he destroyed well-nigh all the
more noble men of the land. Moreover, hating all of
his own family, either by violence or treachery he made
away with every single one that he feared might be
able to succeed him in the kingdom. He further left his
own wife that had borne him the famous youth Ebraucus, and abandoned himself wholly to unclean living,
preferring unnatural intercourse to natural love. At last,
in the twentieth year of his reign, while he was out
hunting, he rode apart from his companions into a certain combe, wherein he was surrounded by a herd of
raging wolves and miserably devoured.

(At that time Saul reigned in Judæa and Eurystheus
in Lacedæmon.)

[7]

AFTER the death of Mempricius, his son Ebraucus, a
man tall of stature and of marvellous strength, undertook the government of Britain, which he held for
thirty-nine years. He was the first after Brute to take a
fleet along the coasts of Gaul, and carrying war into
the country to harass the provinces by the slaughter of
men and the sacking of the cities; returning thence with
victory and enriched with boundless plenty of gold and
silver. He afterwards founded a city beyond the Humber, which, after his own name, he called Kaerebrauc,
that is to say, the City of York. At that time King David
reigned in Judæa, and Silvius Latinus in Italy. Gad,
Nathan, and Asaph prophesied in Israel. Ebraucus
founded also the city of Alclud (Dumbarton) towards
Scotland, and the fortress of Mount Agned, which now
is called the Castle of Damsels, and the Dolorous Mountain.

## [8]

HE begat, moreover, twenty sons by twenty wives that
he had, besides thirty daughters, and for forty years did
he maintain the kingdom of Britain right stoutly. The
names of his sons were these: Brute Greenshield,
Margadud, Sisillius, Regin, Morvid, Bladud, Iagon,
Bodloan, Kincar, Spaden, Gaul, Dardan, Eldad, Ivor,
Cangu, Hector, Kerin, Rud, Assarach, Buel. The names
of the daughters were: Gloigin, Ignogin, Oudas, Guen-
lian, Gaurdid, Angarad, Guenlodoe, Tangustel, Gor-
gon, Medlan, Methael, Ourar, Mailure, Kambreda,
Ragan, Gael, Ecub, Nest, Chein, Stadud, Gladus,
Ebrein, Blangan, Aballac, Angaes, Galaes—the fairest
of all at that time living in Britain or Gaul—,Edra,
Anor, Stadiald, and Egron. These all did their father
cause to be convoyed into Italy unto Silvius Alba, who
reigned after Silvius Latinus. There were they married
with the more noble Trojans with whom the Latin and
Sabine women did refuse to match them. The sons,
moreover, with Assarach their brother for chieftain, took
a fleet into Germany, where with the help of Silvius
Alba, they subdued the people and possessed themselves
of the kingdom.

## [9]

HOWBEIT, Brute, surnamed Greenshield, remained with
his father, and obtaining the government of the kingdom after his father's death, reigned for twelve years.
Him succeeded his son Leil, a lover of peace and justice, who, taking advantage of a prosperous reign,
builded a city in the northern parts of Britain called
after his name Carlisle. At this time did Solomon begin
to build the Temple of the Lord in Jerusalem, and the
Queen of Sheba came thither to hearken unto his wis-

dom. At the same time Silvius Epitus succeeded his father Alba in the kingdom of the Latins. Leil lived five-and-twenty years after that he had come into the kingdom, albeit toward the end he maintained his royalty but feebly. Owing to his sluggard slackness a civil war suddenly arose in the realm. After him reigned his son Hudibras nine-and-thirty years, who, after the civil dissensions, did restore concord among the people and founded Kaerchent, that is, Canterbury. He also founded Kaergueint, which is Winchester, and the fortress of Mount Paladur, which is now called Shaftesbury. There, while the wall was a-building, an eagle spake, the sayings whereof, had I believed them to be true, I would not have shrunk from committing to written memory along with the rest.

(At that time reigned Capys, the son of Epitus, and Haggai, Amos, Jehu, Joel, and Azarias did prophesy.)

[ 10 ]

NEXT succeeded Bladud his son, in whose hands the kingdom remained for twenty years. He builded the city of Kaerbadon, that is now called Bath, and fashioned hot baths therein, meet for the needs of men, the which he placed under the guardianship of the deity Minerva, in whose temple he set fires that could not be quenched, that never turned into ashes, but as they began to fail became as it were round balls of stone.

(At that time did Elijah pray that it might not rain upon the earth, and it rained not for the space of three years and six months.)

Bladud was a right cunning craftsman, and did teach nigromancy throughout the realm of Britain, nor did he stint of his subtle sleights until he had fashioned him wings and tried to go upon the top of the air, when he fell upon the temple of Apollo in the city of London, and was dashed into many pieces.

## [ 11 ]

WHEN Bladud was thus given over to the destinies, his
son Lear was next raised to the kingdom, and ruled the
country after manly fashion for three-score years. He it
was that builded the city on the river Soar, that in the
British is called Kaerleir, but in the Saxon, Leicester.
Male issue was denied unto him, his only children being
three daughters named Goneril, Regan, and Cordelia,
whom all he did love with marvellous affection, but
most of all the youngest born, to wit, Cordelia. And
when that he began to be upon the verge of eld, he
thought to divide his kingdom amongst them, and to
marry them unto such husbands as were worthy to have
them along with their share of the kingdom. But that
he might know which of them was most worthy of the
largest share, he went unto them to make inquiry of
each as to which of them did most love himself. When,
accordingly, he asked of Goneril how much she loved
him, she first called all the gods of heaven to witness
that her father was dearer to her heart than the very
soul that dwelt within her body. Unto whom saith her
father: "For this, that thou hast set mine old age before
thine own life, thee, my dearest daughter, will I marry
unto whatsoever youth shall be thy choice, together
with the third part of Britain." Next, Regan, that was
second, fain to take ensample of her sister and to wheedle her father into doing her an equal kindness, made
answer with a solemn oath that she could no otherwise
express her thought than by saying that she loved him
better than all the world beside. The credulous father
thereupon promised to marry her with the same dignity
as her elder sister, with another third part of the kingdom for her share. But the last, Cordelia, when she saw
how her father had been cajoled by the flatteries of her
sisters who had already spoken and desiring to make

trial of him otherwise, went on to make answer unto him thus: "Father mine, is there a daughter anywhere that presumeth to love her father more than a father? None such, I trow, there is that durst confess as much, save she were trying to hide the truth in words of jest. For myself, I have ever loved thee as a father, nor never from that love will I be turned aside. Albeit that thou art bent on wringing more from me, yet hearken to the true measure of my love. Ask of me no more, but let this be mine answer: So much as thou hast, so much art thou worth, and so much do I love thee." Thereupon forthwith, her father, thinking that she had thus spoken out of the abundance of her heart, waxed mightily indignant, nor did he tarry to make known what his answer would be. "For that thou hast so despised thy father's old age that thou hast disdained to love me even as well as these thy sisters love me, I also will disdain thee, nor never in my realm shalt thou have share with thy sisters. Howbeit, sith that thou art my daughter, I say not but that I will marry thee upon terms of some kind unto some stranger that is of other land than mine, if so be that fortune shall offer such an one; only be sure of this, that never will I trouble me to marry thee with such honour as thy sisters, inasmuch as, whereas up to this time I have loved thee better than the others, it now seemeth that thou lovest me less than they."

Straightway thereupon, by counsel of the nobles of the realm, he giveth the twain sisters unto two Dukes, of Cornwall, to wit, and Scotland, together with one moiety only of the island so long as he should live, but after his death he willed that they should have the whole of the kingdom of Britain. Now it so fell out about this time that Aganippus, King of the Franks, hearing report of Cordelia's beauty, forthwith despatched his envoys to the King, beseeching him that Cordelia might be entrusted to their charge as his bride whom he would marry with due rite of the wedding·

torch. But her father, still persisting in his wrath, made answer that right willingly would he give her, but that needs must it be without land or fee, seeing that he had shared his kingdom along with all his gold and silver betwixt Cordelia's sisters Goneril and Regan. When this word was brought unto Aganippus, for that he was on fire with love of the damsel, he sent again unto King Lear saying that enow had he of gold and silver and other possessions, for that one-third part of Gaul was his, and that he was fain to marry the damsel only that he might have sons by her to inherit his land. So at last the bargain was struck, and Cordelia was sent to Gaul to be married unto Aganippus.

*This is Suggested from the outset in Shakespeare.*

## [12]

SOME long time after, when Lear began to wax more sluggish by reason of age, the foresaid Dukes, with whom and his two daughters he had divided Britain, rebelled against him and took away from him the realm and the kingly power which up to that time he had held right manfully and gloriously. Howbeit, concord was restored, and one of his sons-in-law, Maglaunus, Duke of Scotland, agreed to maintain him with forty knights, so that he should not be without some semblance of state. But after that he had sojourned with his son-in-law two years, his daughter Goneril began to wax indignant at the number of his knights, who flung gibes at her servants for that their rations were not more plentiful. Whereupon, after speaking to her husband, she ordered her father to be content with a service of twenty knights and to dismiss the others that he had. The King, taking this in dudgeon, left Maglaunus, and betook him to Henvin, Duke of Cornwall, unto whom he had married his other daughter, Regan. Here, at first, he was received with honour, but a year had not passed before discord again arose betwixt those of the

King's household and those of the Duke's, insomuch as
that Regan, waxing indignant, ordered her father to
dismiss all his company save five knights only to do him
service. Her father, beyond measure aggrieved thereat,
returned once more to his eldest daughter, thinking to
move her to pity and to persuade her to maintain himself and his retinue. Howbeit, she had never renounced
her first indignation, but swore by all the gods of
Heaven that never should he take up his abode with
her save he contented himself with the service of a single knight and were quit of all the rest. Moreover, she
upbraided the old man for that, having nothing of his
own to give away, he should be minded to go about
with such a retinue; so that finding she would not give
way to his wishes one single tittle, he at last obeyed and
remained content with one knight only, leaving the rest
to go their way. But when the remembrance of his former dignity came back unto him, bearing witness to the
misery of the estate to which he was now reduced, he
began to bethink him of going to his youngest daughter
oversea. Howbeit, he sore misdoubted that she would
do nought for him, seeing that he had held her, as I
have said, in such scanty honour in the matter of her
marriage. Natheless, disdaining any longer to endure
so mean a life, he betook him across the Channel into
Gaul. But when he found that two other princes were
making the passage at the same time, and that he himself had been assigned but the third place, he brake
forth into tears and sobbing, and cried aloud: "Ye destinies that do pursue your wonted way marked out by
irrevocable decree, wherefore was it your will ever to
uplift me to happiness so fleeting? For a keener grief it
is to call to mind that lost happiness than to suffer the
presence of the unhappiness that cometh after. For the
memory of the days when in the midst of hundreds of
thousands of warriors I went to batter down the walls
of cities and to lay waste the provinces of mine enemies
is more grievous unto me than the calamity that hath

overtaken me in the meanness of mine estate, which hath incited them that but now were grovelling under my feet to desert my feebleness. O angry fortune! will the day ever come wherein I may requite the evil turn that hath thus driven forth the length of my days and my poverty? O Cordelia, my daughter, how true were the words wherein thou didst make answer unto me, when I did ask of thee how much thou didst love me! For thou saidst, 'So much as thou hast, so much art thou worth, and so much do I love thee.' So long, therefore, as I had that which was mine own to give, so long seemed I of worth unto them that were the lovers, not of myself but of my gifts. They loved me at times, but better loved they the presents I made unto them. Now that the presents are no longer forthcoming, they too have gone their ways. But with what face, O thou dearest of my children, shall I dare appear before thee, I who, wroth with thee for these thy words, was minded to marry thee less honourably than thy sisters, who, after all the kindnesses I have conferred upon them, have allowed me to become an outcast and a beggar?"

Landing at last, his mind filled with these reflections and others of a like kind, he came to Karitia, where his daughter lived, and waiting without the city, sent a messenger to tell her into what indigence he had fallen, and to beseech his daughter's compassion inasmuch as he had neither food nor clothing. On hearing the tidings, Cordelia was much moved and wept bitterly. When she made inquiry how many armed men he had with him, the messengers told her that he had none save a single knight, who was waiting with him without the city. Then took she as much gold and silver as was needful and gave it unto the messenger, bidding him take her father to another city, where he should bathe him, clothe him, and nurse him, feigning that he was a sick man. She commanded also that he should have a retinue of forty knights well appointed and armed, and that then he should duly announce his arrival to Aganippus and herself. The messenger accordingly forthwith attended King Lear into another city, and hid him there in secret until that he had fully accomplished all that Cordelia had borne him on hand to do.

## [13]

As soon therefore, as he was meetly arrayed in kingly apparel and invested with the ensigns of royalty and a train of retainers, he sent word unto Aganippus and his daughter that he had been driven out of the realm of Britain by his sons-in-law, and had come unto them in order that by their assistance he might be able to recover his kingdom. They accordingly, with the great counsellors and nobles, came forth to receive him with all honour, and placed in his hands the power over the whole of Gaul until such time as they had restored him unto his former dignity.

## [14]

In the meanwhile, Aganippus sent envoys throughout the whole of Gaul to summon every knight bearing arms therein to spare no pains in coming to help him to recover the kingdom of Britain for his father-in-law, King Lear. When they had all made them ready, Lear led the assembled host together with Aganippus and his daughter into Britain, fought a battle with his sons-in-law, and won the victory, again bringing them all under his own dominion. In the third year thereafter he died, and Aganippus died also, and Cordelia, now mistress of the helm of state in Britain, buried her father in a certain underground chamber which she had bidden be made under the river Soar at Leicester. This underground chamber was founded in honour of the two-faced Janus, and there, when the yearly celebration of

the day came round, did all the workmen of the city set
hand unto such work as they were about to be busied
upon throughout the year.

[ 15 ]

Now, when Cordelia had governed the kingdom in
peace for five years, two sons of her sisters began to
harass her, Margan, to wit, and Cunedag, that had been
born unto the Dukes Maglaunus and Henvin, both of
them youths of notable likelihood and prowess, Margan
being son of Maglaunus and Cunedag of Henvin. These,
after the deaths of their fathers, had succeeded them in
their dukedoms, and now took it in high dudgeon that
Britain should be subject to the rule of a woman. They
therefore assembled their hosts and rebelled against the
Queen, nor were they minded to put an end to their
outrages until after laying waste a number of provinces,
they had defeated her in several battles, and had at last
taken her and put her in prison, wherein, overwhelmed
with grief for the loss of her kingdom, she slew herself.
Forthwith the youths divided the island between them,
whereof that part which stretcheth from the Humber
towards Caithness fell to Margan's share, and the other,
on the other side of the river, that vergeth toward the
West, was allotted to Cunedag. After the space of two
years, certain of them that rejoiced in making disturbance in the realm, joined them with Margan and began
to tempt him to walk in crooked paths, saying that foul
shame it was he, the eldest born, should not have dominion over the whole island; so that, what with this
and other grievances, they at last egged him on to
march with an army into Cunedag's territories, and
thus began to heap fuel on the fire they had kindled. On
the war breaking out, Cunedag with all his host marched
out to meet him, and in the battle that was fought inflicted no small slaughter, driving Margan in flight be-

fore him, and afterwards following his flight from province to province, until at last he overtook and slew him
in a village of Wales, which after that Margan was slain
there hath been called by his name, Margan to wit, ever
since by the country folk even unto this day. Cunedag,
accordingly, having won the victory, possessed himself
of the monarchy of the whole island and governed the
same gloriously for three-and-thirty years.

(At that time Isaiah and Hosea prophesied, and Rome
was founded the eleventh of the Kalends of May by the
twin-brethren, Romulus and Remus.)

[16]

AFTERWARDS, upon the death of Cunedag, his son
Rivallo succeeded him, a peaceful youth and fortunate,
who governed the realm with diligence. In his time
there fell a rain of blood three days, and a great swarm-
ing of flies was there, whereof men died. After him succeeded Gurgustius, his son, unto whom Sisillius, and after
him Iago the nephew of Gurgustius, unto whom succeeded Kinmarch the son of Sisillius, and after him Gor-
bodug. Unto him were two sons born, whereof the one
was called Ferrex and the other Porrex. But when their
father began to verge upon eld, a contention arose betwixt the twain as to which should succeed him in the
kingdom. Howbeit, Porrex, spurred on thereunto by a
more grasping covetise, layeth snares for his brother
with design of slaying him, whereupon Ferrex, when
the matter was discovered unto him, betook him across
the Channel into Gaul, and, having obtained the help
of Suard, King of the Franks, returned and fought
against his brother. In this battle betwixt them, Ferrex
was slain together with the entire host that accompanied
him. Thereupon their mother, who was named Iudon,
when she learnt the certainty of her son's death, was beyond measure troubled, and conceived a bitter hatred

of the other, for she loved the one that was slain the
better of the twain, and so hotly did her wrath blaze up
by reason of his death, that she was minded to revenge
it upon his brother. She accordingly took possession of
the tent wherein he was lying fast asleep, and setting
upon him with her waiting-women hacked him all into
little pieces. Thenceforward the people was sore afflicted
by civil war for a long space, and the kingdom was governed by five kings who harried the one another with
mutual forays wherein was much blood spilt.

[ 17 ]

AT last, in after days, arose a certain youth renowned
above all others for his singular prowess, by name Dunwallo Molmutius, the son of Cloten, King of Cornwall.
Excelling all the Kings of Britain in comeliness and
courage, he no sooner undertook the government of the
country upon his father's death than he invaded the
lands of Pinner, King of England, whom after a battle
he defeated and slew. Thereupon Rudauc, the King of
Wales, and Stater, King of Scotland, took counsel together, and after that they had contracted an alliance,
led their armies into Dunwallo's territory to lay waste
town and country and destroy his people. Dunwallo
marched to meet them with thirty thousand men and
gave battle, but after great part of the day had been
spent in fighting and neither party could claim the victory, he called apart six hundred of his bravest youths
and bade them all take and don the arms of the enemies
they had slain. He himself also flung aside the arms he
was wearing and did the like. He then led them into the
press of the enemy's ranks, going in among them as
though he were of their own party, and when he had
reached the place where Rudauc and Stater were leading on their men, gave the word unto his comrades to
charge down upon them. They accordingly dashed for-

ward, and the two Kings were slain in the onset and a number of others along with them. But Dunwallo Molmutius, fearing lest he should be himself slain of his own men, turned back with his comrades and disarmed him. Then, donning again the arms that he had flung aside, he cheereth on his comrades to another charge which he himself led foremost. Scarce a moment later the day was won and the enemy put to flight and scattered. It was then only left for him to march through the lands of the slain, overthrow their cities and fortresses, and subject their people to his dominion. And after that he had thus utterly subjugated the whole island, he fashioned for himself a crown of gold and restored the realm unto the former estate thereof.

This King it was that did establish amongst the Britons the laws that were called the Molmutine laws, the which even unto this day are celebrated amongst the English. For among other things which, long time after, the Blessed Gildas did write of him, he ordained that the temples of the gods and the cities should enjoy such privilege, as that in case any runaway or guilty man should take refuge therein, he should depart thence forgiven of his adversary. He ordained, moreover, that the ways which led unto the foresaid temples and cities, no less than the ploughs of the husbandmen, should by the same law be held inviolable. In his days, therefore, the knife of the cut-throat was blunted and the cruelties of the robber ceased in the land, for nowhere was any that durst do violence unto other. At last, after that forty years were fulfilled sithence that he had taken the crown, he departed and was buried in the city of Trinovantum anigh the Temple of Concord, which he had builded to the confirmation of his law.

# BOOK III

## [1]

AFTER Dunwallo's death, his two sons, Belinus, to wit, and Brennius, both desirous of succeeding him in the kingdom, clashed the one upon the other with a mighty shock. For the contention between them was which of the twain should wear the diadem of the realm. But after they had fought many battles thereanent betwixt themselves, the friends of both did intervene between them and restored them to concord, covenanting that the kingdom should be shared between them on this condition, that Belinus should have the crown of the island along with England, Wales, and Cornwall to boot, forasmuch as he was the elder born, and Trojan custom did demand that the dignity of the inheritance should fall unto him, while Brennius, for that he was the younger, should be subject to his brother, and should hold Northumbria from the Humber as far as Caithness. These covenants being duly confirmed by treaty, they governed the country for a space of five years in peace and justice. But, for that discord doth ever seek to intermeddle with prosperity, certain forgers of falsehoods were not lacking that found access to Brennius, saying unto him: "What sluggard sloth hath thus beset thee to hold thee in subjection unto Belinus, when the same father and mother and the same nobility have made thee his peer? Add to this, moreover, how in many a hard-fought battle thou hast over and over again shown how thou couldst withstand Cheulf, Duke of Flanders, and put him to flight when he would have made good his landing upon the shores of our province. Break, therefore, this covenant that is a disgrace unto thee, and

46

take to wife the daughter of Elsing, the King of Norway, and by his help recover the dignity thou hast lost." After that they had corrupted the youth's mind with these and other like conceits, he at last assented unto their counsel, sailed away to Norway, and married the King's daughter, even as he had been advised by these same sycophants.

[2]

MEANWHILE, when this was reported to his brother, he took it in dudgeon that without asking leave or licence he had thus acted against him. He therefore marched into Northumbria and took the cities of them of that province, garrisoning them with his own men. Whereupon Brennius, hearing a rumour that notified him of his brother's doings, fitted out a fleet and returned to Britain, bringing with him a strong force of Norwegians. But whilst that he was cleaving the level fields of the sea with a fair wind and without misgiving, Guichtlac, King of the Danes, who had followed him, fell upon him suddenly, he himself being desperately enamoured of the damsel that Brennius had married. Aggrieved, therefore, beyond measure at his loss of her, he had fitted forth his ships and men and started in pursuit of him full sail. In the battle at sea that followed it so happened that he came alongside the ship wherein was the foresaid damsel, and making the vessel fast to his own with grappling hooks, fetched the damsel out of the one aboard the other and set her down in the midst of his own shipmates. But whilst the barks were thus grappled together, and were swaying about hither and thither in the deep sea, foul winds rise of a sudden, and in the squall the ships are parted, and driven by stress of weather upon different coasts. The King of Denmark, after drifting for five days out of his course before the tempest in continual terror, made land at last with the

damsel on the coast of Northumbria, knowing not upon
what shores he had been cast by this unlooked-for disaster. And when the men of the country learned what
had fallen out, they took and brought them to Belinus,
who was awaiting his brother's arrival in the parts by
the sea. There were also along with Guichtlac's ships
three other ships, whereof one was of them that Brennius had fitted out. Glad enough was the King when
he heard who they were, but yet more exceedingly glad
that this had befallen him just at the very moment he
was most desirous of being revenged upon his brother.

[3]

AFTER a space of some days, Brennius had got his ships
together again, and, lo and behold ye, landeth on the
coast of Scotland. Forthwith, as soon as he heareth how
his bride and they that were with her have been taken
captive, and that in his absence his brother hath wrested
from him the kingdom of Northumbria, he sendeth messengers unto him, demanding that his kingdom and his
bride shall be at once restored unto him, otherwise he
will lay the whole island waste from sea to sea, and slay
his brother whensoever and wheresoever he may meet
him withal. Which when Belinus understood, he flatly
refused his demand, and summoning all the host of the
island marcheth into Scotland to do battle with him.
But Brennius, when he knew that he had only asked to
be denied, and that his brother was thus coming against
him, went to meet him in the forest that is called Calaterium, there to meet and do battle with him. Both, accordingly, took up a position on the same field, each
dividing his fellows into companies, and advancing the
one upon the other, began the engagement at close
quarters. Great part of the day was spent in fighting, for
they of greater prowess on both sides met hand to hand.
Great was the bloodshed on the one side and on the

other, for sore deadly were the wounds they dealt with their brandished weapons, and the wounded fell before the onset of the companies as they had been corn before the reaper's sickle. At last the Britons prevail, and the Norwegians flee with their maimed and mangled companies to their ships. Belinus pursueth them as they flee, making slaughter without pity. In that battle fell 15,000 men, nor of the residue was there a single thousand that escaped unharmed. Brennius, just making shift to reach one ship that fortune threw in his way, betook him to the coast of Gaul. But the rest who had come with him could only skulk away to the best hiding-place they could find as chance might guide them.

## [4]

WHEN Belinus had achieved the victory, he summoned all the nobles of the realm to meet him at York, to take counsel with him as to what he should do with the King of the Danes. For the King had sent him word from his prison that he would submit himself and the kingdom of Denmark unto him, and pay him yearly tribute, so he were allowed to depart freely along with his mistress. He sent word further that he would confirm the covenant by solemn oath, and give hostage for its fulfilment. When this offer was laid before the assembled nobles, all of them signified their willingness that Belinus should grant Guichtlac's petition on these terms. He himself also agreed, and Guichtlac, released from prison, returned to Denmark with his mistress.

## [5]

BELINUS, moreover, finding none in the kingdom of Britain that was minded to withstand him, and that he was undisputed master of the island from sea to sea,

confirmed the laws which his father had ordained, and
commanded that even and steadfast justice should be
done throughout the realm. Especially careful was he to
proclaim that the cities and the highways that led unto
the city should have the same place that Dunwallo has
established therein. But a dissension arose as concerning
the highways, for that none knew the line whereby
their boundaries were determined. The King therefore,
being minded to leave no loophole for quibbles in the
law, called together all the workmen of the whole island,
and commanded a highway to be builded of stone and
mortar that should cut through the entire length of the
island from the Cornish sea to the coast of Caithness,
and should run in a straight line from one city unto another the whole of the way along. A second also he bade
be made across the width of the kingdom, which,
stretching from the city of St. Davids on the sea of South
Wales as far as Southampton, should show clear guidance to the cities along the line. Two others also he
made be laid out slantwise athwart the island so as to
afford access unto the other cities. Then he dedicated
them with all honour and dignity, and proclaimed it
as of his common law, that condign punishment should
be inflicted on any that shall do violence to other thereupon. But if that any would fain know all of his ordinances as concerning them, let him read the Molmutine
laws that Gildas the historian did translate out of the
British into Latin, and King Alfred out of Latin into
the English tongue.

## [6]

IN the meanwhile that Belinus was reigning in peace
and tranquillity, his brother Brennius, driven forth, as
hath been said, to the shores of Gaul, was sore tormented of inward tribulation. For he took it grievously
to heart that he was banished from his country, without

any means of returning thither so as to enjoy again the
dignity he had lost. Not knowing therefore what to do,
he betook him unto the Princes of Gaul, with a company of twelve knights only. And when he had laid
open his ill-fortune unto them all, and found that no
succour could he obtain from any, he came at last unto
Segin, Duke of the Burgundians, and of him was right
honourably received. And whilst that he was still sojourning with him, he entered into so close familiarity
with the Duke, as that none other was there in his court
that was preferred before him. For in all matters,
whether of peace or of war, such prowess did he show
that the Duke loved him with a father's love. For he
was comely to look upon, tall and big of limb, and, as
was meet, well-taught in hawking and venery. And for
that he had fallen into so near friendship with the
Duke, Segin determined that he should take unto him
his only daughter in lawful wedlock. And if thereafter
it should so be that the Duke were without heir male,
he granted Brennius that after his own death he should
have the kingdom of the Burgundians along with his
daughter. But in case a son should be born unto the
Duke, he promised his assistance in raising him to the
kingship of Britain, and this was promised him not only
by the Duke but by all the champion knights that were
of the Duke's allegiance, so great was the friendship
they bare towards him. Straightway thereupon the damsel is given in marriage to Brennius, the princes of the
land become his men, and the throne of the country is
conferred upon him. Nor had the full twelvemonth
elapsed wherein these matters were settled, before the
Duke's last day arrived, and he departed out of this life.
Then Brennius neglected not the occasion to bind unto
himself yet more closely those princes of the land whose
friendship he had aforetime secured, by distributing largesse among them from the Duke's treasure that had
been hoarded from the time of his ancestors. And, that
which the Burgundians did hold of yet higher esteem,

he was right bountiful in his gifts of victual and never shut his door against any man.

## [7]

HAVING thus drawn the affection of every man unto himself, he deliberated inwardly in what manner he might take his revenge upon his brother Belinus, and when he announced his plans unto the people that were his lieges, they all with one accord declared that they would go with him into whatsoever land he might design to lead them. Nor did he linger, for, assembling a mighty host, he entered into covenant with the Gauls for leave to pass unmolested through their provinces on his way towards Britain. Forthwith he fitted out a fleet on the shore of Normandy, and launching into the deep, with a fair wind made good his landing on the island. As soon as the tidings of his arrival was bruited abroad, his brother Belinus, mustering all the youth of the kingdom, marched forth to meet him. But while their companies were still standing in orderly rank on the two sides just ready to begin the engagement, the mother of both, who was still living, pressed her hastily forward in the midst of the serried ranks. Her name was Conwenna, and the desire of her heart was to look again upon her son whom she had not seen of so long a time. Accordingly, so soon as she had reached with trembling steps the place where he was standing, she flung her arms about his neck, and stayed the yearning of her heart by kissing him again and yet again. Then, baring her bosom, she spake unto him on this wise in a voice broken by her sobs: "Remember, my son, remember these breasts that thou hast sucked and the womb that bare thee wherein the Maker of all things hath created thee man of man and brought thee forth into the world through the throes of childbirth. Remember all the anxieties that I have suffered for thee, and grant thou this

my petition! Yield thy pardon unto thy brother, and
constrain the wrath that thou hast conceived against
him, for no revenge is thine of right as against one that
hath never offered thee either insult or injury. Even
this that thou dost urge against him, to wit, that
through him thou hast been banished from thy kingdom, if so be that thou wilt more narrowly look into
the bearings of the case, nought wilt thou find therein
that thou canst call a wrong. For he banished thee not
that any worse thing might befall thee, but he compelled thee to forego the worser things that thou
mightest be exalted unto the better. For whereas thou
didst only possess thy share of the kingdom as his vassal,
now that thou hast lost it, thou art his peer in that thou
hast obtained the realm of the Burgundians. What else
hath he done herein, save that from being a needy
knight, he hath promoted thee to be a high and mighty
king? Add to this that the quarrel which hath risen betwixt ye was none of his seeking, but was begun by thee
when, trusting to the King's help of Norway, thou didst
burn to rebel against him!"

Moved, therefore, by the prayer unto which she had
thus given utterance, in a chastened spirit he yielded
obedience to her will, and doing off his helmet, walked
forward with her to his brother. Belinus, when he saw
him thus coming towards him with a countenance of
peace, flung aside his arms and ran into his embrace
with a kiss. The brothers made friends forthwith, and
with their disarmed troops made their way unto the city
of London. There taking counsel what they should do,
they made them ready to lead their common army into
Gaul, and to subject all the provinces thereof to their
dominion.

[8]

AT the end of the year they passed the Channel into
Gaul, and began to lay the country waste. When the

tidings thereof were bruited abroad among the various nations, all the knights of the Franks came to meet them and fight against them. But the victory falling to Belinus and Brennius, the Franks fled with their wounded companies in all directions. But the Britons and Burgundians, so soon as they had won the day, ceased not to follow up the fleeing Gauls until they had taken captive their Kings and compelled them to surrender. Setting garrisons in the cities they overthrew, they reduced the whole kingdom to submission within a single twelvemonth. Lastly, when they had forced all the provinces to yield, they started for Rome with all their host, and ravaged the cities and farms throughout Italy.

## [9]

AT that time there were two Consuls at Rome, Gabius and Porsenna, unto whose government the country had been committed, who, when they saw that no people were so strong they might withstand the fierce fury of Belinus and Brennius, came unto them with consent of the Senate, to bespeak their goodwill and friendship. They offered, moreover, presents of much gold and silver, and a tribute every year so they might be allowed to hold their own in peace. Taking hostages, therefore, to secure their loyalty, the Kings granted them pardon, and led their troops into Germany. Natheless, so soon as ever they had set them to work ravaging that country, the Romans repented them of the foresaid covenant, and taking courage afresh, marched forth to help the Germans. When the Kings found it out, they took it in grievous dudgeon, and held counsel how best to meet the attack of the two peoples together, for so huge a multitude of Italians had arrived that they were in no small jeopardy. Wherefore, after taking counsel together, Belinus with his Britons remained in Germany to carry on the war against the enemy, while Brennius

with his armies marched upon Rome to take revenge
for the broken covenant. Howbeit, the Italians coming
to know thereof, deserted the Germans, and hurried
back to Rome, doing their best to out-march the advance of Brennius and get there first. But when their
design was notified to Belinus, he called back his army,
and starting off as soon as night was past, took possession of a certain valley through which the enemy
would have to pass, and lying in ambush there, waited
for their arrival. On the morrow at dawn, the Italians,
who had begun their march, reached the same spot, and
when they beheld before them the valley glittering with
the arms of their enemies, at once surmised in dismay
that they who were there were Brennius and his Seno-
nian Gauls. Thereupon, as soon as the enemy were well
in sight, Belinus suddenly charged down upon them and
dashed swiftly into their midst. In a moment the Romans, marching disorderly and without arms, were utterly taken aback, and skurried off the field in headlong
flight, followed hard by Belinus, who never once stinted
of slaughtering them without mercy till night came on
and he could no longer see to make an end of the bloodshed. After this victory he followed in search of Brennius, who had already been three days besieging Rome.
They joined forces, accordingly, and the common army
made a general assault upon the city, doing their
utmost to breach the walls. Moreover, by way of adding
terror to slaughter, they set up gibbets in front of the
city gates, and sent word to the besieged that they would
hang up the hostages they had given on the gallows-tree
in case they were minded not to surrender. Natheless,
the Romans, persisting in their purpose, scorned to take
pity on their sons and grandsons, and determined to defend themselves and drive the enemy back from the
walls, at one time shattering their besieging engines
either with appliances devised for defence or with
counter engines of the same kind, and at another with
weapons and missiles of all sorts. So, when the brethren

saw that they were thus loath to yield, in a fit of insolent wrath they bade hang four-and-twenty of the noblest among the hostages in sight of their kinsfolk. But the Romans only thereby provoked to a yet more insolent stubbornness, and relying on a message they had received from the Consuls Gabius and Porsenna to the effect that they would come to their succour on the morrow, resolved to make a sally from the city and to battle with the besiegers. And even as they were prudently arranging their troops, lo the aforesaid Consuls arrived ready to do battle, having rallied their allies who had been dispersed. Advancing accordingly, in close file, they made a sudden assault upon the Burgundians, and Britons, and the citizens also issuing forth in concert with them, helped them to do no small slaughter at the outset. Natheless, the brethren when they saw so sudden a discomfiture inflicted on their fellow-soldiers, were right sore uneasy, and with redoubled vigour cheered them on, reformed their ranks, and leading on one assault after another compelled them to give ground. At the last, after many thousand fighting men had been slain, the victory rested with the brethren; Gabius was slain, Porsenna made prisoner, the city was taken. Nought remained for them but to distribute the hidden treasures of the citizens in largesse to their comrades.

## [10]

AFTER he had won this victory, Brennius abode still in Italy, and trampled upon the people thereof with tyranny unheard of. But of his other deeds and of his end, for that they be written in the Roman histories, I do in no wise care to treat, seeing that thereby I should import too great a prolixity into my work, and that in going over ground, which others have already beaten, I should be turning aside from my present purpose.

Howbeit Belinus returned to Britain and ruled the
kingdom all the rest of his life in peace. Wheresoever
the cities that had aforetime been builded had fallen
into decay he restored them, and many new ones did he
found. Amongst others he did lay out one upon the
river Usk nigh the Severn sea, that was of many ages
called Kaerusk, that was the mother city of South Wales.
But after that the Romans came hither, the old name
was done away and it was called the City of the Legions
(Caerleon), drawing the name from the Roman legions
that wont to winter there. In the city of London made
he a gate of marvellous workmanship upon the banks
of Thames, the which the citizens do still in these days
call Billingsgate after his name. He builded, moreover,
a tower of wondrous bigness, with a quay at the foot
whereunto ships could come alongside. He renewed his
father's laws everywhere throughout the kingdom, rejoicing always in doing steady and even-handed justice.
In his days, therefore, did he cause such wealth to accrue
unto his people as that the like hath never been heard
tell of in any age neither before nor since. At the end,
when his last day did snatch him away from this life, his
body was burnt and his ashes were enclosed in a golden
urn which they placed with wondrous skilful artifice
upon the top of the foresaid tower in the city of
London.

## [11]

AFTERWARD, his son succeeded him, Gurguint Barbtruc,
a sober man and a prudent, who, imitating his father's
deeds in all things, did love peace and justice, and when
his neighbours rebelled against him, taking fresh courage by ensample of his father, he fought sundry right
bloody battles against them, and forced his enemies back
into subjection due. Amongst other matters it so fell out
that the King of Denmark who had paid tribute in his

father's days did eschew making the same payment unto himself, denying that he owed him any subjection. He thereupon, taking the matter in high choler, led a fleet into Denmark, and after afflicting the people with grievous deadly havoc, slew the King and imposed his ancient yoke upon the country.

[ 12 ]

AT that time, when he was returning home after the victory by the Isles of Orkney, he fell in with thirty ships thronged with men and women, and when he made inquiry as to the reason of their coming thither, their Duke, Partholoim by name, came unto him, and, doing him much worship, besought pardon of him and peace. He had been banished, he said, from the parts of Spain, and was cruising in those waters in search of a land wherein to settle. He made petition, moreover, that some small share of Britain might be allotted unto them wherein to dwell, so as that they need no longer rove the irksome highways of the sea. Wherefore, when Gurguint Barbtruc had learnt that they came out of Spain and were called Basques, and that this was the drift of their petition, he sent men with them to Ireland which at that time was desert without a single inhabitant, and made them a grant thereof. Thenceforward they did there increase and multiply, and have held the island even unto this day. But Gurguint Barbtruc, when that he had fulfilled the days of his life in peace, was buried in Caerleon which after his father's death he had made it his care to beautify with public buildings and walls.

[ 13 ]

AFTER him, Guithelin won the crown of the kingdom which all the days of his life he governed in kindly and

sober wise. His wife was a noble woman named Marcia,
learned in all the arts. She, among many other and unheard-of things that she had found out of her own natural wit, did devise the law which the Britons call
Marciana. This also did King Alfred translate along
with the others and called it in the Saxon tongue the
Mercian law. And when Guithelin died, the rule of the
kingdom fell unto the foresaid Queen and her son who
was called Sisillius. For, at that time, Sisillius was but
of seven year, nor did his age warrant that the rule of
the kingdom should be given up into his hands.

## [14]

For which reason, his mother being wise in counsel and
politic beyond the common, did obtain the empire of
the whole island. When she departed out of the light of
this world, Sisillius took the crown, and held the helm
of state. After him, Kimar his son held rule, unto whom
succeeded Danius his brother, and after his death was
Morvid crowned, who was son of his father Danius by
Tangustela his concubine. He would have been of
highest renown for his prowess had he not given way to
exceeding great cruelty, for no man would he spare in
his wrath, but would slay him on the spot had he any
weapon at hand. Natheless was he comely of aspect and
profuse in giving of largesse, nor was there another of
so great valour in the land as that he could withstand
him in single combat.

## [15]

In his days did a certain King of the Flemings land
with a great force on the shore of Northumbria and began to ravage the country. Morvid, thereupon collecting together all the youth of his dominions, marched

forth against them and did battle with him. He was of more avail in fighting singly than was the greater part of the army of his dominions put together, and when he had won the victory not a soul was left alive that he did not slay. For he commanded them to be brought unto him one after the other that he might glut his blood-thirst by putting them to death; and when he ceased for a time out of sheer weariness, he ordered them be skinned alive, and burnt after they were skinned. But in the midst of these his cruel outrages a calamity befell him that put an end to his wickedness. For a beast, more fell than any monster ever heard of before, came up from the Irish sea and preyed continually upon the seafaring folk that dwelt in those parts. And when Morvid heard tidings thereof he came unto the beast and fought with her single-handed. But when he had used up all his weapons against her in vain, the monster ran upon him with open jaws and swallowed him up as he had been a little fish.

### [16]

FIVE sons had been born unto him, whereof the eldest-born, Gorbonian, succeeded to the throne. None at that time was a man more just, nor more a lover of upright dealing, nor none that ruled his people with greater diligence. For it was ever his custom to pay first due honour unto the gods, and then right justice to the commonalty. He restored the temples of the gods throughout all the cities of Britain and builded many new. All his days did the island abound in a plenty of riches such as none of the neighbouring countries did enjoy. For he enjoined the husbandmen to till their lands, and protected them against the oppressions of their landlords. His young men of war, moreover, he did maintain with gold and silver in such sort as none of them should have need to do an injury unto any

other. In the midst of these and many other deeds that
bare witness unto his inborn goodness, he paid the debt
of nature, and, departing from the light of this world.
was buried in the city of London.

[17]

AFTER him, Arthgallo his brother wore the crown of the
kingdom, a man in all he did the very contrary of his
brother. For he made it his business everywhere to
smite down the noble and upraise the base; to take
away from the rich that which was their own, and to
heap up untold treasure for himself. The which the barons of the realm refusing to put up with any longer,
raised an insurrection against him, and deposed him
from the throne of the kingdom. They then raised
thereunto Elidur his brother, who for the pity that he
afterward showed unto his brother was called the Pious.
For after that Elidur had held the kingdom a space of
five years, whilst he was hunting in the forests of Calaterium, it so fell out that he met his brother who had
been deposed. Arthgallo had wandered through sundry
of the provincial kingdoms seeking for help to recover
his lost honours, but help nowhere could he find, and
when he could no longer endure the poverty that had
overtaken him, had returned to Britain with a company
of ten knights only. Seeking out, therefore, such as had
aforetime been his friends, he was passing through the
foresaid forest when Elidur his brother espied him in
such unhoped-for wise. As soon as he saw him he ran
up to him and embraced him, kissing him again and
again. And when he had wept long time over his brother's mean estate, he brought him with him to the city
of Dumbarton and hid him in his own chamber. He
then feigned that he himself was there lying sick and
sent his messengers throughout the whole kingdom to
intimate unto those princes that were vassals of the

crown that he was fain they should come to visit him.
And when all had come together in the city where he
lay, he bade that each one of them should come severally into his chamber without making any noise. For
he said that the sound of many voices would be hurtful
to his head in case they all came in together in a crowd.
Each one, therefore, believing the story, obeyed his bidding and came into the house orderly, the one after another. Elidur, the meanwhile, had given order unto his
sergeants that were there all ready, to take each one as
he came in, and, save he were minded to swear allegiance unto Arthgallo his brother, to smite off his head.
Thus did he deal severally with them all, and so, by
fear of death, reconciled them all unto Arthgallo. When
the covenant was duly confirmed, Elidur brought Arthgallo unto the city of York, and taking the crown off
his own head set it upon that of his brother. Hence it
was that the name of the Pious was bestowed upon him,
for that he had shown, as I have said, this pity towards
his brother. Arthgallo, accordingly, reigned ten years,
and did so amend him of his former misdeeds, as that
now he did begin to abase the baser sort and to exalt
the gentler, to allow every man to hold his own, and
to do right justice. After a time, falling into a lethargy,
he died and was buried in the city of Carlisle.

[ 18 ]

THEREAFTER Elidur was again made King, and was restored unto his former dignity. But whilst that he was
following his eldest brother Gorbonian in all good
deeds, his twain other brothers, Iugenius and Peredur,
assembling armed men from every quarter, march forth
to fight against him. Having won the victory, they took
him and shut him up within the tower of the city of
London, setting a guard to watch. Afterward, they
shared the kingdom in twain, whereof that part which

stretcheth westward from Humber fell to the lot of
Iugenius, but the other with the whole of Scotland to
Peredur. At last, after seven years had slipped away,
Iugenius died and the whole kingdom fell unto Peredur. When the sceptre was set in his hand, he did ever
thereafter govern the kingdom mildly and soberly, insomuch that it was said of him that he did excel his
brothers who had gone before him, nor was any mention made of Elidur. But, for that death knoweth not
to spare any man, she came upon him unawares and
snatched him away from life. Then straightway is Elidur led forth from prison and a third time raised to
the throne, who, after that he had fulfilled his time in
bounty and justice, passing forth from the light of this
world left his piety as an ensample unto them that
should come after him.

[19]

AFTER Elidur's death, Regin, a son of Gorbonian, took
the crown of the kingdom, and did imitate his uncle in
wisdom as in wit. For, eschewing all tyranny, he exercised justice and mercy towards his people, nor turned
aside from the path of righteousness. After him reigned
Margan, the son of Arthgallo, who, taking ensample
by the gentleness of his kinsfolk, ruled the nation of the
Britons in tranquillity. Him succeeded Enniaun, his
brother, who departed so widely from his father's wont
in his treatment of the people, that in the sixth year of
his reign he was deposed from the throne of the realm.
In his place was set his kinsman Idwallo, the son of
Iugenius, who, admonished by the fate that had befallen Enniaun, did pursue the paths of justice and
righteousness. Unto him succeeded Runno, son of Peredur, and him Gerontius, son of Elidur. After him came
Catell his son, and after Catell, Coill; after Coill, Porrex, and after Porrex, Cherin. Unto him were born

three sons, Fulgentius, to wit, Eldad, and Andragius, who reigned the one after the other. Thenceforward, Urian, son of Andragius, succeeded, unto whom Eliud, unto whom Eliduc, unto whom Cloten, unto whom Gurgintius, unto whom Merian, unto whom Bledud, unto whom Cap, unto whom Owen, unto whom Sisillius, unto whom Bledgabred. He surpassed all the singers of the forepast age, both in measures of harmony and in the fashioning of all manner of musical instruments, so as that he might seem the very god of all minstrels. After him reigned Arthinail his brother, and after Arthinail Eldol, unto whom succeeded Redion, unto whom Rhydderch, unto whom Samuil-Penissel, unto whom Pir, unto whom Capoir. Then succeeded Cligueill, the son of Capoir, a man in all his acts moderate and prudent, and who above all things did exercise right justice among his peoples.

[ 20 ]

AFTER him succeeded his son Hely, and ruled the kingdom for forty years. Unto him were born three sons, Lud, Cassibelaunus, and Nennius, whereof the eldest born, Lud, to wit, took the kingdom on his father's death. Thereafter, for that a right glorious city-builder was he, he renewed the walls of Trinovantum, and girdled it around with innumerable towers. He did likewise enjoin the citizens that they should build houses and stately fabrics therein, so as that no city in far-off kingdoms should contain fairer palaces. He himself was a man of war, and bountiful in giving of feasts. And, albeit that he had many cities in his dominion, yet this did he love above all other, and therein did he sojourn the greater part of the whole year, whence it was afterward named Kaerlud, and after that, by corruption of the name, Kaerlondon. In a later day, by the changing of the tongues, it was called London, and yet later, after the landing of the foreign folk that did subdue the country unto themselves, hath it been called Londres. After the death of Lud, his body was buried in the foresaid city nigh unto that gate, which even yet is called Porthlud in British, but in Saxon Ludgate. Two sons were born unto him, Androgeus and Tenuantius, but for that by reason of their infancy they were unable to rule the kingdom, their uncle Cassibelaunus was raised to the throne of the kingdom in their stead. So soon as he was crowned King, he did so abound alike in bounty and in prowess, as that his fame was bruited abroad, even in far-off kingdoms. Whence it came to pass that the kingship of the whole realm did fall unto him and not unto his nephews. Howbeit, Cassibelaunus, yielding willingly to natural affection, was not minded that the youths should be without kingdoms of their own, wherefore he allotted a large share of the realm unto each. For the city of London did he grant to Androgeus along with the duchy of Kent, and the duchy of Cornwall unto Tenuantius. He himself, howbeit, as wearing the sovereign dignity of the crown, was mindful to hold them along with all the princes of the whole island in vassalage unto himself.

# BOOK IV

## [1]

IN the meantime it so fell out, as may be found in the Roman histories, that after he had conquered Gaul, Julius Cæsar came to the coast of Flanders. And when he had espied from thence the island of Britain, he asked of them that stood around what land it might be and who were they that dwelt therein? Whilst that he was still looking out to seaward after he had learnt the name of the kingdom and of the people, "By Hercules," saith he, "we Romans and these Britons be of one ancestry, for we also do come of Trojan stock. For after the destruction of Troy, Æneas was first father unto us, as unto them was Brute, whom Silvius, son of Ascanius, son of Æneas, did beget. But, and if I mistake not, they be sore degenerate from us, and know not what warfare meaneth, seeing that they lie thus sundered from the world in the outer ocean. Lightly may they be compelled to give us tribute, and to offer perpetual obedience unto the dignity of Rome. Natheless, first of all let us send them word, bidding them pay us toll and tallage unvisited and untouched of the Roman people, and, like the rest of the nations, do homage to the Senate, lest haply, by shedding the blood of these our kinsmen, we should offend the ancient nobility of Priam, father of us all." Having sent this message in a letter to King Cassibelaunus, Cassibelaunus waxed indignant and sent him back an epistle in these words.

[2]

"CASSIBELAUNUS, King of the Britons, to Gaius Julius Cæsar. Marvellous, Cæsar, is the covetousness of the Roman people, the which, insatiable of aught that is of gold or silver, cannot even let us alone that have our abode beyond the world and in peril of the ocean, but must needs presume to make a snatch at our revenues, which up to this time we have possessed in quiet. Nor is even this enow for them, save we also cast away our freedom for the sake of becoming subject unto them and enduring a perpetual bondage. An insult unto thyself, Cæsar, is this which thou dost ask of us, seeing that the same noble blood that flowed in the veins of Æneas beateth in the heart of Briton and of Roman alike, and that those very same glorious links that unite us in a common kindred ought also no less closely to bind us in firm and abiding friendship. That friendship it was that thou shouldst have asked of us, not slavery. We know how to bestow our friendship freely; we know not how to bear the yoke of bondage. For such freedom have we been wont to enjoy, that bowing the neck unto slavery is a thing wholly unknown amongst us. Yea, should even the gods themselves think to snatch it from us, we would withstand them to the last gasp, and it should go hard but that we would hold to it in their despite. Be it therefore clearly understood, Cæsar, that in case, as thou hast threatened, thou dost emprise the conquest of this island of Britain, thou shalt find us ready to fight both for our freedom and for our country."

[3]

WHEN he readeth this letter, Gaius Julius Cæsar fitteth out his fleet and only waiteth for a fair wind to adven-

ture on the enterprise of carrying into effect the message he had sent to Cassibelaunus. As soon as the
wished-for wind began to blow, he hoisted sail and
came with a fair course into the mouth of the Thames
with his army. They had already landed from the boats,
when, lo, Cassibelaunus with all his strength cometh to
meet him. On reaching the town of Dorobellum he
there held counsel with his barons how best to keep the
enemy at a distance. There were with him Belinus, his
Commander-in-Chief of the army, by whose counsel the
whole kingdom was governed; his two nephews, Androgeus to wit, Duke of London, and Tenuantius, Duke of
Cornwall. There were, moreover, three kings that were
his vassals, Cridiocus, King of Scotland, Gueithaet of
North Wales, and Brithael of South Wales, who, as they
had encouraged the rest to fight, and all were eager for
the fray, gave counsel that they should forthwith march
upon Cæsar's camp, and before that he had taken any
fortress or city, dash in upon him and drive him out,
for that, so he once were within any of the garrisoned
places of the country, it would be all the harder to dis-
lodge him, as he would then know whither he and
his men might repair for safety. All having signified
their assent, they accordingly marched to the coast
where Julius had set up his camp and his tents, and
there, both armies in battle-array, engaged in combat
hand-to-hand with the enemy, spear-thrust against spear-
thrust and sword-stroke against sword-stroke. Forthwith on this side and on that the wounded fell smitten
through the vitals, and the ground is flooded with the
gore of the dying, as when a sudden south-wester drives
back an ebbing tide. And in the thick of the melly, it so
chanced that Nennius and Androgeus, who commanded
the men of Kent and the citizens of London fell upon
the bodyguard of the Emperor himself. When they came
together, the Emperor's company was well-nigh scattered by the close ranks of the British assailants, and
whilst they were confusedly battling together, blow on

blow, good luck gave Nennius a chance of encountering Julius himself. Nennius accordingly ran in upon him, glad beyond measure that it should lie in his power to strike even one blow at a man so great. Cæsar, when he saw him making a rush at him, received him on the shield he held before him, and smote him on the helmet with his naked sword as hard as his strength would allow. Then, lifting the sword again, he was fain to follow up the first by a second blow that should deal a deadly wound, but, Nennius, seeing his intention, lifted his shield between, and Cæsar's blade, glancing off his helmet, stuck fast in the shield with so passing great force, that when they could no longer maintain the combat for the press of the troops rushing in upon them, the Emperor had not strength to wrench it forth. Howbeit, Nennius, when he had laid hold on Cæsar's sword on this wise, hurled away his own that he held, and tugging forth the other, falleth swiftly on the enemy. Whomsoever he smote therewith, he either smote off his head or wounded him so sore at the passing, as that no hope was there of his living thereafter. At last, whilst he was thus playing havoc with the enemy, Labienus the tribune came against him, but was slain by Nennius at the first onset. At last, when the day was far spent, the Britons pressed forward in close rank, and charging on undaunted time after time, by God's grace won the day, and Cæsar with his wounded Romans retreated to the beach betwixt the camp and the ships. During the night he got together all that were left of his troops and betook him to his ships, glad enough to make the deep sea his camp of refuge. And when his comrades dissuaded him from continuing the campaign, he was content to abide by their counsel, and returned unto Gaul.

[4]

CASSIBELAUNUS, rejoicing in the victory he had achieved, gave thanks unto God, and calling together his comrades in success, bestowed exceeding abundant largesse upon each according to the merits of his prowess. On the other hand, his heart was wrung with sore grief for that his brother Nennius had been hurt mortally, and was then lying in jeopardy of death. For Julius, in the combat aforesaid, had stricken him a wound beyond help of leechcraft, and within the fortnight after the battle he departed the light of this world by an untimely death, and was buried in the city of London nigh the north gate. At his funeral were kingly honours paid unto him, and they set by his side, in his coffin, the sword of Cæsar that had stuck in his shield in the fight. And the name of that sword was Saffron Death, for that no man smitten thereby might escape on live.

[5]

WHEN Julius thus turned his back to the enemy and landed on the shores of Gaul, the Gauls made great effort to rebel and to cast off the dominion of Julius. For they made count that he had been so enfeebled as that they need no longer dread his power. For amongst them all was there but one same story, that the whole sea was seething over with the ships of Cassibelaunus, ready to pursue the flight of Julius himself. Whence the bolder spirits amongst the Gauls busied them in taking thought how best to drive him beyond their frontiers, which Julius getting wind of, he had no mind to take in hand a doubtful war against so fierce a people, but chose rather to open his treasuries and wait upon certain of the chief nobles, so as to bring back the receivers of his bounty to their allegiance. Unto the common folk he promiseth freedom; unto the disinherited the restoration of their losses, and even to the bondsman liberty. Thus he that aforetime had stripped them of all they possessed and roared at them with the fierceness of a lion, hath now become a gentle lamb, and humbly bleateth out what a pleasure it is unto him to be able to restore them everything; nor doth he stint his wheedling until such time as he hath recovered the power he had lost. In the meanwhile not a day passed but he chewed the cud over his flight and the victory of the Britons.

## [6]

AFTER a space of two years he again maketh ready to cross the ocean-channel and revenge him upon Cassibelaunus, who on his part, as soon as he knew it, garrisoned his cities everywhere, repaired their ruined walls and stationed armed soldiers at all the ports. In the bed of the river Thames, moreover, whereby Cæsar would have to sail unto the city of London, he planted great stakes as thick as a man's thigh and shod with iron and lead below the level of the stream so as to crash into the bows of any of Cæsar's ships that might come against them. Assembling, moreover, all the youth of the island, he constructed cantonments along the coast and waited for the enemy's arrival.

## [7]

JULIUS, meanwhile, after providing everything necessary for his expedition, embarked with a countless multitude of warriors on board, eager to wreak havoc upon the people who had defeated him, and wreaked, no doubt, it would have been, so only he could have reached dry land without damage to his fleet—a feat, howbeit, that he failed to achieve. For whilst that he was making way up Thames towards the foresaid city, his ships ran upon the fixed stakes and suffered sore and sudden jeopardy. For by this disaster not only were his soldiers drowned to the number of many thousands, but his battered ships sank foundered by the inrush of the river. When Cæsar found how matters were going, he made all haste to back sail, and setting all hands to work, to run inshore. They, moreover, who had made shift to escape the first peril by the skin of their teeth, crawled up with him unto dry land. Cassibelaunus, who stood on the bank all the time looking on, was glad enough of the peril of them that were drowned, but had little joy over the safety of the rest. He gave the signal to his fellow-soldiers, and charged down upon the Romans. But the Romans, albeit they had suffered this jeopardy in the river, so soon as they stood on dry land, withstood the charge of the Britons like men, and having hardihood for their wall of defence, made no small slaughter of their enemies, albeit that the slaughter they suffered was more grievous than that they inflicted, for the disaster at the river had sore thinned their companies, while the ranks of the Britons, multiplied every hour by fresh reinforcements, outnumbered them by three to one. No marvel, therefore, that the stronger triumphed over the weaker. Wherefore when Cæsar saw that he was thoroughly routed, he fled with his minished numbers to his ships, and reached the shelter of the sea exactly as he wished, for a timely wind blew fair, and hoisting sail he made the coast of Flanders in safety. He then threw himself into a certain tower he had constructed at a place called Odnea before he went this time to Britain, for his mind misgave him as to the loyalty of the Gauls, and he feared they might rise against him a second time, as they did when he first showed his back to the Britons. It was in view of this likelihood that he had builded this tower as a place of refuge, so that in case the people should raise an insurrection he might be able to withstand any rebellion.

[8]

CASSIBELAUNUS, after winning this second victory, was mightily elated, and issued an edict that all the barons of Britain and their wives should assemble in the city of London to celebrate the solemnities due unto their country's gods who had granted them the victory over so mighty an Emperor. They accordingly all came without tarrying and made sacrifice of divers kinds, and profuse slaying of cattle. Forty thousand kine did they offer, a hundred thousand sheep, and of all manner fowl a number not lightly to be reckoned, besides thirty thousand in all of every sort of forest deer. And when they had paid all due honour unto the gods, they feasted them on the remainder as was the wont on occasion of solemn sacrifices; and the day and the night they spent in playing games of divers kinds. Now, while the sports were going on, it fell out that two noble youths whereof the one was nephew of the King and the other of Duke Androgeus, had tried conclusions man to man in a wrestling bout, and fell out as to which had had the upper hand. The name of the King's nephew was Hirelglas, and of the other Cuelin. And after many insults had been bandied about betwixt them, Cuelin snatched up a sword and smote off the King's nephew's head, whereupon was a mighty ferment in the court, and the news of the murder forthwith flying abroad soon reached Cassibelaunus. Grievously troubled at his kinsman's fate, Cassibelaunus commanded Androgeus to bring his nephew into court before him, and that when so brought he should be ready to undergo such sentence as the barons might pronounce, so that Hirelglas should not remain unavenged in case they should find that he had been unjustly slain.

Howbeit, for that Androgeus had a suspicion as to the King's mind in the matter, he made answer that he himself had his own court, and that whatsoever claim any might have as against any of his men ought to be heard and decided therein. If, therefore, Cassibelaunus were resolved to have the law of Cuelin, he ought by custom immemorial to have sought it in Androgeus's own court in the city of London. Cassibelaunus, thereupon, finding that he could not obtain the satisfaction he meant to have taken, threatened Androgeus with a solemn oath that he would waste his duchy with sword and fire, save he agreed to allow his claim. Howbeit, Androgeus, waxing wroth, withheld obedience to his demand, and Cassibelaunus waxing wroth no less, made haste to ravage his dominions. Natheless, Androgeus, through his friends and kinsfolk about the court, besought the King to lay aside his wrath, but finding that he could in no wise allay his fury, began to take thought whether he might not make shift to devise some other means of withstanding him. At last, despairing utterly of compassing his purpose otherwise, he resolved to call in Cæsar to his succour, and sent his letters unto him conceived in these words:—

"To Gaius Julius Cæsar, Androgeus, Duke of London, after aforetime wishing him death, now wisheth health. I do repent me of that I wrought against thee when thou didst battle with my King, for, had I eschewed such enterprise, thou wouldst have conquered Cassibelaunus, upon whom hath crept such pride of his triumph as that he is now bent on driving me beyond his frontiers—me, through whom he did achieve the triumph. This is the reward that he holdeth due unto my merits. I have saved him his inheritance, he now seeketh to disinherit me. I have restored him a second time his kingdom, he now desireth to reave me of mine own kingdom. For in fighting against thee all these benefits have I bestowed upon him. I call the gods of heaven to witness that never have I deserved his wrath, save

I can be said to deserve it for refusing to deliver up
unto him my nephew whom he doth earnestly desire to
condemn to an unjust death. And that the truth hereof
may be clearly manifest to your discernment, take note
in what manner the quarrel did arise. It so fell out
that for joy of our victory we were celebrating a festival
unto our country's gods, unto whom when we had duly
offered sacrifice, our youth did pass the time in sports
one with another. Among the rest our nephews, taking
ensample of the others, did engage in a wrestling bout.
And when my nephew had won the bout, the other,
burning with unjust wrath, ran up to strike him. But
he, avoiding the blow, took him by the forearm, thinking to snatch the sword out of his fist. In the struggle
the King's nephew fell upon the point of the sword and
dropped down stricken to the death. When, therefore,
this was reported unto the King, he commanded me to
deliver up my nephew to suffer punishment for the
manslaughter. The which when I refused to do, he
came with all his host into my provinces and hath most
grievously harried them. For which reason, praying thy
mercy, I do beseech thy help that I may be restored,
and by my means thou shalt be master of all Britain.
In me hast thou no cause for misgiving, for here is no
treason. The motives of men are swayed by events, and
it may well be that some may become friends that have
aforetime been at strife, and some there be that after
flight may yet achieve the victory."

[9]

WHEN he had read this letter, Julius Cæsar took counsel
with his familiars and was advised by them not to go to
Britain simply upon the Duke's verbal invitation, but
to demand hostages in addition enough to ensure his
good faith before starting on the expedition. Androgeus
accordingly forthwith sent his son Scæva along with

thirty noble youths that were nigh kinsfolk of his own. When the hostages were delivered, Cæsar was reassured, and recalling his troops, sailed with a stern wind to the haven of Richborough. Cassibelaunus in the meanwhile had begun to besiege the city of London and to sack the manor houses in the country round. Howbeit, as soon as he heard that Julius had landed, he raised the siege and hurried away to meet the Emperor. And, as he was marching into a valley near Canterbury, he caught sight of the Roman army pitching their camp and the tents therein, for Androgeus had led them thither so as to fall upon them there by ambuscade. In a moment, the Romans, understanding that the Britons were upon them, armed them as swiftly as they might, and stationed their men in companies. On the other side, the Britons don their arms and advance together in squadrons. Howbeit, Androgeus with five thousand men in arms lay concealed in the forest nigh at hand ready to run to Cæsar's assistance and make a stealthy and sudden onslaught upon Cassibelaunus and his comrades. As they came together in this order on the one side and the other, never a moment did they slack of flinging javelins that carried death into the enemies' ranks, and dealing wounds as deadly with blow on blow of their swords. The squadrons clash together, and mighty is the shedding of blood. On both sides the wounded drop like leaves of the trees in autumn. And while the battle is at the hottest, forth issueth Androgeus from the forest and falleth on the rear of Cassibelaunus's main army, whereupon depended the fate of the battle. Presently, his vanguard already in part cut down and disordered by the onset of the Romans, and his rear thus harassed by their own fellow-countrymen, he could stand his ground no longer; and his broken and scattered forces flee routed from the field. By the side of the valley rose a rocky hill with a thick hazel wood at the top, whereunto Cassibelaunus with his men fled for cover when they found themselves defeated on the level, and taking their stand in the wood, defended them like men and slew a number of the enemy that pursued them. For the Romans and the men of Androgeus were hard after them, cutting up the squadrons in their flight, and skirmishing heavily with them on the hillside without being able to force their way to the top. For the rocks on the hill and the steepness of the ridge afforded such good cover to the British that they could make sallies from the heights and still carry slaughter among the enemy. Cæsar, therefore, beleaguered the hill all that night, for it was dark already, and cut off every means of retreat, thinking to wring from the King by hunger what he could not force from him by arms. O, but in those days was the British race worthy of all admiration, which had twice driven in flight before them him who had subjected the whole world beside unto himself, and even in defeat now withstood him whom no nation of the earth had been able to withstand, ready to die for their country and their freedom! To their praise it was that Lucan sang how Cæsar,

"Scared when he found the Britons that he sought for,
 Only displayed his craven back before them."

At the end of the second day, Cassibelaunus, who had all this time had nought to eat, began to fear that he must yield him captive to hunger and submit him to the prison of Cæsar. He sent word accordingly to Androgeus to make peace for him with Julius, lest the dignity of the race whereof he was born should suffer by his being led into captivity. He sent word also, that he had not deserved he should desire his death, albeit that he had harassed his country. And when the messengers had told him their errand, saith Androgeus:

"Not to be beloved is the prince that in war is gentle as a lamb, but in peace fierce as a lion. Gods of heaven and earth! My lord beseecheth me now that aforetime did command me: Doth he now desire to make peace

with Cæsar and to do him homage, of whom Cæsar did
first desire peace? Forsooth, he might have known that
he who drove an Emperor so mighty out of his kingdom could also bring him back. Why am I to be treated
unfairly who could render my service either to him or
to another? Led blindfolded of his own folly is he that
doth exasperate with injuries and insults the fellow-
soldiers unto whom he oweth his victories. For no victory is won by the commander alone, but by them that
shed their blood for him in the battle. Natheless will I
make his peace with him if I may, for the injury that
he hath done me is enough revenged in this that he
hath prayed my mercy."


[ 10 ]


THEREUPON Androgeus went straightway to Julius, and
clasping his knees, spake unto him on this wise:

"Behold, already hast thou enough revenged thee
upon Cassibelaunus. Have mercy now upon him!
Nought more remaineth for him to do save only that
he render homage unto thee and pay due tribute unto
the dignity of Rome." And when Cæsar answered him
never a word, Androgeus spake again:

"This thing only, Cæsar, have I promised unto thee,
and nought more than this, that I would do mine utmost to make Cassibelaunus acknowledge him thy man
and to subdue Britain unto thy sovereignty. Lo, now,
Cassibelaunus is vanquished and Britain subdued unto
thee by mine assistance. What more owe I unto thee?
May He that did create all things forbid that I should
suffer lord of mine that prayeth me of mercy and hath
done me right as touching the wrong he had done unto
me, to be thrust into prison or chained in fetters. No
light thing is it to slay Cassibelaunus while I am alive,
nor shall I blush to render him all service that I may
save thou hearken unto my counsel."

Julius thereupon, his eagerness somewhat slackened by fear of Androgeus, accepted the allegiance of Cassibelaunus on condition of his paying annual tribute, the amount of the tribute he pledged himself to pay being three thousand pounds of silver. Thenceforward Julius and Cassibelaunus made friends together, and bestowed gifts of courtesy the one upon the other. Afterwards Cæsar wintered in Britain, and with the return of spring crossed the Channel into Gaul. Some time later, after collecting an army of men of all nations, he marched to Rome against Pompey.

### [11]

AFTER seven years had passed by, Cassibelaunus died and was buried in the city of York. Unto whom succeeded Tenuantius, Duke of Cornwall, the brother of Androgeus, for Androgeus himself had gone to Rome along with Cæsar, so that Tenuantius was crowned King, and governed the realm with diligence. He was a man of warlike spirit and dealt out strong-handed justice. After him, his son Cymbeline was raised to the kingly dignity, a strenuous knight that had been nurtured in the household of Augustus Cæsar. He had contracted so nigh a friendship with the Romans that albeit he might well have withheld the tribute from them, yet, natheless, did he pay the same of his own freewill.

(In those days was born our Lord Christ Jesus, by whose precious blood was mankind redeemed, that aforetime had been bound in the chains of the devils.)

### [12]

CYMBELINE, after that he had ten years governed Britain, begat two sons, whereof the elder born was named

Guiderius and the other Arviragus. And when the days
of his life were fulfilled, he gave up the helm of state to
Guiderius. But when Guiderius refused to pay the tribute which the Romans demanded, Claudius, who had
been raised to the Empire, made a descent upon the
island. There was with him his commander-in-chief of
his army who was called in the British tongue Lelius
Hamo, by whose counsel all campaigns that were
undertaken were directed. This man, accordingly, when
he had disembarked at the city of Porchester, began by
building up the gates of the city with a wall so as to
shut all issue for the citizens, his design being either to
compel the hunger-starven burgesses to surrender or
otherwise to slay them without mercy.

[13]

WHEN the tidings of Claudius Cæsar's arrival was
spread abroad, Guiderius assembled every armed man
in the realm and marched against the Roman army,
and when the battle began, at first stoutly made head
against the enemy, slaying more men with his own
single sword than the greater part of his army put together. Already Claudius was betaking him to his ships,
already were the Romans well-nigh scattered, when the
crafty Hamo, casting aside the armour he was wearing,
did on the arms of a Briton, and in guise of a Briton
fought against his own men. Then he cheered on the
Britons to the pursuit, promising them a speedy victory.
For he had learned their tongue and their customs, seeing that he himself had learnt nurture along with the
British hostages at Rome. By this device he made shift
by degrees to come close up to the King, and when he
found an opening to get at him, just when he least suspected any peril of the kind, slew him by the edge of
the sword, and slipping away betwixt the companies of
his enemies, rejoined his own men with his ill-omened

victory. But Arviragus, as soon as he espied that his
brother was slain, straightway cast aside his own armour
and did on that of the King, hurrying hither and
thither and cheering on his men to stand their ground
as though it had been Guiderius himself. They, not
knowing that the King was dead, took fresh courage
from his cheering, at once held their ground and bat-
tled on, doing no small slaughter among the enemy. At
the last the Romans gave way, and abandoning the
field, flee shamefully in two divisions, Claudius, in the
one, betaking him unto the shelter of his ships, and
Hamo, not having time to reach the ships slipping away
into the forest. Arviragus, therefore, weening that Claudius was fleeing along with him, hurried in pursuit, and
never once stinted of chasing him from point to point,
until he came to a stand on the seacoast, at the place
that is now called Southampton, after the name of the
said Hamo. There was a haven there, suitable for ships
to lade and unlade, and a number of merchant carracks
were then lying therein. Hamo was mighty keen to get
aboard of them, but Arviragus was too quick for him,
and unexpectedly coming down upon him slew him on
the sudden. The haven, accordingly, hath from that day
unto this been called Hamo's Port.

[14]

MEANWHILE Claudius, as soon as he could get his men
together again, attacked the city aforesaid, which at that
time was called Kaerperis, but now Porchester. It was
not long before he cast down the walls, and after defeating the citizens pursued Arviragus to Winton,
within which city he had taken refuge. He then besieged that city, and endeavoured to take it by divers
devices. But Arviragus, when he beheld himself besieged, mustered his forces, and opening the gates sallied forth to fight. Howbeit, just as he was preparing to

charge, Claudius sent messengers unto him bearing word that he was minded to make peace. For he feared the hardiness of the King and the valour of the Britons, and chose rather to subdue him by prudence and policy than to run the hazard of a doubtful encounter. He therefore proposed a reconciliation, and promised to give him his daughter, so only he would acknowledge the kingdom of Britain to be a fief of the Roman Empire. The aldermen of his court accordingly counselled him to lay aside his warlike preparations and accept the promise of Claudius. For no disgrace was it, they said, unto him to become a vassal of the Romans, seeing that they had possessed them of the empire of the whole world. Assuaged by these and many other considerations, he complied with their advice and yielded to the emperor. Claudius accordingly sent to Rome for his daughter forthwith, and availing him of Arviragus's assistance, brought the Orkneys and the outlying islands into subjection to himself.

[15]

At the end of winter the envoys returned with his daughter and delivered her unto her father. The damsel's name was Genuissa, and of so surpassing beauty was she that she was the admiration of all that beheld her. And after that they were joined in lawful wedlock, she did kindle so fervent love in the heart of the King as that he held her, and her only, dearer than all the world beside. Whence, being fain that the place where he was first wedded unto her should be made famous for ever, he proposed unto Claudius that he should build thereon a city which might perpetuate to future times the remembrance of so happy a marriage. Claudius gladly received the proposal, and commanded a city to be builded, which, after his own name, he called Kaerglou, or Gloucester, by which name it is known even unto this day, situate upon the bank of the Severn, which is the boundary betwixt Wales and England. Howbeit some do say that it hath the name from one Gloius, the duke that was born unto Claudius in that city, unto whom after the death of Arviragus the dukedom of Wales did fall. After the city was builded and the island was at peace, Claudius returned to Rome, and granted the rule of the islands of the province unto Arviragus.

(At that time Paul the Apostle did found the Church of Antioch, and coming afterward unto Rome did there hold the bishopric thereof, sending Mark the Evangelist into Egypt to preach the Gospel he had written.)

[ 16 ]

AFTER Claudius had returned to Rome, Arviragus began to show his policy and his prowess, to rebuild cities and castles, and to hold the people of the realm in check, with such justice as that he was a terror even unto kings afar off. Howbeit his pride did therewithal wax so great as that he despised the Roman power, and was minded no longer to be bound by his homage to the Senate, but to arrogate all things unto himself. Upon hearing these tidings, Vespasian was sent by Claudius either to bring about a reconciliation with Arviragus or to reimpose his subjection to the Romans. But when Vespasian began to draw nigh unto the haven of Richborough, Arviragus met him and forbade him to enter thereinto. And so vast a multitude of men in arms had he brought with him as that the Romans were scared, and durst not attempt to land lest he should attack them. Vespasian accordingly drew away from that port, and backing sail made for Totnes. As soon as he reached dry land, he marched upon Kaerpenhuelgoit, that is called Exeter, to besiege it. And when he had beleaguered it for seven days, Arviragus with

his army arrived and did battle with him. On that day
the armies of both were sore cut up, but neither obtained the victory. But at morn upon the morrow, by
the mediation of Genuissa the Queen, the leaders made
friends and despatched their fellow-soldiers into winter
quarters. When the winter was over, Vespasian returned
to Rome, and Arviragus remained in Britain. At last,
on the verge of old age, he began to show greater regard for the Senate, and ruled his kingdom in peace
and quietness, confirmed the ancient customary laws
and established others new, bestowing, moreover, passing great largesse on all such as he held worthy thereof.
His fame being bruited abroad throughout all Europe,
the Romans both loved and feared him in such wise
that of all kings was there none of whom was there so
much talk at Rome as of him. Whence Juvenal in his
book doth record how a certain blind man, when he
was speaking to Nero about the huge turbot that had
been caught, said:

> "Some king shalt thou lead captive,
> Or from the draught-tree of his British chariot
> Headlong shall fall Arviragus."

None was more stark than he in war, in peace none
more gentle, none jollier, none more bountiful in largesse. When he had fulfilled the days of his life, he was
buried at Gloucester in a certain temple which he had
builded and dedicated in honour of Claudius.

## [17]

His son Marius succeeded him in the kingdom, a man
of marvellous prudence and wisdom. In his reign, after
a time, came a certain King of the Picts, named Rodric,
with a great fleet from Scythia and landed in the northern part of Britain which is called Scotland, beginning
to ravage the province. Assembling his people, Marius

accordingly came to meet him, and after sundry battles obtained the victory. He then set up a stone in token of his triumph in that province which was afterward called Westmoreland after his name, whereon is graven a writing that beareth witness unto his memory even unto this day. After that Rodric was slain, he gave unto the conquered people that had come with him that part of Scotland which is called Caithness wherein to inhabit. For the land was wilderness, seeing that none had dwelt therein to till the land for many a long day. And for that they had no wives, they besought of the Britons their daughters and kinswomen, but the Britons disdained to match their children with such manner of folk. Whereupon, finding that they did only meet with denial in this quarter, they betook them over the Channel to Ireland and brought back with them women from thence, of whom were born a mixed breed that did hugely multiply their numbers. But enough as concerning them, for I purpose not to treat of their history, nor of that of the Scots who derive their origin from them and the Hibernians. But Marius, when that he had settled the island in absolute peace, began to manifest his affection for the Roman people, paying the tribute that they demanded, and, provoked thereunto by ensample of his father, did exercise justice, law, and peace, and all things honourable throughout his kingdom.

## [18]

BUT when he had ended the course of his life, his son Coill guided the helm of state. Coill from childhood had been brought up at Rome, and having been taught Roman ways, had conceived a mighty liking for the Romans. Wherefore he also paid them the tribute and eschewed all wrangling about it, for that he saw the whole world was subject unto them, and that their

power did surpass the power of any one province or of
any alliance among the smaller nations. He paid therefore that which was demanded, and in peace held that
which was his own. None of all the kings ever showed
greater honour unto his nobility, for them that were
rich did he allow to live in peace, and them that were
poor did he maintain with unfailing bounty.

## [19]

UNTO Coill was born one single son whose name was
Lucius, who, upon the death of his father, had succeeded to the crown of the kingdom, and did so closely
imitate his father in all good works that he was held
by all to be another Coill. Natheless, being minded that
his ending should surpass his beginning, he despatched
his letters unto Pope Eleutherius beseeching that from
him he might receive Christianity. For the miracles that
were wrought by the young recruits of Christ's army in
divers lands had lifted all clouds from his mind, and
panting with love of the true faith, his pious petition
was allowed to take effect, forasmuch as the blessed Pon-
tiff, finding that his devotion was such, sent unto him
two most religious doctors, Fagan and Duvian, who,
preaching unto him the Incarnation of the Word of
God, did wash him in holy baptism and converted him
unto Christ. Straightway the peoples of all the nations
around came running together to follow the King's example, and cleansed in the same holy laver, were made
partakers of the kingdom of Heaven. The blessed doctors, therefore, when they had purged away the pagan-
ism of well-nigh the whole island, dedicated the temples that had been founded in honour of very many
gods unto the One God and unto His saints, and filled
them with divers companies of ordained religious.
There were then in Britain eight-and-twenty flamens as
well as three archflamens, unto whose power the other

judges of public morals and officials of the temple were subject. These also, by precept of the Pope, did they snatch away from idolatry; and where there were flamens there did they set bishops, and archbishops where there were archflamens. The seats of the archflamens were in the three noblest cities, in London, to wit, and in York and in Caerleon, whereof the ancient walls and buildings still remaining on the Usk, in Glamorgan, do bear witness to the former dignity thereof. From these three was superstition purged away, and the eight-and-twenty bishops, with their several dioceses, were subordinated unto them. Unto the Metropolitan of York Deira was subject, along with Scotland, both of which the great river Humber doth divide from England. Unto the Metropolitan of London England and Cornwall were subject. These two provinces the Severn doth bound from Cambria, that is, Wales, which was subject unto Caerleon.

[20]

At last, when everything had been thus ordained new, the prelates returned to Rome, and besought the most blessed Pope to confirm the ordinances they had made. And when the confirmation had been duly granted they returned into Britain with a passing great company of others, by the teaching of whom the nation of the British was in a brief space established in the Christian faith. Their names and acts are to be found recorded in the book that Gildas wrote as concerning the victory of Aurelius Ambrosius, the which he hath handled in a treatise so luminous as that in nowise is there any need to write it new in a meaner style.

# BOOK V

## [1]

MEANWHILE King Lucius the Glorious, when he saw
how the worship of the true faith had been magnified
in his kingdom, did rejoice with exceeding great joy,
and converting the revenues and lands which formerly
did belong unto the temples of idols unto a better use,
did by grant allow them to be still held by the churches
of the faithful. And for that it seemed him he ought to
show them yet greater honour, he did increase them
with broader fields and fair dwelling-houses, and confirmed their liberties by privileges of all kinds. Amidst
these and other acts designed to the same purpose he
departed this life, and was right worshipfully buried in
the church of the first See in the year from the Incarnation of Our Lord one hundred and fifty-six. No issue
left he to succeed him, whence at his death dissension
arose amongst the Britons and the power of the Romans
was sore enfeebled withal.

## [2]

WHEN these tidings were brought unto Rome, the Senate sent as legate Severus the senator and two legions
along with him to recover the country to the Roman
power. So soon as he had landed, he did battle with the
Britons, and one part of them surrendered unto him,
but the rest, whom he could not subdue, he did so
harass with continual slaughter and defeat, as that he
drove them to take refuge beyond Deira in Scotland.

Natheless, under their Duke, Sulgenius, they withstood
him with all their might, and many a time inflicted
passing sore slaughter both upon their fellow-countrymen and upon the Romans. For Severus took with him
as auxiliaries all the island people whomsoever he could
find, and thus oftentimes returned with victory. But
their Emperor, grievously annoyed at these incursions,
bade build a wall betwixt Deira and Scotland so as to
hinder his making any nigher attack upon him. A wall
accordingly they wrought at the common charge from
sea to sea that did for a long space bar every opening
against the inroads of the enemy. Howbeit, when Sulgenius could no longer stand his ground, he crossed over
into Scythia to beseech the help of the Picts in restoring
him to his dignity. And when he had there assembled
all the youth of the country, he returned with a passing
great fleet into Britain, and laid siege unto York. Which
matter coming to be bruited abroad amongst the other
nations, the greater part of the Britons deserted Severus
and went over to Sulgenius. But not for that did
Severus slacken in his emprise. He mustered his Romans
and the other Britons that still stuck to him, marched
off to the beleaguered city and gave battle to Sulgenius.
But when the battle had been hotly fought out to the
end, Severus and a multitude of his men had been slain,
and Sulgenius himself wounded to the death. Severus
was buried just afterwards at York, whereof his legions
had taken possession. He left two sons, Bassianus and
Geta, whereof Geta was born of a Roman mother while
Bassianus was son of a British lady. When their father
was dead, the Romans accordingly raised Geta to the
kingship, favouring him the rather for that he was Roman of both sides. But the Britons refused to accept
him, and elected Bassianus for that he was of their kindred by his mother's blood. Straightway the brethren
fall to fighting, wherein Geta being slain Bassianus ob-
taineth possession of the kingdom.

## [3]

AT that time was there in Britain a certain youth by name Carausius, born of low degree, who after that he had approved his prowess in many encounters, made his way to Rome, and besought leave of the Senate to defend with his fleets the coasts of Britain against the incursions of the barbarians, the which of it were granted unto him he promised that he would achieve so many and such great matters as that the Republic should be more magnified thereby, than it could be were the kingdom of Britain delivered into their hands. These fine promises he made cajoled the Senate, and he succeeded in obtaining that which he had asked for, returning to Britain with charters sealed. Forthwith, swiftly collecting a number of ships, he made choice of a number of daring youngsters and putting to sea went round all the shores of the kingdom and raised a passing great disturbance among the people. Meanwhile, landing in the neighbouring islands, he ravaged the fields, sacked the towns and cities, and plundered all that they possessed from the islanders. Whilst he was carrying on in this wise, all they that hanker after other men's goods began to flock about him, whereby presently such an army had he got together as that none of the neighbouring princes could have withstood him. Presently his spirit was so puffed up at having such a force at his command that he told the Britons, so they would make him king, he would slay the Romans to a man and free the whole island of that race of barbarians. And when he had obtained his demand, he forthwith gave Bassianus battle and slew him, taking the rule of the kingdom into his own hands. Howbeit, it was the Picts whom Sulgenius, his mother's brother, had brought into Britain that did betray Bassianus, for just in the pinch of the battle,

when it was their bounden duty to come to Bassianus'
rescue, they had been so corrupted by the promises and
bribes of Carausius, that they fell upon the allies of
Bassianus. Whereby the rest, who could not tell which
were their allies and which their enemies, fled away, hot
foot, and victory remained with Carausius. He, when
he had won the day, gave the Picts a place wherein
they might dwell in Scotland, and there abode they
through after ages, mixed up with the Britons.


## [4]

WHEN this usurpation of Carausius was reported at
Rome, the Senate sent Allectus as legate with three legions to slay the tyrant and restore the kingdom of
Britain to the power of Rome. Straightway, as soon as
he was landed, Allectus did battle with Carausius, and
after he had slain him mounted the throne of the kingdom. He then visited the Britons with exceeding bloody
slaughter for that they had deserted the Republic and
had stuck to an alliance with Carausius. Howbeit, the
Britons, grievously indignant thereat, raised up Asclepiodotus, Duke of Cornwall, to be King, and making
common cause, pursued Allectus and challenged him
to battle. He was then in London and was celebrating
a festival to the gods of the country. But the moment he
was aware of Asclepiodotus' arrival, he quitted the sacrifice and issuing forth with all his forces against him
right stoutly delivered his attack. Howbeit, Asclepiodotus was too strong for him, and after scattering his
troops compelled Allectus to flee in such sort as that
following hard on his heels he at last overtook and slew
him, along with many thousand men to boot. And
when the victory had thus fallen unto him, Livius
Gallus, that was colleague of Allectus, called together
the remainder of the Romans into the city and shut the

gates, setting garrisons in the towers and other places of defence, weening that he could thus make stand against Asclepiodotus, or at leastwise escape the death that threatened him. But Asclepiodotus, espying this that he had done, straightway laid siege to the city and sent word to all the Dukes of Britain that he had slain Allectus with many of his men, and was now besieging Gallus with the residue of the Romans within London; wherefore he did most earnestly pray and beseech each one of them to hasten as speedily as might be to his assistance. For the whole race of the Romans might lightly be exterminated out of Britain so only they all joined in a common assault upon the besieged. In answer to his summons accordingly came they of North and South Wales, of Deira, and of Scotland, together with all other whatsoever of British race. And when all had come together before the Duke's own eyes, he bade innumerable engines to be made wherewith to batter down the walls of the city. Every single man setteth him to the work, daring and hardy, and doeth all that one man may do to storm the city. Forthwith the walls are battered down and a breach is made whereby they force an entrance and put the Romans to the sword. But the Romans, seeing that they were being slaughtered without a moment's stay, persuaded Gallus to surrender and deliver himself and them up to Asclepiodotus, praying him of his mercy that they might be allowed to depart with their lives. For well-nigh all of them were already slain save one single legion that still survived. Gallus yielded his assent thereunto, and gave up his men and himself unto Asclepiodotus, but when he did greatly desire to have mercy upon them, up came the North Welsh and forming themselves in rank about them smote off every one of their heads on that one day, over a brook within the city that was afterward called after the Duke's name in British, Nantgallim, but in Saxon, Walbrook.

[5]

THE Romans thus trampled underfoot, Asclepiodotus
took the crown of the kingdom, and with the assent of
the people set it upon his own head. Thenceforward he
ruled the country in right justice and peace ten years,
checking the cruelties of robbers and the murders
wrought by the knives of the highwaymen. In his days
arose the persecution of the Emperor Diocletian,
wherein Christianity was well-nigh blotted out of the
whole island, wherein it had remained whole and in-
violate from the days of King Lucius. For Maximianus
Herculius, chief of the armies of the foresaid tyrant, had
conquered the country, and by his command all the
churches were thrown down, and all the sacred scrip-
tures that could be found were burnt in the market-
places. The priests, moreover, that had been elected,
along with the faithful committed to their charge, were
put to death, insomuch as that a thronging fellowship
of Christians did hasten to vie with one another which
should first reach the kingdom of Heaven and the delight thereof, as though it had been their own abiding
place. God did therefore magnify His mercy upon us,
and in the day of persecution, lest the British people
should lose their way utterly in the thick darkness of
that dreadful night, did of His own free gift enlumine
lamps of exceeding brightness in His holy martyrs,
whose tombs and places where they suffered would kindle no feeble glow of divine charity in the hearts of
their beholders, had not all knowledge thereof been
lost unto their fellow-countrymen through the grievous
perversity of the barbarians. Amongst others of both
sexes that with undaunted courage stood firm in the
ranks of Christ suffered Alban of Verulam and Julius
and Aaron of Caerleon, whereof Alban, glowing with
the grace of charity, when his confessor Amphibalus was

pursued by his persecutors and was just on the very
verge of being taken, did first hide him in his own
house and afterwards offer himself to suffer death in his
place, herein following the ensample of Christ laying
down His life for His sheep. The other twain were torn
limb from limb and mangled in unheard-of wise, and
fled forth without tarrying unto the gates of the Jerusalem that is above, crowned with the garlands of their
martyrdom.

[ 6 ]

MEANWHILE Coel, Duke of Kaercolun, that is, Colches-
ter, raised an insurrection against King Asclepiodotus,
and after slaying him in a pitched battle, did set the
crown of the kingdom upon his own head. When the
tidings thereof were announced at Rome, the Senate
rejoiced greatly over the death of the King, who had
throughout been so sore a trouble unto the Roman
power. Calling to mind withal the disaster they had suffered in the loss of the kingdom, they sent as legate
Constantius the senator, who had subdued Spain unto
their dominion, a wise man and a hardy, who had
wrought more than any other to magnify the power of
the commonweal. Now Coel, Duke of the Britons, when
he was aware that Constantius was arrived, durst not
venture to do battle against him for that he had heard
tell of him how no King might make stand against him.
Accordingly, so soon as Constantius set foot within the
island Coel sent his messengers unto him, and besought
him of peace, promising fealty and homage on condition that he might possess the kingdom of Britain and
pay nought beyond the wonted tribute unto the Roman
sovereignty. This message delivered, Constantius thereunto agreed, and peace was duly confirmed by the giving of hostages. A month afterward Coel was overtaken
of a right grievous malady, whereof within eight days

he died. After his death, Constantius took unto himself
the crown of the kingdom and therewithal the daughter
of Coel unto wife. Her name was Helena, and all the
damsels of the kingdom did she surpass in beauty, nor
was none other anywhere to be found that was held
more cunning of skill in instruments of music nor better
learned in the liberal arts. None other issue had her father to succeed him on the throne of the kingdom,
wherefore he had made it his special care that she
should be so instructed as that she might the more easily
take in hand the government of the realm after her father's death. And after that Constantius had taken her
as his Queen, she bare unto him a son, and called his
name Constantine. Sithence that time, eleven years had
passed away, when Constantius died at York and be-
queathed the kingdom unto his son. Who, when he was
raised to the honours of the throne, within a few years
did begin to manifest passing great prowess, showing
the fierceness of a lion in maintaining justice among his
people, restraining the ravening of robbers and treading
underfoot the cruelties of them that did use oppression,
being resolved that everywhere his peace should be
made new and firmly stablished.

[7]

AT that time was there a certain tyrant at Rome,
Maxentius by name, who strove to oust every upright
citizen from his inheritance, and with most hateful tyranny did oppress the commonweal. They upon whom
his cruelty fell, driven out of their own lands and country, fled away unto Constantine in Britain, and by him
were received with honour. At last, when many such
had flocked about him, they did stir him up into hatred
of the said tyrant, and did full often exclaim against
him in speeches such as this:

"How long, O Constantine, wilt thou endure this our

calamity and exile? Wherefore delayest thou to restore
us to our native land? Thou art the only one of our
blood strong enough to give us back that which we have
lost and to drive Maxentius forth. For what prince is
there that may be compared unto the King of Britain,
whether it be in the valour of his hardy soldiers or in
the plenty of his gold and silver? We do adjure thee,
give us back our possessions, give us back our wives and
children, by emprising an expedition to Rome with
thine army and ourselves."

[8]

PROVOKED thereunto by these and other words, Constantine accordingly went to Rome and subdued it unto
himself, and thereafter did obtain the sovereignty of the
whole world. He had taken with him three uncles of
Helena, Joelin, to wit, Trahern, and Marius, and raised
them unto the order of Senators. In the meanwhile
Octavius, Duke of Gwent, raised an insurrection against
the proconsuls of the Roman sovereignty unto whom
the government of the island had been entrusted, and
after slaying them, himself assumed the throne of the
kingdom. And when tidings of this had been brought
unto Constantine, he sent hither Trahern, the uncle of
Helena, with three legions to recover the island unto
the Roman sovereignty. Trahern, accordingly, landing
on the coast nigh the city of Porchester that in British
is called Kaerperis, made an assault thereupon, and
within two days took it. The which, being bruited
abroad amongst all the nations, King Octavius gathered
together the whole armed strength of the island and
met him no great way from Winchester, in the field that
in British is called Maisurian, and, delivering battle,
obtained the victory. Trahern with his wounded troops
betook him to his ships, and embarking, made for Scotland by sea voyage, where he busied him in ravaging

the provinces. When this news was brought back again
by his messenger, King Octavius reassembled his companies in pursuit of him, and did battle with him in the
province that was called Westmoreland; but this time
he had to flee without the victory. But Trahern, when
he saw that victory was his own, pursued Octavius and
gave him no rest until he had wrested from him his
cities and his crown. Octavius, therefore, in sore trouble
at the loss of his kingdom, repaired with a fleet to Norway to seek for help from King Gombert. Meanwhile
he had by edict bidden his familiars use every effort to
compass the death of Trahern. The Earl of a certain
municipal fortified town, who loved Octavius above all
other, accordingly, was not slow in fulfilling the command. For when on a day Trahern issued forth of London, he lay in wait for him with a hundred soldiers in
a certain combe of the forest wherethrough he had to
pass, and as he was going by, sallied out unexpectedly
upon him and slew him in the midst of his own fellow-
soldiers. So, when this was reported unto Octavius, he
returned unto Britain, and after scattering the Romans,
recovered the throne of the kingdom. Hence, after a
brief space, such was his prowess and so great plenty of
gold and silver had he, as that no man was there of
whom he was afeard, and he held the kingdom of
Britain happily from that time forward until the days
of Gratian and Valentinian.

[9]

At last, worn out with eld, and desirous of making provision for his people at his death, he inquired of his
counsellors which of his family they would most gladly
raise to be king after that he himself were departed. For
he had but one single daughter, and was without heir
male unto whom he might hand down the rule of the
country. Some, accordingly, proposed that he should

give his daughter to wife along with the kingdom unto
some Roman noble, so as that thereby they should enjoy the firmer peace. But others gave their voice that
Conan Meriadoc, his nephew, should be declared heir
to the throne of the kingdom, and that his daughter
should be given in marriage with dowry of gold and
silver unto the prince of some other kingdom. Whilst
that they were debating these matters amongst themselves, in came Caradoc, Duke of Cornwall, and gave it
as his counsel that they should invite Maximian the
Senator and give him the King's daughter and the kingdom, that so they might enjoy perpetual peace. For his
father was a Welsh Briton, he being the son of Joelin,
uncle of Constantine, of whom mention hath been made
above. By his mother and by birth, howbeit, he was Roman, and by blood was he of royal pedigree on both
sides. Caradoc held therefore that this marriage did
promise an abiding peace, for that he knew Maximian,
being at once of the family of the Emperors and also by
origin a Briton, would have good right to the kingdom
of Britain. But when the Duke of Cornwall had thus
delivered his counsel, Conan, the King's nephew, waxed
indignant, for his one endeavour was to make a snatch
at the kingdom for himself, and aiming at this end only,
stuck not to run counter to the whole court beside. But
Caradoc, being in nowise minded to change his purpose,
sent his son Maurice to Rome to sound Maximian on
the matter. Maurice himself was a big man and a
comely, as well as of great prowess and hardiment, and
if any would gainsay aught that he laid down, he would
prove the same in arms in single combat. When, therefore, he appeared in presence of Maximian, he was received in becoming wise, and honoured above the
knights that were his fellows. At that time was there a
mighty quarrel toward betwixt Maximian himself and
the two Emperors Gratian and his brother Valentinian,
for that he had been denied in the matter of one third
part of the empire which he had demanded. When

Maurice, therefore, saw that Maximian was being put upon by the twain Emperors, he spake unto him in these words:

"What cause hast thou, Maximian, to be afeard of Gratian, when the way lieth open unto thee to snatch the empire from him? Come with me into the island of Britain and thou shalt wear the crown of the kingdom. For King Octavius is sore borne down by eld and lethargy and desireth nought better than to find some man such as thyself unto whom he may give his kingdom and his daughter. For heir male hath he none, and counsel hath he sought of his barons unto whom he should give his daughter to wife, with the kingdom for dower. And, for that his barons would fain give obedient answer unto his address, his high court hath made resolve that the kingdom and the damsel should be granted unto thee, and unto me have they given commission that I should notify thee of the matter. If, therefore, thou wilt come with me into Britain, thou shalt achieve this adventure; the plenty of gold and silver that is in Britain shall be thine, and the multitude of hardy men of war that dwell therein. Thus wilt thou be enough strong to return unto Rome, and, after that thou hast driven forth these Emperors, then mayst thou enjoy the empire thereof thyself. For even thus did Constantine thy kinsman before thee, and many another of our kings that hath ere now raised him unto the empire."

[ 10 ]

MAXIMIAN, therefore, giving assent unto his words, came with him into Britain. On his way he sacked the cities of the Franks, and thereby purveyed him of heaps of gold and silver wherewith to pay the men of arms he mustered from every quarter. Soon afterward he put to sea and made for Southampton with a fair wind. And when tidings thereof were brought unto the King, he

was dismayed with sore amazement, weening that an
enemy's army was upon him. Wherefore calling unto
him Conan his nephew, he commanded him to summon
every man in arms throughout the country and to
march against the enemy. Conan accordingly assembled
all the youth of the kingdom and came to Southampton, where Maximian had pitched his tents. He, when
he perceived how huge a multitude they were that had
arrived, was in a grievous quandry, for what was there
he could do? They that had come with him were a far
smaller company—he dreaded the number and the
courage of Conan's fighting men, and of peace had he
no hope. Wherefore, calling unto him the elders of his
host along with Maurice, he bade them say what they
thought best to be done in such an overtake? Unto
whom saith Maurice:

"Not for us, certes, is it to do battle with such an army
of knights and warriors, nor came we hither for any
such purpose as an invasion of Britain by force of arms.
Behoveth us ask for peace and leave to abide in the
land until such time as we know the King's mind. Let
us say that we be envoys from the Emperors, and bear
their mandates to Octavius, so as to humour these folk
and wheedle them with politic words." So, all of them
approving this scheme, he took with him twelve of the
barons, hoary-headed and of sounder wit than the rest,
all with boughs of olive in their right hands, and came
to meet Duke Conan. When the Britons beheld these
men of reverend age bearing the olive in token of peace,
they uprose from their seats to do them honour, and
made way for them to pass freely unto the Duke.
Straightway, standing in the presence of Conan Meriadoc, when they had saluted him on behalf of the Emperors and the Senate, they said that Maximian had
commission unto King Octavius to bear him the mandates of Gratian and Valentinian. Unto whom Conan:
"Wherefore, then, is he followed by so large a company?
This is not the guise wherein legates wont to appear,

but rather that of an invading army that is minded to
do us a mischief." Then saith Maurice: "Unmeet had
it been for a man of so high rank to come hither save in
seemly state and with due escort of knights and men;
and all the more for that as representing the Roman
empire, and also by reason of deeds done by his forefathers, he may haply be hated of many kings. Were he
to march through the land with a lesser company, like
enow he might be slain by the enemies of the commonweal. In peace he cometh, and in peace he doth beseech,
as in truth ought well to be believed from that which
he hath done. For from the time that here we landed
have we so behaved us as that we have done no wrong
unto no man. All our charges have we paid like peaceful folk; we have bought fairly that which we needed,
and nought have we taken from any man by force."
And whilst that Conan was still wavering as to whether
he would make choice of peace or war, Caradoc, Duke
of Cornwall, accosted him, as also did other of the barons, and persuaded him not to enter upon a war after
listening unto such a petition. Wherefore, albeit that he
were fainer to fight, he laid down his arms and granted
peace, himself escorting Maximian to the King in London, and setting forth unto him the whole matter in
order as it had fallen out.

## [11]

THEN Caradoc, Duke of Cornwall, taking with him his
son Maurice, bade that the bystanders should withdraw
them, and addressed the King in these words:
"Behold, that which they who do with truer affection
observe their obedience and fealty towards thee have so
long time desired, hath, by God's providence, now been
brought unto a happy issue. For thou didst ordain that
thy barons should give thee counsel as to what were best
to do as concerning both thy daughter and thy kingdom,

forasmuch as that in these days thine eld doth so sore
let and hinder thee of governing thy people any longer.
Some there were that counselled delivering up the
crown unto Conan thy nephew and marrying thy daughter worthily elsewhere, as fearing the ruin of our countrymen should a prince of foreign tongue be set over
them. Others would have granted the realm unto thy
daughter so she were matched with some noble of our
own speech who might succeed thee on thy departure.
But the more part gave it as their counsel that some
man of the blood of the Emperors should be sent for,
unto whom might be given thy daughter and thy crown.
For they promised that a firm and abiding peace would
ensue therefrom, seeing that they would be protected
by the power of Rome. Now, therefore, behold, God
hath deigned that this youth should be wafted to thy
shores, who is born not only of the blood of the Romans
but of the blood royal of the Britons, and unto him, by
my counsel, wilt thou not tarry to give thy daughter in
wedlock. For, put case thou shouldst deny him in this,
what right canst thou confer upon any other as against
him to the realm of Britain? For a kinsman is he of Constantine, and nephew of Coel our King, whose daughter Helena none can deny to have possessed the kingdom by right hereditary." And when Caradoc had thus
made report of the counsel of the barons, Octavius
agreed thereunto and by common consent forthwith
gave the kingdom of Britain together with his daughter
unto Maximian. The which Conan Meriadoc beholding,
he did wax indignant beyond all telling and betook him
privily unto Scotland where he busied him in raising
an army to harass Maximian. When he had assembled
his troops together he crossed the Humber river and
ravaged the provinces both on the hither side thereof
and on the further. When this was reported unto Maximian he assembled his whole strength, and hurrying
forth to meet him defeated him in battle and returned
home with victory. Natheless was Conan not so enfee-

bled thereby that he could not again rally his men, and when he had got them together he set him again to harrying the provinces. Maximian accordingly returned, and fought several battles with him, wherein at one time he would come back victorious and at another worsted. At last, after each had inflicted sore loss upon the other, the friends of both did come betwixt, and a reconciliation was brought about.

[12]

FIVE years later Maximian puffed up with pride and surquedry by reason of the passing great store of gold and silver that did daily flow in upon him, fitted out an exceeding mighty fleet and assembled every single armed warrior in Britain. For the realm of Britain was not enough for him, but he must needs seek also to subjugate the Gauls. Crossing the Channel, he went first into the kingdom of Armorica, that now is called Brittany, and made war upon the Gaulish folk that did then inhabit therein. But the Gauls under Duke Inbalt coming to meet him, did battle against him, wherein the more part finding themselves in sore jeopardy did fettle them to flee, for Duke Inbalt had fallen and fifteen thousand men-at-arms that had come together from all parts of the kingdom. And when Maximian had achieved so notable a slaughter, he was overjoyed beyond all measure, for well knew he that after the death of so many fighting men he should soon subdue the country. He therefore called Conan unto him without the ranks, and saith unto him, somewhat smiling the while: "Lo, we have won us one of the fairest realms of Gaul, and herein, behold, lieth good hope that we be able to win the rest. Hasten we, therefore, to take the cities and strong places thereof, before the tidings of this jeopardy fly forth unto further Gaul and call the rest of the peoples to arms. For, so we can hold this kingdom, I mis-

doubt me not but we can subdue the whole of Gaul
unto our dominion. Nor let it irk thee to have yielded
the kingdom of Britain unto me, albeit that thou hadst
hope of possessing it thyself, for whatsoever thou hast
lost therein will I make good unto thee in this country,
for in this kingdom will I make thee King, and it shall
be another Britain that we will replenish with men of
our own race after that we have driven out them that
do now abide therein. For the land is fruitful of corn
and the rivers of fish. The forests be passing fair, and
the glades and launds thereof right pleasant, insomuch
as that in my judgment is there nowhere to be found a
land that is more delightful." And therewithal did
Conan bow his head before him and con him thanks,
promising that, so long as he should live, he would do
him homage and fealty as his loyal vassal.

[13]

AFTER this they called out their troops and marched
upon Rennes, taking it the same day. For when they
heard how cruel were the Britons and how they had
slain their fellow-countrymen, the citizens fled the
swiftest they might, leaving behind them the women
and children. Others in the other cities and other towns
did follow their ensample, whereby was easy entrance
made for the Britons, who into whatsoever place they
entered, slew all that therein was of male kind, sparing
only the women. At last, when they had utterly done
away every single male that dwelt in the whole of the
provinces, they garrisoned the cities and towns with
British warriors and established camps in divers places
upon the headlands. Accordingly, so soon as Maximian's
cruelness was bruited abroad throughout the other provinces of Gaul, a mighty consternation fell upon every
duke and every prince, so as none other hope had they
save only in offering prayers and oblations to their gods.

From every country quarter they fled unto the cities and strongholds and whatsoever places seemed to offer a safe refuge. Maximian, therefore, finding himself so mighty a terror unto them, took fresh hardihood and made haste to multiply his army by offer of swingeing bounties unto recruits. For whomsoever he knew to be greedy of other men's goods, him did he enlist, and stinted not to stuff their wallets with gold or silver, or largesse of one kind or another.

## [14]

THEREBY did he gather such a host about him as he weened was enow for him to be able to subjugate the whole of Gaul. Howbeit, he did put off practising further severities for a brief space, until the kingdom he had taken began to settle down and he should have replenished it with a British folk. He accordingly issued an edict that a hundred thousand of the common folk in the island of Britain should be collected and should come to him, besides thirty thousand soldiers who should safeguard them that were to remain in the country from any incursion of the enemy. And when all these things were accomplished and the Britons had arrived, he distributed them amongst all the nations of the kingdom of Brittany, and did thus create a second Britain the which he did bestow upon Conan Meriadoc. But he himself with the rest of his fellow-soldiers went into further Gaul, and after divers most grievous battles did subdue the same, as well as the whole of Germany, having obtained the victory in every single battle. Then, stablishing the throne of his empire at Trier, he did so furiously wreak his revenge upon the two Emperors Gratian and Valentinian, that he slew the one and put the other to flight from the city of Rome.

## [ 15 ]

In the meanwhile the Gauls and Aquitanians did sore
harass Conan and the Armorican Britons, and annoy
them continually with repeated incursions, which
Conan withstood, repaying slaughter with slaughter and
right manfully defending the country committed unto
him. And when the victory had fallen unto him, he was
minded to give wives unto his comrades-in-arms so that
unto them might be born heirs that should possess that
land in perpetuity. And that they might make no mix-
ture with the Gauls, he issued decree that women
should come from the island of Britain to be married
unto them. He therefore sent messengers into the island
unto Dionotus, King of Cornwall, who had succeeded
his brother Caradoc in the kingdom, that he should
take charge of this business. For he himself was noble
and exceeding powerful, and unto him had Maximian
entrusted the rule of the island while he himself was
busied in the aforesaid emprises. Now Dionotus had a
daughter of marvellous beauty whose name was Ursula,
whom Conan did desire above all things beside.

## [ 16 ]

Dionotus accordingly, upon seeing Conan's messenger,
being desirous of obeying his wishes, assembled together
from the divers provinces the daughters of nobles to the
number of eleven thousand, and of others born of the
common people sixty thousand, and bade them all meet
together within the city of London. He commanded further that ships should be brought thither from the various coasts wherein they might be sent oversea unto the
husbands that awaited them. For albeit that in so vast a
company many there were that were well-pleased with

their lot, yet were there more unto whom it was displeasing, for that they loved their kinsfolk and their
country with a greater affection. Nor, haply, were lacking some who preferring chastity to marriage would
rather have lost their life even in some foreign nation
than obtain wealth and a husband on this wise. For
albeit that few were of the same mind, yet would well-
nigh all have chosen somewhat different could they
have had their own way in the matter. When the fleet
was ready, the damsels go aboard and dropping down
the river Thames make for the high seas. At last, just as
they were tacking to make the shore of Brittany, a contrary wind sprang up in their teeth and very soon scattered all their company. The ships were all in sore jeopardy in the midst of the sea. The more part of them
foundered, and those that did escape utter shipwreck
were driven on to barbarous islands, where they were
either slain or sold into bondage by the uncouth people,
inasmuch as they had fallen among the detestable sol-
diery of Guanius and Melga, who by command of
Gratian did ravage all the nations along the coast and
Germany itself with dreadful slaughter. Guanius was
King of the Huns and Melga of the Picts, whom
Gratian had specially commissioned and sent into Germany to harass and slay them that favoured Maximian.
Whilst these were roving along the seaboard plundering
and murdering, they met the damsels as they were
driven on to the shore in those parts. These marauders,
beholding the beauty of the damsels, would fain have
wantoned with them, but meeting denial, fell upon
them and slaughtered by far the most part of them
without mercy. Then the detestable Dukes of the Picts
and Huns, Guanius and Melga, who favoured the cause
of Gratian and Valentinian, when they learnt that the
island of Britain had been emptied of all its men-at-arms
hurriedly steered thitherward, and taking them of the
neighbour islands into their alliance made straight for
Scotland. Setting their men in marching order they ac-

cordingly invaded the kingdom wherein was neither ruler nor defender, and slaughtered the helpless common folk, for Maximian, as hath been said, had taken with him all the young fighting men that he could find and had left behind none but the unarmed and witless tillers of the soil. So when Guanius and Melga found that these could make no stand against them, they made no small slaughter amongst them, never ceasing to sack and ravage the cities and provinces as they had been so many sheepfolds. When, therefore, this so grievous calamity was reported unto Maximian, he sent Gratian the Burgess with two legions to their assistance, who as soon as they landed in the island gave battle to the enemy and drove them forth into Hibernia with sore slaughter. In the meanwhile Maximian was slain at Rome by the friends of Gratian, and the Britons whom he had brought with him were slain or scattered. They that made shift to escape betook them to their fellow-countrymen in Armorica that now was called the Other Britain (Brittany).

# BOOK VI

## [1]

Now Gratian the Burgess, when he heard of Maximian's being murdered, assumed the crown of the kingdom, and made himself King. Thenceforth such tyranny wrought he over the people, as that the common folk, banding them together, fell upon him and slew him. This news being bruited abroad among the other kingdoms, the enemies already spoken of returned from Hibernia, and bringing with them Scots, Norwegians, and Danes, did lay waste the realm from sea to sea with sword and fire. On account of this devastation and most cruel oppression, messengers are sent with letters to Rome, begging and entreating that in answer to this tearful petition an armed force may be sent to avenge them, and promising faithful subjection for ever, so only the Romans will drive their enemies away. A legion accordingly that had not suffered in their former disasters is placed under their command, and after disembarking from the ships wherein it was carried across the ocean, soon came to close quarters with the enemy. At last, after that a passing great multitude of them had been stricken down, the Romans drove them all out of the country and freed the wretched commonalty from this outrageous havoc. They then bade the Britons make a wall from sea to sea betwixt Scotland and Deira builded of turfs, that should be a terror to warn off the enemy and a safeguard to the men of the country. For Scotland was utterly wasted by the barbarians that haunted therein, and whatsoever enemies made descent upon the land did there find a convenient shelter.

Wherefore the native-born indwellers of the land did set them to work right diligently, and partly at the public charge and partly at private did complete the building of the wall.

## [2]

THE Romans thereupon gave public notice to the country that thenceforward they could in no wise be troubled again to undertake any more laborious expeditions of this kind, and that such and so great an army by land and sea as was that of the Romans held it disgrace to endure fatigue-work for the sake of a pack of cowardly, pilfering vagabonds. Wherefore henceforth they must look to fighting their own battles single-handed, and the best thing they could do was to inure them in arms and fight like men with all their might to defend their land and substance, their wives and children, and that which is even dearer than these—their freedom and their lives. And at the same time as they gave this public warning, they bade every man in the island that could bear arms come to an assembly in London, for that the Romans were making ready to embark for home. And when all were come together, Guethelin, Metropolitan of London, was charged to make a speech unto them, the which he did in these words:

"At the bidding of the princes standing here present, my bounden duty it is to speak unto you, yet needs must I weep rather than make appeal unto ye in any lofty discourse. For sore it grieveth me of the feebleness and orphanhood that hath overtaken us sithence that Maximian hath stripped the realm of every single fighting man and youth. For ye were but the remnant, a folk that knew nought of the ways of war, but were employed in other toil, tillers of the soil and craftsmen in the several handicrafts of trade. Wherefore, when your foemen of foreign nations did fall upon ye, they drave ye forth

of your sheepcotes into the wilderness as ye had been
sheep straying without a shepherd, until such time as
the Roman power did restore ye unto your holdings.
Now, therefore, will ye always set your hopes upon
being safeguarded by the foreigner? Will ye even yet not
teach your hands to fight with shield and sword and
spear against these thieves and robbers, no whit stronger
than ye be yourselves, save for your own listlessness and
lethargy? The Romans are aweary of the travail of
these voyages to and fro for nought save to fight your
battles. They have now chosen rather to lose the whole
of the tribute ye pay than any longer to endure these
fatigues by land and sea. What though ye were only
common folk in the days when ye had soldiers, ween ye
therefore that manhood hath departed from ye? Cannot
men be born in thwart order, so as that a soldier may
be the son of a farm-labourer, or a farm-labourer son
of a soldier, the son of a shopkeeper a soldier, or the soldier's son a shopkeeper? And sithence that of common
wont the one doth beget the other, I trow not that aught
of manhood is lost by any. But if that men ye be, quit
ye like men, and pray Christ He give ye hardihood to
defend your freedom." And when he had made an end
of speaking, such a cheering and shouting arose that
ye would have said they were all brimming over with
valour.

[3]

AFTER this the Romans encourage the timid folk with
brave counsel, and leave them patterns whereby to fashion their arms. They did likewise ordain that towers
should be set at intervals overlooking the sea all along
the ocean seaboard of the southern districts where they
had their shipping, for that here was most peril to be
dreaded from the barbarians. But easier is it to make
a hawk of a haggard than presently to make a scholar

of a ploughman, and he that poureth forth deep learning before them doth but scatter pearls before swine. For so soon as ever the Romans had bidden them farewell as they that never should return thither, behold the Dukes Guanius and Melga issue forth again from the ships wherein they had fled into Ireland, along with the rest of the companies of Scots and Picts, as well as of the Norwegians, Danes and others that they brought with them, and take possession of the whole of Scotland as far as the wall. For knowing that the Romans had left the island, and had vowed never to return, they set to work to lay waste the island with more than their wonted assurance. And in face of all this, nought could the Britons find to do but to post their slow-witted yokels on the top of the wall, too clumsy to fight, and too addle-pated with the quaking of their midriffs to run away, who so stuck there day and night squatting on their silly perches. Meanwhile the long hooked weapons of the enemy are never idle, wherewithal they dragged down the thrice-wretched clowns from the walls and dashed them to the ground. And well was it for them that were slain by this untimely death, for that by their speedy departure they avoided being snatched away by the same grievous and lingering torments as their brethren and their children. O, the vengeance of God upon past sins! Such was the doom that befel through the wicked madness of Maximian that had drained the kingdom of so many gallant warriors, who, had they been present in so sore a strait, no people could have fallen upon them that they would not have forced to flee, as was well seen, so long as they remained in the land. For long they controlled the realms subject to their sway and held Britain peacefully. Thus it is when a realm is abandoned to the safekeeping of yokels. But enough hath been said. Forsaking the cities and the high wall, again the country folk are put to flight, again are they scattered, even more hopelessly than they were wont; again are they pur-

sued by the enemy, again are they overtaken by a yet
bloodier slaughter, and the wretched common folk are
torn to pieces by their foes as sheep are rent by the
wolves. Yet once again therefore do the miserable remnant send letters unto Agitius, the chief commander of
the Roman forces, appealing unto him on this wise:
"Unto Agitius, thrice consul, the groans of the Britons."
Then, after some few words, the complaint proceedeth:
"The sea driveth us upon the barbarians, the barbarians drive us back again unto the sea. Betwixt the twain
we be thus but bandied from one death unto another,
for either we be drowned or slain by the sword." Natheless, nought the more might they obtain the succour
they sought. Sad and sorry return they home to tell their
fellow-countrymen how ill their petition hath sped.

[4]

AFTER taking counsel hereupon, Guethelin, Archbishop
of London, passed across the Channel into Lesser Britain, which at that time was called Armorica or Letavia,
to seek help of their brethren oversea. At that time
Aldroen was the King thereof, the fourth from Conan,
unto whom, as hath been said, Maximian had given
the kingdom. Aldroen seeing a man so reverend, received him with honour and asked of him wherefore he
had come. Unto whom Guethelin:

"Your Highness ere now hath been acquainted with
the misery—a misery, in truth, that may well move thee
unto tears—which we, thy fellow Britons, have suffered from the time that Maximian did despoil our island of all her warriors, and commanded that the realm
which thou dost possess—and long in peace mayst thou
possess the same—should be by them inhabited. For all
they of the neighbour islands of the province have risen
up against us, the poverty-stricken remnant of our
name, and have so made void our island, of old replen-

ished with abundant wealth of every kind, as that all
the nations thereof are utterly destitute of the staff of
food, save only such meat as they can kill by hunting
to stay their hunger; nor was there any to help it, for
not one strong man, not a single warrior was left unto
us of our own people. For the Romans have conceived
a weariness of us, and have utterly denied us their succour. Bereft of all other hope, we have now thrown us
upon thy mercy, beseeching thee to grant us thy protection, and to defend the kingdom, of right thine own,
from the incursions of the barbarians. For, if it be that
thou thyself are unwilling, what other is there that
ought of right to be crowned with the diadem of Constantine and Maximian, the diadem that hath been
worn by thy grandsires and great-grandsires? Make
ready thy fleets and come! Behold, into thy hands do I
deliver the kingdom of Britain!"

Thereupon Aldroen thus made answer:

"The time hath been when I would not have refused
to accept the island of Britain, had any offered it unto
me, for other country, I wot, is there none more fruitful
whilst it enjoyeth peace and tranquillity. But now that
so sore calamity hath overtaken it, the value thereof is
sore diminished, and hateful hath it become unto myself and unto other princes. But more than all other
evil hath the power of the Romans done hurt thereunto, forasmuch as that no man may hold enduring
sovereignty therein but that needs must he lose his freedom and bear the yoke of bondage. Who would not,
therefore, choose rather to possess less elsewhere with
liberty, than to hold all the riches thereof under the
yoke of slavery? This realm that is now subject unto my
dominion do I possess as sovereign, not as vassal unto
any sovereign lord unto whom my homage is due. This
single kingdom therefore have I chosen to prefer before all other nations, for that I can govern it in freedom; yet natheless, sithence that my grandsires and
great-grandsires and their forefathers have held right

in the island, I do commit unto thy charge my brother
Constantine and two thousand men, who, if God so
will, may free the land from the inroads of the barbarians, and crown him with the diadem thereof. For a
brother I have of this name, skilled in warfare and of
good conditions. Him will I not fail to commit unto
thee with so many men as I have said, if it please thee
to accept him. But as of a greater number I do deem
it right to hold my peace, for that an inroad of the
Gauls doth daily threaten me."

Scarce had Aldroen made an end of his speaking,
when the Archbishop rose up to thank him, and when
Constantine was called unto him, smiled upon him in
exultation, crying out: "Christ conquereth! Christ is
Emperor! Christ is King! Behold here the King of forsaken Britain! Only be Christ with us, and lo, here is
he that is our safety, our hope, our joy!" No need of
more. The ships are made ready on the coast, the men
are chosen from divers parts of the kingdom, and delivered unto Guethelin.

[5]

AND when everything was ready they put to sea and
made for the haven of Totnes. Forthwith they assembled what was left of the youth of the island, and attacking the enemy, through the merits of the blessed
man, obtained the victory. Thereupon the Britons that
afore were scattered flocked unto them from every quarter, and a great council was held at Silchester, where
they raised Constantine to be King and set the crown
of the realm upon his head. They gave him also unto
wife a damsel born of a noble Roman family, whom
Archbishop Guethelin had brought up, who in due
course did bear unto him three sons, whose names were
Constans, Aurelius Ambrosius and Uther Pendragon.
Constans, the eldest born, he made over to the church

of Amphibalus in Winchester, that he might there be
admitted into the order of monks. The other twain,
Aurelius, to wit, and Uther, he gave in charge to
Guethelin to be brought up. At last, after ten years had
passed away, a certain Pict that was Constantine's vassal came unto him, and feigning that he did desire to
hold secret converse with him, when all had gone apart,
slew him with a knife in a spring-wood thicket.

## [6]

On the death of Constantine a dissension arose among
the barons whom they should raise to the throne. Some
were for Aurelius Ambrosius, others for Uther Pendragon, and others for others of the blood royal. At last,
while they were still contending now for this one and
now for that, Vortigern, Earl of Gwent, who was himself panting to snatch the crown at all hazards, went
unto Constans the monk and spake unto him on this
wise: "Behold, thy father is dead, and neither of thy
brethren can be made King by reason of their childish
age, nor none other of thy family do I see whom the
people can raise to be King. Now, therefore, if thou
wilt be guided by my counsel, and wilt multiply my
substance, I will bring the people into such a mind as
that they shall choose thee for King, and albeit that
thy religious order be against it, I will free thee from
this habit of the cloister." When Constans heard him
speak thus, he rejoiced with exceeding great joy, and
promised with a solemn oath that he would do whatsoever he might will. So Vortigern took him and led
him to London clad in royal array and made him King,
albeit scarce with the assent of the people. At that time,
Guethelin the Archbishop was dead, nor was there none
other that durst presume to anoint him King, for that
he had been monk and might not of right be so translated. Natheless, not for that did he refuse the crown

that Vortigern with his own hands did set upon his
head in lieu of a bishop.

## [7]

WHEN Constans was thus raised to the throne, he committed unto Vortigern the whole ordinance of the kingdom, and gave him up utterly unto his counsel in such
sort as that nought did he do without his bidding. And
this did he out of sheer feebleness of wit, for that in
the cloister nought had he learnt of the governance of
a kingdom. The which when Vortigern understood, he
began to take thought within himself by what means
he might be made King in his stead, for of a long time
this was that he had coveted above all other thing, and
he now saw that this was a fitting time when his wish
might lightly be carried into effect. For the whole realm
had been committed unto his ordinance, and Constans,
who was called King, was there as nought save the
shadow of a prince. For nought of stern stuff had he in
him, nor no will to do justice, insomuch as that of
none was he dreaded, neither of his own people nor of
the nations around. His brethren, moreover, the two
children, to wit, Uther Pendragon and Aurelius Ambrosius, were not yet out of the cradle, and incapable of
the rule of the kingdom. A further mischance, moreover, had befallen inasmuch as that all the elder barons of the realm were dead, and Vortigern alone, politic and prudent, seemed the only counsellor of any
weight, for the rest were well-nigh all of them but mere
lads and youths that had come into their honours as it
might happen when their fathers and uncles had been
slain in the battles that had been fought aforetime. Vortigern, accordingly, finding all these things favourable,
took thought by what contrivance he might most easily
and craftily depose Constans the monk and step into
his shoes with most renown. He therefore chose rather

to put off his scheme for a time, until he had better
stablished his power in the divers nations of the kingdom and accustomed them unto his rule. He began,
therefore, by demanding that the King's treasures
should be given into his custody, as well as the cities
with their garrisons, saying that there was talk of the
out-islanders intending an attack upon them. And when
this demand was granted, he set everywhere familiars
of his own to hold the cities in allegiance unto himself.
Then, scheming in furtherance of the treason he designed, he went unto Constans, and told him that needs
must he increase the number of his household that he
might the more safely withstand the enemies that were
coming against him. Unto whom Constans: "Have I
not committed all things unto thy disposition? Do,
therefore, whatsoever thou wilt, so only that they abide
in mine allegiance." Whereupon Vortigern: "It hath
been told me that the Picts are minded to lead the
Danes and Norwegians against us so as that they may
harry us to the uttermost. Wherefore I propose, and
unto me seemeth it the safest counsel, that thou
shouldst retain certain of the Picts in thy court that
may serve as go-betweens to bring us witting from them
that be without. For, and it be true that already they
have begun to rebel, they will spy out the contrivances
and crafty devices of their fellows in such sort as that
lightly mayst thou escape them." Herein behold the
secret treachery of a secret enemy! For not in this wise
did he counsel Constans as having regard unto his
safety, but rather for that he knew the Picts to be a
shifty folk and swift to every crime. When that they
were drunken, therefore, or moved to wrath, they
might full easily be egged on against the King, and so
murder him out of hand. Whence, if aught of the kind
should happen, the way would be open unto him of
advancing himself unto the kingdom even as he had
so often coveted to do. Sending messengers, therefore,
into Scotland, he invited a hundred Pictish soldiers

from thence and received them into the King's retinue.
And after that they were received, he showed them
honour above all other, filling their pouches with all
manner of bounties and their bellies with meats and
drinks beyond measure, in such sort as that they held
him to be a very king. Accordingly, they would wait
upon him through the streets singing songs in his
praise, saying: "Worthy is Vortigern of the empire!
Worthy is he of the sceptre of Britain, whereof Constans is unworthy!" Upon this, Vortigern would bestow
more and more largesse upon them that he might be
yet more pleasing in their eyes. But when he had won
the hearts of them all, he made them drunken, saying
that he was minded to retire from Britain that he
might acquire more abundant treasure of his own, for
that the scanty allowance he had could not possibly be
enow to keep fifty soldiers in his pay. Then, in sor-
rowful-seeming wise he betook him privily unto his
own lodging and left them drinking in the hall. Upon
seeing this, the Picts, believing that what he said was
true, were aggrieved beyond telling and began to mut-
ter one with another, saying: "Wherefore suffer we this
monk to live? Why do we not rather slay him, so that
Vortigern may possess the throne of the kingdom? For
who but he ought to succeed him in the kingdom? For
worthy is he of all dominion and honour, worthy is he
of all sovereignty, that stinteth not to bestow such largesse upon us!"

## [8]

THEREUPON they burst into the sleeping-chamber, and
fall suddenly upon Constans, and smiting off his head,
bare it to show to Vortigern, who when he beheld it
burst into tears as one overborne by sorrow, albeit that
never aforetime was he so beside himself with joy. Calling together the citizens of London, for it was there

that all this befel, he bade all the traitors be first set
in fetters and then beheaded for presuming to perpe-
trate a crime so heinous. Some there were that deemed
the treason had been devised by Vortigern, for that the
Picts never durst have done the deed save with his
knowledge and consent. Others again stuck not a moment to purge him of so black a crime. At last, the matter not being cleared up, they unto whom had been
committed the nurture of the two brethren, Aurelius
Ambrosius and Uther Pendragon, fled away with them
into Little Britain, fearing lest they should be slain of
Vortigern. There King Budec received them and
brought them up in due honour.

[9]

Now Vortigern, when he saw that there was none his
peer in the kingdom, set the crown thereof upon his
own head and usurped precedence over all his fellow-
princes. Howbeit, his treason at last being publicly
known, the people of the neighbouring out-islands,
whom the Picts had led with them into Scotland, raised
an insurrection against him. For the Picts, indignant
that their comrades-in-arms had been thus put to death
on account of Constans, were minded to revenge them
upon Vortigern, who was thereby not only sore troubled in his mind, but suffered heavy loss amongst his
fighting-men in battle. On the other hand, he was still
more sorely troubled in his mind by his dread of Aurelius Ambrosius and his brother Uther Pendragon, who,
as hath been said, had fled into Little Britain for fear
of him. For day after day was it noised in his ears that
they were now grown men, and had builded a passing
huge fleet, being minded to adventure a return unto
the kingdom that of right was their own.

## [10]

In the meanwhile three brigantines, which we call "long-boats," arrived on the coasts of Kent full of armed warriors and captained by the two brethren Horsus and Hengist. Vortigern was then at Dorobernia, which is now called Canterbury, his custom being to visit that city very often. When his messengers reported unto him that certain men unknown and big of stature had arrived, he took them into his peace, and bade them be brought unto him. Presently, when they came before him, he fixed his eyes upon the two brethren, for that they did surpass the others both in dignity and in comeliness. And, when he had passed the rest of the company under review, he made inquiry as to the country of their birth and the cause of their coming into his kingdom. Unto whom Hengist, for that he was of riper years and readier wit than the others, thus began to make answer on behalf of them all:

"Most noble of all the Kings, the Saxon land is our birthplace, one of the countries of Germany, and the reason of our coming is to offer our services unto thee or unto some other prince. For we have been banished from our country, and this for none other reason than for that the custom of our country did so demand. For such is the custom in our country that whensoever they that dwell therein do multiply too thick upon the ground, the princes of the divers provinces do meet together and bid the young men of the whole kingdom come before them. They do then cast lots and make choice of the likeliest and strongest to go forth and seek a livelihood in other lands, so as that their native country may be disburdened of its overgrown multitudes. Accordingly, owing to our country being thus overstocked with men, the princes came together, and casting lots, did make choice of these young men that here thou seest before thee, and bade them obey the custom that hath been ordained of time immemorial. They did appoint, moreover, us twain brethren, of whom I am named Hengist and this other Horsus, to be their captains, for that we were born of the family of the dukes. Wherefore, in obedience unto decrees ordained of yore, have we put to sea and under the guidance of Mercury have sought out this thy kingdom."

At the name of Mercury the King lifted up his countenance and asked of what manner religion they were. Unto whom Hengist:

"We do worship our country's gods, Saturn, Jove and the rest of them that do govern the world, but most of all Mercury, whom in our tongue we do call Woden. Unto him have our forefathers dedicated the fourth day of the week that even unto this day hath borne the name of Wednesday after his name. Next unto him we do worship the goddess that is most powerful above all other goddesses, Frea by name, unto whom they dedicated the sixth day, which we call Friday after her name." Saith Vortigern: "Right sore doth it grieve me of this your belief, the which may rather be called your unbelief, yet natheless, of your coming do I rejoice, for either God or some other hath brought ye hither to succour me in mine hour of need. For mine enemies do oppress me on every side, and so ye make common cause with me in the toils of fighting my battles, ye shall be worshipfully retained in my service within my realm, and right rich will I make ye in all manner of land and fee."

The barbarians forthwith agreed, and after the covenant had been duly confirmed, remained in the court. Presently thereupon, the Picts issuing from Scotland, mustered a huge army and began to ravage the northern parts of the island. As soon as ever Vortigern had witting thereof, he called his men together and marched forth to meet them on the further side Humber. When the men of the country came into close quarters with the enemy, both sides made a passing sharp onset; but little need had they of the country to do much of the fighting, for the Saxons that were there did battle in such gallant fashion as that the enemies that aforetime were ever wont to have the upper hand were put to flight, hot foot, without delay.

## [ 11 ]

VORTIGERN accordingly, when he had won the victory by their means, increased his bounties upon them and gave unto their duke, Hengist, many lands in the district of Lindsey for the maintenance of himself and his fellow-soldiers. Hengist therefore, as a politic man and a crafty, when that he found the King bare so great a friendship towards him, spake unto him on this wise:

"My lord, thy foemen do persecute thee on every side, and few be they of thine own folk that bear thee any love. They all do threaten thee and say that they will bring in hither thy brother Aurelius Ambrosius from the shores of Brittany, that, after deposing thee, they may raise him to be King. May it therefore please thee that we send unto our own country and invite warriors thence so that the number of our fighting men may be increased. Yet is there one thing further that I would beseech of the discretion of thy clemency, were it not that I misdoubt me I might suffer a denial thereof." Upon this saith Vortigern: "Send therefore thine envoys unto Germany and invite whomsoever thou wilt, and, as for thyself, ask of me whatsoever thou wilt, and no denial thereof shalt thou suffer." Thereupon Hengist bowed his head before him and gave him thanks, saying: "Thou hast enriched me of large dwelling-houses and lands, yet withal hast thou withheld such honour as may beseem a Duke, seeing that my forefathers were dukes in mine own land. Wherefore, methinketh amongst so much beside, some city or castle might have been given unto me, whereby I might have been held of greater account by the barons of thy realm. The rank of an Earl or a Prince might have been granted unto one born of a family that hath held both these titles of nobility." Saith Vortigern: "I am forbidden to grant any boon of this kind upon thee, for that ye be foreigner and heathen men, nor as yet have I learnt your manners and customs so as that I should make ye the equals of mine own folk; nor yet, were I to hold ye as mine own very countryfolk, could I set precedent of such a grant so the barons of the realm were against it." Whereunto Hengist: "Grant," saith he, "unto thy servant but so much only as may be compassed round about by a single thong within the land that thou hast given me, that so I may build me a high place therein whereunto if need be I may betake me. For loyal liegemen unto thee I have been and shall be, and in thy fealty will I do all that it is within my mind to do." Whereupon the King, moved by his words, did grant him his petition, and bade him send his envoys into Germany forthwith, so that the warriors he invited thence might hasten at once unto his succour. Straightway, as soon as he had despatched his envoys into Germany, Hengist took a bull's hide, and wrought the same into a single thong throughout. He then compassed round with his thong a stony place that he had right cunningly chosen, and within the space thus meted out did begin to build the castle that was afterwards called in British, Kaercarrei, but in Saxon, Thongceaster, the which in the Latin speech is called *Castrum corrigiæ*.

[12]

MEANTIME the envoys returned from Germany, bringing with them eighteen ships full of chosen warriors. They convoyed also the daughter of Hengist, Ronwen by name, whose beauty was unparagoned of any. When they were arrived, Hengist invited King Vortigern into his house to look at the new building and the new warriors that had come into the land. The King accordingly came privily forthwith, and not only praised the work so swiftly wrought, but received the soldiers that had been invited into his retinue. And after that he had been entertained at a banquet royal, the damsel stepped forth of her chamber bearing a golden cup filled with wine, and coming next the King, bended her knee and spake, saying: "Laverd King, was heil!" But he, when he beheld the damsel's face, was all amazed at her beauty and his heart was enkindled of delight. Then he asked of his interpreter what it was that the damsel had said, whereupon the interpreter made answer: "She hath called thee 'Lord King,' and hath greeted thee by wishing thee health. But the answer that thou shouldst make unto her is 'Drinc heil.'" Whereupon Vortigern made answer: "Drinc heil!" and bade the damsel drink. Then he took the cup from her hand and kissed her, and drank; and from that day unto this hath the custom held in Britain that he who drinketh at a feast saith unto another, "Wassail!" and he that receiveth the drink after him maketh answer, "Drink hale!" Howbeit, Vortigern, drunken with the divers kinds of liquor, Satan entering into his heart, did wax enamoured of the damsel, and demanded her of her father. Satan entering into his heart, I say, for that he, being a Christian, did desire to mate him with a heathen woman. Hengist, a crafty man and a prudent, herein discovering the inconstancy of the King's mind, forthwith held counsel with his brother Horsus and the rest of the aldermen that were with him what were best to be done as touching the King's petition. But they all were of one counsel, that the damsel should be given unto the King, and that they should ask of him the province of Kent in return for her. So the matter was settled out of hand. The damsel was

given unto Vortigern, and the province of Kent unto
Hengist without the knowledge of Gorangon the Earl
that of right was lord thereof. That very same night
was the King wedded unto the heathen woman, with
whom thenceforth was he beyond all measure well-
pleased. Natheless, thereby full swiftly did he raise up
enemies against him amongst the barons of the realm
and amongst his own children. For aforetime had three
sons been born unto him, whereof these were the
names: Vortimer, Katigern, and Pascentius.

[13]

At that time came St. Germanus, Bishop of Auxerre,
and Lupus, Bishop of Troyes, to preach the word of
God unto the Britons. For their Christianity had been
corrupted, not only on account of the King having set
a heathen folk in their midst, but on account of the
Pelagian heresy, by the venom whereof they had long
time been infected. Natheless, by the preaching of the
blessed men the religion of the true faith was restored
amongst them, the which they did daily make manifest
by many miracles, for many miracles were wrought of
God by them, as Gildas hath set forth in his tractate
with abundant clearness and eloquence. Now, when
the damsel was given unto the King as hath been told,
Hengist said unto him: "Behold, I am now thy father,
and meet is it that I be thy counsellor; nor do thou
slight my counsel, for by the valour of my folk shalt
thou subdue all thine enemies unto thyself. Let us invite also hither my son Octa with his brother Ebissa,
for gallant warriors they be; and give unto them the
lands that lie in the northern parts of Britain nigh
the wall betwixt Deira and Scotland, for there will
they bear the brunt of the barbarians' assaults in such
sort that thou upon the hither side of Humber shalt
abide in peace." So Vortigern obeyed, and bade them

invite whomsoever they would that might bring him
any strength of succour. Envoys accordingly were sent,
and Octa, Ebissa, and Cerdic came with three hundred
ships all full of an armed host, all of whom did Vortigern receive kindly, bestowing upon them unstinted
largesse. For by them he conquered all his enemies and
won every field that was fought. By little and little
Hengist invited more and more ships and multiplied
his numbers daily. So when the Britons saw what he
was doing, they began to be adread of their treason
and spake unto the King that he should banish them
forth of his realm, for that Paynims ought not to com-
municate with Christians nor be thrust into their
midst, for that this was forbidden by the Christian
law; and, moreover, that so huge a multitude had already arrived as that they were a terror to the folk of
the country, insomuch as that none could tell which
were the Paynims and which Christians, for that the
heathens had wedded their daughters and kinswomen.
Upon these and the like grounds of objection they did
urge the King to dismiss them from his retinue, lest
at any time they should deal treacherously with him
and overrun the folk of the country. But Vortigern
did eschew giving heed unto their counsel, for he loved
the Saxons above all other nations on account of his
wife. Which when the Britons understood, they forthwith forsook Vortigern and with one accord raised up
Vortimer his son to be their King, who accepting their
counsel, at once began to drive out the barbarians
everywhere, fighting against them and continually harassing them with fresh incursions and slaughter. Four
pitched battles he fought with them; the first on the
river Derwent, the second at the ford of Episford,
where Horsus and Catigern, another son of Vortigern,
met hand to hand, both falling in the encounter, each
wounded to the death by the other. The third battle
was on the seacoast, when the Saxons fled, sneaking
away like women to their ships and taking refuge in

the Isle of Thanet. But Vortimer there beleaguered
them, and harassed them day after day by attacking
them from his ships. And when they could no longer
withstand the attack of the Britons, they sent King Vortigern who had been with them in all their battles to
his son Vortimer to petition for leave to depart and to
repair unto Germany in safety. And while a conference
was being held upon the matter, they took the occasion
to embark on board their brigantines, and returned
into Germany leaving their women and children behind them.

## [14]

VORTIMER thus having won the victory, at once began
to restore their possessions unto the plundered countrymen, to treat them with affection and honour, and
to repair the churches at the bidding of St. Germanus.
But the devil did straightway wax envious of his goodness, and entering into the heart of his step-mother
Ronwen, did egg her on to compass his destruction.
She, calling to her aid all the sleights of witchcraft,
gave him by a certain familiar of his own, whom she
had corrupted with bribes innumerable, a draught of
poison. No sooner had the noble warrior drunk thereof
than he was smitten with a sudden malady so grievous
that hope of his life was none. Forthwith he bade all
his soldiers come unto him, and making known unto
them that death was already upon him, distributed
amongst them his gold and silver and all the treasure
that his forefathers had heaped together. He did comfort, moreover, them that were weeping and groaning
around him, telling them that this way along which
he was now about to journey was none other than the
way of all flesh. The brave young warriors, moreover,
that wont to fight at his side in every battle, he did
exhort to fight for their country and to defend the

same against all attacks of their enemies. Moved by an
impulse of exceeding hardihood, moreover, he commanded that a brazen pyramid should be wrought for
him, and set in the haven wherein the Saxons were
wont to land, and that after his death his body should
be buried on the top thereof, so as that when the barbarians beheld his image thereupon they should back
sail and turn them home again to Germany. For he
said that not one of them durst come anigh so they did
even behold his image. O, the passing great hardihood
of the man who was thus desirous that even after
death he might be dreaded by those unto whom while
living he had been a terror! Natheless, after his death,
the Britons did otherwise, for they buried his corpse in
the city of London.

## [ 15 ]

AFTER the death of his son, Vortigern was restored unto
his kingdom, and at the earnest instance of his wife
sent his envoys to Hengist in Germany, bidding him to
come back again to Britain, but privily and with but
few men only, as he was afeard, in case he came over
otherwise, a quarrel might arise betwixt the barbarians and the men of the country. Howbeit, Hengist,
hearing of Vortimer's death, raised an army of three
hundred thousand armed men, and fitting out a fleet
returned unto Britain. But as soon as the arrival of so
huge a host was reported to Vortigern and the princes
of the realm, they took it in high dudgeon, and taking
counsel together, resolved to give them battle and drive
them forth of their coasts. Tidings of this resolve were
at once sent to Hengist by messengers from his daughter, and he forthwith bethought him what were best to
do by way of dealing a counter-stroke. After much
brooding over divers devices, the one that he made
choice of in the end was to betray the people of the

kingdom by approaching them under a show of peace. He accordingly sent messengers unto the King, bidding them bear him on hand that he had not brought with him so mighty an armament either with any purpose that they should remain with him in the country, or in any way do violence unto any that dwelt therein. The only reason he had brought them with him was that he believed Vortimer to be still alive, and that in case Vortimer had opposed his return he was minded to be able to withstand him. Howbeit, now that he had no longer any doubt as to Vortimer being dead, he committed himself and his people unto Vortigern to dispose of as he should think best. So many of their number as he might wish to retain with him in the kingdom might stay, and so many as he might desire to dismiss he was quite willing should return to Germany forthwith. And, in case Vortigern were willing to accept these terms, he himself besought him to name a day and place for them to meet, and they would then settle everything in accordance with his wishes. When such a message was brought unto Vortigern, passing well pleased was he, for he had no mind that Hengist should again depart. So at last he bade that the men of the country and the Saxons should meet together nigh the monastery of Ambrius on the Kalends of May, then just drawing on, that then and there the matter might be solemnly settled. When this had been agreed on both sides, Hengist, having a mind to put in use a new manner of treason, made ordinance unto his comrades that every single one of them should have a long knife hidden in his legging, and when the Britons were without any suspicion discussing the business of the meeting, he himself would give the signal, "Nimeth eoure saxas" ("Take your daggers"), whereupon each of them should be ready to fall boldly upon the Briton standing next him, and drawing forth his knife to cut his throat as swiftly as might be. Accordingly on the day appointed all met together in the city

aforesaid, and began to talk together over the terms
of peace, and when Hengist espied that the hour had
come when his treachery might most meetly be carried
into effect he shouted out, "Nimeth eoure saxas!" and
forthwith laid hold on Vortigern and held him fast
by his royal robe. The moment the Saxons heard the
signal they drew forth their long knives and set upon
the princes that stood around, thinking of nought less
at the instant, and cut the throats of about four hundred and sixty amongst the barons and earls, whose
bodies the blessed Eldad did afterward bury and place
in the ground after Christian fashion not far from
Kaercaradoc, that is now called Salisbury, within the
church-yard that lieth about the monastery of Abbot
Ambrius, who of yore had been the founder thereof.
For all of them had come unarmed, nor never deemed
of aught save treating as touching the peace. Whence
it came to pass that the others, which had come for
nought but treachery, could lightly slay them as having
done off their arms. Howbeit the Paynims wrought not
their treason unavenged, for many of themselves were
slain whilst that they were putting the others to death
the Britons snatching the stones and sticks that were
on the ground, and in self-defence doing no little exe-
cution upon their betrayers.


[ 16 ]


AMONG others that were there was Eldol, Earl of
Gloucester, who, seeing this treachery, took up a stake
that he had found by chance and defended himself
therewithal. Whomsoever he got at, he brake him the
limb he struck and sent him to hell forthwith. Of some
the head, of others the arms, of others the shoulders,
and of many more the legs did he shatter, causing no
small terror wheresoever he laid about him, nor did
he stir from the place before he had slain seventy men

with the stake he wielded. But when he could no
longer stand his ground against so great a multitude,
he made shift to get away and betook him to his own
city. Many fell on the one side and the other, but the
Saxons had the upper hand, as well they might, seeing
that the Britons, never suspecting aught of the kind,
had come without arms and so were the less able to
defend them. Natheless, they were not minded to slay
Vortigern, but bound him and threatened him with
death, and demanded his cities and strong places as
ransom for his life; he straightway granting all they
had a mind to, so he were allowed to escape on live.
And when he had confirmed this unto them by oath,
they loosed him from his fetters, and marching first of
all upon London, took that city, taking next York and
Lincoln as well as Winchester, and ravaging the country at will, slaying the country folk as wolves do sheep
forsaken of their shepherd. When therefore Vortigern
beheld so terrible a devastation, he betook him privily
into the parts of Wales, not knowing what to do against
this accursed people.


[ 17 ]


Howbeit, he at last took counsel of his wizards, and
bade them tell him what he should do. They told him
that he ought to build him a tower exceeding strong,
as all his other castles he had lost. He sought accordingly in all manner of places to find one fit for such a
purpose and came at last unto Mount Snowden, where,
assembling a great gang of masons from divers countries, he bade them build the tower. The stonemasons,
accordingly, came together and began to lay the foun-
dations thereof, but whatsoever they wrought one day
was all swallowed up by the soil the next, in such sort
as that they knew not whither their work had van-

ished unto. And when word was brought hereof unto
Vortigern, he again held counsel with his wizards to
tell him the reason thereof. So they told him that he
must go search for a lad that had never a father, and
when he had found him should slay him and sprinkle
his blood over the mortar and the stones, for this, they
said, would be good for making the foundation of the
tower hold firm. Forthwith messengers are sent into all
the provinces to look for such manner of man, and
when they came into the city that was afterward called
Carmarthen, they saw some lads playing before the
gate and went to look on at the game. And being
weary with travel, they sate them down in the ring and
looked about them to see if they could find what they
were in quest of. At last, when the day was far spent, a
sudden quarrel sprang up betwixt a couple of youths
whose names were Merlin and Dinabutius. And as they
were wrangling together, saith Dinabutius unto Merlin: "What a fool must thou be to think thou art a
match for me! Keep thy distance, prithee! Here am I,
born of the blood royal on both sides of the house;
and thou? None knoweth what thou art, for never a
father hadst thou!" At that word the messengers lifted
up their faces, and looking narrowly upon Merlin,
asked the bystanders who he might be. They told them
that none knew his father, but that his mother was
daughter of the King of South Wales, and that she
lived along with the nuns in St. Peter's Church in that
same city.

[18]

THE messengers hurried off to the reeve of the city,
and enjoined him in the King's name that Merlin and
his mother should be sent unto the King. The reeve,
accordingly, so soon as he knew the errand whereon

they came, forthwith sent Merlin and his mother unto Vortigern for him to deal withal as he might list. And when they were brought into his presence, the King received the mother with all attention as knowing that she was of right noble birth, and afterward began to make inquiry as to who was the father of the lad. Unto whom she made answer: "As my soul liveth and thine, O my lord the King, none know I that was his father. One thing only I know, that on a time whenas I and the damsels that were about my person were in our chambers, one appeared unto me in the shape of a right comely youth and embracing me full straitly in his arms did kiss me, and after that he had abided with me some little time did as suddenly vanish away so that nought more did I see of him. Natheless, many a time and oft did he speak unto me when that I was sitting alone, albeit that never once did I catch sight of him. But after that he had thus haunted me of a long time, he lay with me for some while in the shape of a man and left me heavy with child. So much, my lord King, is my true story, and so much leave I unto thee to interpret aright, for none other have I known that is father unto this youth." Amazed at her words, the King commanded that Maugantius should be called unto him to declare whether such a thing might be as the lady had said. Maugantius was brought accordingly, and when he had heard the story from first to last, said unto Vortigern: "In the books of our wise men and in many histories have I found that many men have been born into the world on this wise. For, as Apuleius in writing as touching the god of Socrates doth make report, certain spirits there be betwixt the moon and the earth, the which we do call incubus dæmons. These have a nature that doth partake both of men and angels, and whensoever they will they do take upon them the shape of men, and do hold converse with mortal women. Haply one of these hath appeared unto this lady, and is the father of the youth."

## [19]

AND when Merlin had hearkened unto all this, he came unto the King and said: "Wherefore have I and my mother been called into thy presence?" Unto whom Vortigern: "My wizards have declared it unto me as their counsel that I should seek out one that had never a father, that when I shall have sprinkled his blood upon the foundation of the tower my work should stand firm." Then said Merlin: "Bid thy wizards come before me, and I will convict them of having devised a lie." The King, amazed at his words, straightway bade his wizards come and set them down before Merlin. Unto whom spake Merlin: "Since ye know not what it is that doth hinder the foundation being laid of this tower, ye have given counsel that the mortar thereof should be slacked of my blood, that so the tower should stand forthwith. Now tell me, what is it that lieth hid beneath the foundation, for somewhat is there that doth not allow it to stand?" But the wizards were adread and held their peace. Then saith Merlin, that is also called Ambrosius: "My lord the King, call thy workmen and bid delve the soil, and a pool shalt thou find beneath it that doth forbid thy tower to stand." And when this was done, straightway a pool was found under the earth, the which had made the soil unconstant. Then Ambrosius Merlin again came nigh unto the wizards and saith: "Tell me now, ye lying flatterers, what is it that is under the pool?" But they were all dumb and answered unto him never a word. And again spake he unto the King, saying: "Command, O King, that the pool be drained by conduits, and in the bottom thereof shalt thou behold two hollow stones and therein two dragons asleep." The King, believing his words for that he had spoken true as touching the pool, commanded also that the pool should be drained. And when he

found that it was even as Merlin had said he marvelled
greatly. All they that stood by were no less astonished
at such wisdom being found in him, deeming that he
was possessed of some spirit of God.

# BOOK VII

## OF THE PROPHECIES OF MERLIN

### [1]

I HAD not come so far as this place of my history, when by reason of the much talk that was made about Merlin my contemporaries did on every side press me to make public an edition of his prophecies, and more especially Alexander, Bishop of Lincoln, a man of the highest piety and wisdom. Nor was there none other, whether he were cleric or layman, that did retain so many knights or nobles in his household, whom his gentle holiness of life and bountiful kindliness did allure into his service. Wherefore, for that he it was whom I did most earnestly desire to please above all other, I did translate the prophecies and did send them unto him along with a letter unto this effect.

### [2]

"THE affection I bear unto thy nobility, Alexander, Prelate of Lincoln, hath compelled me to translate the *Prophecies of Merlin* out of the British into Latin before I had made an end of the *History* I had begun as concerning the acts of the British Kings; for my purpose was to have finished that first, and afterward to have published this present work, for fear lest, both labours hanging on my hands at once, my wit should scarce be sufficient for either. Howbeit, sithence that I am well assured aforehand of pardon being granted unto me

according to the discretion of thine own subtile wit, I
have set my rustic reed to the writing of these little
books, and have interpreted for thee this unknown language. Greatly, natheless, do I marvel that thou hast
deigned to commit this task unto my poor pen, seeing
that the wand of thy power might have commanded the
services of so many more learned and more wealthy
than am I to charm the ears of thy Minerva with the
delight of a sublimer song. And, to say nothing of all
the philosophers of the whole island of Britain, this I
blush not to confess, that thou art the one man who
hast it in thee to chant more excellently than they all
unto this adventurous lyre. Howbeit, sith it so pleaseth
thee that Geoffrey of Monmouth should sound his pipe
in these vaticinations, eschew thou not to show favour
unto his minstrelsies, and if so be that he carol out of
time or tune do thou with the ferule of thine own
muses chastise him back into keeping true harmony and
measure."

# [3]

ACCORDINGLY, while Vortigern, King of the Britons, was
yet seated upon the bank of the pool that had been
drained, forth issued the two dragons, whereof the one
was white and the other red. And when the one had
drawn anigh unto the other, they grappled together in
baleful combat and breathed forth fire as they panted.
But presently the white dragon did prevail, and drave
the red dragon unto the verge of the lake. But he, grieving to be thus driven forth, fell fiercely again upon the
white one, and forced him to draw back. And whilst
that they were fighting on this wise, the King bade
Ambrosius Merlin declare what this battle of the dragons did portend. Thereupon he straightway burst into
tears, and drawing in the breath of prophecy, spake,
saying:

"Woe unto the Red Dragon, for his extermination draweth nigh; and his caverns shall be occupied of the White Dragon that betokeneth the Saxons whom thou hast invited hither. But the Red signifieth the race of Britain that shall be oppressed of the White. Therefore shall the mountains and the valleys thereof be made level plain and the streams of the valleys shall flow with blood. The rites of religion shall be done away and the ruin of the churches be made manifest. At the last, she that is oppressed shall prevail and resist the cruelty of them that come from without. For the Boar of Cornwall shall bring succour and shall trample their necks beneath his feet. The islands of the Ocean shall be subdued unto his power, and the forests of Gaul shall he possess. The house of Romulus shall dread the fierceness of his prowess and doubtful shall be his end. Renowned shall he be in the mouth of the peoples, and his deeds shall be as meat unto them that tell thereof. Six of his descendants shall follow his sceptre, but after them shall rise up the German Worm. The Wolf of the sea shall exalt him, unto whom the woods of Africa shall bear company. Again shall religion be done away, and the Sees of the Primates shall be transmuted. The dignity of London shall adorn Canterbury and men shall resort unto the seventh shepherd of York in the realm of Brittany. St. Davids shall be robed in the pall of Caerleon and a preacher of Ireland shall be stricken dumb on account of an infant in the womb. It shall rain a shower of blood, and a baleful famine shall prey upon mortal men. When these things befal, then shall the Red one grieve, yet when he hath undergone his travail shall he wax strong. Then shall the calamity of the White be hastened and that which is builded in his little garden shall be overthrown. Seven sceptre-bearers shall be slain, and one thereof shall be canonised a saint. Children shall perish in the wombs of their mothers, and dread shall be the torments of men that thereby may they that were born in the land be restored unto their own. He that shall do these things shall clothe him in the brazen man, and throughout many ages shall keep guard over the gates of London sitting upon a brazen horse. Thereafter shall the Red Dragon turn him back into his own ways, and labour to wreak his wrath upon himself. Wherefore the vengeance of the Thunderer shall overtake him, for that every field shall fail the tiller of the soil. Death shall snatch away the people and all nations shall be made void. The remnant that are left shall forsake their native soil and sow seed in plantations of foreign lands. The Blessed King shall fit forth a navy and shall be reckoned twelfth in the court amongst the saints. A grievous desolation of the land shall there be, and the threshing-floors of harvests shall return unto the forests fruitful in mast and acorn. Then again shall the White Dragon arise and invite hither the daughter of Germany. Again shall our little gardens be filled of foreign seed, the Red one shall pine away at the furthest end of the pool. Thereafter shall the German Worm be crowned and the Brazen Prince be buried. A term hath been assigned unto him that he shall not be able to overpass. A hundred and fifty years shall he remain in disquiet and subjection, but three hundred shall he be seated therein. Then shall the North wind rise against him and snatch from him the flowers that the West wind had brought forth. There shall be gilding in the temples and the edge of the sword shall not cease. Scarce shall the German Worm find refuge in his caves for the vengeance of his treason that shall overtake him. Yet at the last for a little while shall he wax strong albeit that the decimation of Normandy shall do him a hurt. For a people in wood and jerkins of iron shall come upon him and take vengeance upon him for his wickedness. He shall restore their dwelling-places unto them that did inhabit them aforetime, and the ruin of the foreigner shall be made manifest. The seed of the White Dragon shall be rooted out of our little gardens and the remnant of his generation shall be decimated. The yoke of bondage shall they bear and their mother shall they wound with spades and ploughs. Two dragons shall succeed, whereof the one shall be slain by the arrow of envy, but the other shall return under the shadow of a name. The Lion of Justice shall succeed, at whose warning the towers of Gaul and the dragons of the island shall tremble. In those days shall gold be wrung forth from the lily and the nettle, and silver shall flow from the hooves of them that low. They that go crisped and curled shall be clad in fleeces of many colours, and the garment without shall betoken that which is within. The feet of them that bark shall be cropped short. The wild deer shall have peace, but humanity shall suffer dole. The shape of commerce shall be cloven in twain; the half shall be round. The ravening of kites shall perish and the teeth of wolves be blunted. The Lion's whelps shall be transformed into fishes of the sea, and his Eagle build her nest upon Mount Aravius. North Wales shall be red with mother's blood and six brethren shall the house of Corineus slay. The island shall be drenched in nightly tears, whence all men shall be provoked unto all things. Woe unto thee, Normandy, for the brain of the Lion shall be poured forth upon thee; and with mangled limbs shall he be thrust forth of his native soil. They that come after shall strive to outsoar the highest, but the favour of the newcomers shall be exalted. Piety shall do hurt unto him that doth possess through impiety until he shall have clad him in his father. Wherefore, girdled about with the teeth of wolves, shall he climb over the heights of the mountains and the shadow of him that weareth a helmet. Scotland shall be moved unto wrath, and calling unto them that are at her side shall busy her only in the shedding of blood. A bridle-bit shall be set in her jaws that shall be forged in the Bay of Brittany. This shall the Eagle of the broken covenant gild over, and the Eagle shall rejoice in her third nesting.

The roaring whelps shall keep vigil, and forsaking the forests shall follow the chase within the walls of cities. No small slaughter shall they make of them that withstand them, and the tongues of bulls shall they cut out. They shall load with chains the necks of them that roar, and the days of their grandsire shall they renew. Thenceforward from the first unto the fourth, from the fourth unto the third, from the third unto the second the thumb shall be rolled in oil. The sixth shall overthrow the walls of Ireland and change the forests into a plain. He shall unite the divers shares into one, and with the head of the Lion shall he be crowned. His beginning shall be subject unto roving affection, but his end shall soar up to those above. For the seats of the blessed shall he renew throughout the lands, and shepherds shall he set in places befitting. Two cities shall he robe in two palls, and virgin bounties shall he bestow upon virgins. Thereby shall he merit the favour of the Thunderer, and his place shall be amongst the blessed. Of him shall issue forth the Lynx that seeth through all things, and shall keep watch to bring about the downfall of his own race, for through him shall Normandy lose both islands and be despoiled of her ancient dignity. Then shall the men of the country be turned back into the island for that strife shall be kindled amongst the foreigners. An old man, moreover, snowy white, that sitteth upon a snow-white horse, shall turn aside the river of Periron and with a white wand shall measure out a mill thereon. Cadwallader shall call unto Conan, and shall receive Scotland into his fellowship. Then shall there be slaughter of the foreigners: then shall the rivers run blood: then shall gush forth the fountains of Brittany and shall be crowned with the diadem of Brutus. Wales shall be filled with gladness and the oaks of Cornwall shall wax green. The island shall be called by the name of Brutus and the name given by foreigners shall be done away. From Conan shall issue forth the warlike Boar that shall try the sharpness of his tushes within the forests of Gaul. For the greater oaks shall he stub short each one, but unto the smaller shall he grant protection. The Arab and the African shall be adread of him, for even into furthest Spain shall sweep the swiftness of his career. The He-goat of the Castle of Venus shall succeed, having horns of gold and a beard of silver, and a cloud shall he breathe forth of his nostrils so dark as that the face of the island shall be wholly overshadowed. There shall be peace in his time, and the harvests shall be multiplied by the bounty of the soil. Women shall become serpents in their gait, and all their steps be full of pride. The castles of Venus shall be builded new, nor shall Cupid's arrows cease to wound. The fountain of Amne shall be turned into blood, and two Kings shall encounter in nigh combat for the Lioness of the ford of the staff. Every soil shall riot in luxury, neither shall mankind cease to follow after lust. All these things shall three ages see, until the buried Kings be brought to light in the city of London. Again shall famine return; again mortality return; and the citizens shall mourn over the desolation of their cities. Then shall the Boar of commerce arrive in the land, who shall recall the scattered flocks unto the pastures they have lost. His breast shall be meat unto the hungry and his tongue as drink unto them that thirst. From his mouth shall issue forth rivers that shall slake the parching gullets of men. Thereafter shall a tree rise up above the Tower of London, that thrusting forth three branches only shall overshadow all the face of the whole island with the spreading breadth of the leaves thereof. Against it shall come the Northwind as an adversary, and an evil blast thereof shall tear away the third branch, but the two that shall remain shall occupy his place until the one shall bring to nought the other by the multitude of his leaves. But when this shall be, then shall he himself hold the places of the twain, and offer sustenance unto birds from the lands that are

without. And it shall be accounted hurtful unto native
fowl, for they shall lose the freedom of their flight by
reason of their dread of the shadow thereof. The Ass
of wickedness shall succeed, swift to fall upon the
workers of gold but slow against the ravening of wolves.
In those days the oaks of the forest shall burn, and
acorns shall grow upon the boughs of the linden tree.
The Severn sea shall flow forth by seven mouths, and
the river of Usk shall seethe for seven months. The
fishes thereof shall die for the heat, and of the fishes
shall serpents be engendered. The baths of the city of
Bath shall wax cold, and the wholesome waters thereof
shall breed death. London shall mourn the slaughter
of twenty thousand, and the Thames river shall be
turned into blood. They that wear the cowl shall be
provoked unto marriage, and their outcry shall be heard
in the mountains of the Alps.

## [4]

"THREE fountains shall well forth in the city of Winchester, whereof the streams shall dispart the island
into three portions. Whosoever shall drink of the one
shall rejoice in the length of his days, neither shall he
be overtaken nor afflicted of any malady. He that shall
drink of the second shall perish of hunger unappeas-
able, and wanness and dread shall sit manifest in his
face. He that shall drink of the third shall be slain by
hazard of sudden death, neither shall his body be a
corpse that men may bury. They that would fain escape
so deadly a swallow-pit will strive to hide it with divers
coverings. But whatsoever bulk be cast thereon shall
take the shape of other substance. For if earth be
heaped thereupon, the earth shall be turned into stones,
stones into liquid, wood into ashes, ash into water.
Moreover, a damsel shall be sent forth of the City of
Canute's Forest to work healing by leechcraft, and

when she shall have put forth all her arts, by her breath only shall she dry up the hurtful fountains. Thereafter, when she shall have refreshed her with the wholesome water, in her right hand shall she carry the forest of Caledon and in her left the bulwarks of the walls of London. Whithersoever she shall walk, her footsteps shall smoke of brimstone that shall burn with a twofold flame, and the smoke thereof shall arouse the Flemings, and make meat for them that be under the sea. She herself shall overflow with tears of compassion, and shall fill the island with the shrieks of her lamenting. He that shall slay her shall be a Stag of ten branches, whereof four shall wear crowns of gold, but the remaining six shall be turned into horns of wild oxen that shall arouse the three islands of Britain with their accursed bellowing. The Forest of Dean shall waken, and bursting forth into human speech shall cry aloud:

" 'Hither, thou Wales, and bringing Cornwall with thee at thy side, say unto Winchester: "The earth shall swallow thee: transfer the see of the shepherd thither where ships do come to haven, and let the rest of the members follow the head." For the day is at hand wherein thy citizens shall perish for their crimes of perjury. The whiteness of wools hath done thee hurt, and the diversity of the dyes thereof. Woe unto the perjured race, for by reason of them shall the renowned city fall into ruin.' The ships shall be glad at the greatness of increase, and out of two shall one be made. The Hedgehog that is loaden with apples shall rebuild her, and unto the smell of the apples the fowls of many forests shall fly together. He shall add thereunto a mighty palace, and wall it around with six hundred towers. London shall behold it with envy and trebly increase her walls. The Thames river shall compass her round on every side, and the report of that work shall pass beyond the Alps. Within her shall the Hedgehog hide his apples and shall devise ways under ground. In that day shall

stones speak, and the sea whereby men sail into Gaul
shall be narrowed into a straiter channel. Upon each
bank thereof shall one man be heard of another, and
the soil of the island shall be made broad. The hidden
things of them that are beneath the sea shall be
revealed, and Gaul shall tremble for dread. Thereafter
shall a Heron issue forth of the forest Calaterium, and
shall fly around the island for a space of two years. By
her cries at night shall she call the fowls of the air together and all winged things shall she assemble in her
company. They shall fall upon the tillage of mortal
men and every grain of the harvests shall they devour.
A famine shall follow the people, and a baleful mortality the famine. And when this sore calamity hath
come to an end, then shall the accursed fowl go unto
the Valley Galabes, and uplift it so that it shall be a
high mountain. Upon the top thereof, moreover, shall
she plant an oak and build her nest in the branches
thereof. Three eggs shall be laid in the nest, where-
from shall issue forth a fox, a wolf, and a bear. The
Fox shall devour her mother, and an ass's head shall
she wear. In this guise shall she affright her brethren
and make them flee into Normandy. But they shall
awaken the tusky Boar, and borne back together in a
boat, shall do battle with the Fox. And when the fight
hath begun, she shall feign her dead and move the
Boar to pity her. Presently he shall go unto her corpse,
and standing over her shall breathe upon her eyes and
her face. But she, not forgetful of her ancient cunning,
shall bite his left foot and rend it away utterly from his
body. Leaping, moreover, upon him, she shall snatch
away from him his right ear and his tail, and slink away
into the caverns of the mountains. Thus befooled, the
Boar shall demand of the Wolf and the Bear that they
restore unto him the members he hath lost. The twain
accordingly, when they shall have entered into his cause,
shall promise him two feet of the Fox, both her ears
and her tail, the which they will compound into hog's

flesh wherewith to make him whole. Hereunto shall the
Boar agree, and shall await his promised restoration.
In the meantime shall the Fox come down from the
mountains and change herself into a Wolf, and making
believe that she is fain to speak with the Boar, shall
come unto him and craftily eat all of him up. Thereafter shall she turn herself into the Boar, and feigning
that she hath lost the missing members shall abide the
coming of her twain brethren. But after that they shall
come unto her, them also with sudden-snapping tooth
shall she slay, and shall be crowned with the head of a
lion.

"In her days shall be born a serpent that shall be
bent wholly upon the destruction of mankind. He shall
encompass London with his length, and all them that
pass by shall he devour. The Mountain Ox shall take
upon him the head of a wolf and shall whiten his teeth
in the workshop of the Severn. He shall gather unto his
company the flocks of them of Scotland and Wales that
shall drink dry the river Thames. The Ass shall call
unto the Goat of the long beard and shall change
shapes with him. Thereupon shall the Mountain Ox
wax wroth, and calling unto him the Wolf, shall become a horned Bull against them. And when he shall
let loose his cruelty upon them, flesh and bones shall
he devour them, yet shall he be burned upon the top
of Urian. The ashes of his funeral pyre shall be turned
into swans that shall swim upon the dry as it had been
a river. They shall devour fishes in fishes, and men in
men shall they swallow up. But when they shall be
stricken with eld, they shall become wolves of the sea,
and within the depths of the sea shall they devise their
treacheries. They shall swamp out the dockyards, and
no little silver shall they gather together thereby. Again
the Thames shall flow, and calling his streams together
shall overpass the limits of his bed. The neighbouring
cities shall he hide out of his sight and overwhelm the
mountains that seek to oppose him. Fulfilled of guile

and wickedness, he shall make recourse unto the fountain of Galabes, and from thence shall seditions arise that shall provoke the North Welsh to battle. The oaks of the forest shall come together and engage in conflict with the rocks of the people of Gwent. The raven shall be there with the kite and shall devour the carcases of the slain. The owl shall build her nest upon the walls of Gloucester, and in the nest thereof shall an ass be brought forth. The serpent of Malvern shall nurture him, and many deceits shall he urge him to contrive. When he hath taken the crown, he shall transcend the highest and shall affright the folk of the land with the hoarseness of his bray. In his days shall the mountains of Pachaia totter, and the provinces shall be despoiled of their forests. For a Worm the breath whereof is fire shall come upon them and burn up the trees with the vapour he shall breathe forth. Out of him shall issue forth seven lions disfigured by heads of goats. With the stench of their nostrils shall they corrupt women, and their own wives shall they cause to be as harlots. The father shall not know his own son, for that they shall live in common even as brute beasts. But a Giant of iniquity shall arise that shall daunt all by the keenness of his eyes. Against him shall rise up the Dragon of Worcester, and shall strive to bring him unto nought. And in the battle shall he prevail against the Dragon, who shall suffer oppression under the wickedness of the conqueror. For he shall mount upon the Dragon, and putting off his garment shall sit upon him naked. The Dragon shall bear him aloft, and swingeing his tail shall beat him upon his naked body. Then shall the Giant, again renewing his strength, pierce his gullet with his sword, and at last shall the Dragon die poisoned, entangled within the coils of his tail.

"After him shall succeed the Boar of Totnes, and with baleful tyranny shall he oppress the people. Gloucester shall send forth a Lion that in divers battles shall harass him even as he rageth. He shall trample him under his feet, and affright him with his yawning jaws. At last the Lion shall wrangle with the realm, and climb above the backs of the nobles. A Bull shall appear in the midst of the conflict, and shall smite the Lion with his right foot. He shall drive him forth through all the taverns of the kingdom, but his horns shall he break against the walls of Exeter. The Fox of Kaerdubali shall wreak revenge upon the Lion, and shall wholly devour him with her teeth. But the Adder of Lincoln shall coil about her, and betoken his presence unto many dragons by his dreadful hissing. Then shall the dragons encounter and one shall tear other into pieces. He that hath wings shall oppress him that hath none, and fix his poisonous claws in his cheeks. Others shall gather together to the battle and one shall slay other therein. A fifth shall succeed unto them that are slain, and by various devices shall break the residue in pieces. Upon the back of one shall he climb with a sword and sever his head from his body. Then, putting off his garment, shall he climb upon another and grasp his tail in his right hand and his left, for naked shall he vanquish him against whom when clad he might nought prevail. The rest shall he torment and drive them all the kingdom round.

"Thereafter shall a roaring Lion come forth and dread shall be the cruel fellness thereof. Thrice five portions shall he bring into one, and he only shall possess the people. A Giant shall glitter in white array and spread him abroad over the white people as a tree. Luxury shall waste the strength of princes and of a sudden shall they be turned into beasts. Amongst them shall arise a Lion, swollen with the blood of men. Under him shall be set a reaper with a sickle in the standing corn, and even as he toileth at his reaping shall he be oppressed of him. The charioteer of York shall appease them, and thrusting forth his lord, shall mount the chariot he driveth. With his drawn sword shall he threaten the East, and the rut of his chariot wheels shall he fill with blood. Then shall he become a fish of the sea that shall mate with a serpent that shall allure him by her hissing. Thence shall be born three thundering bulls, who, when they have eaten up their pastures, shall be turned into trees. The first shall carry a scourge of vipers, and shall turn his back upon the nextborn, who shall strive to snatch away the scourge, but by the last shall it be seized and carried off. They shall turn away their faces the one from other until they have cast away the poisoned cup. Unto him shall succeed the Husbandman of Scotland, at whose back shall a serpent overhang. He shall busy him in turning of the soil so that the land may be white unto harvest. The serpent shall weary him in spilling of his venom, that the green blade may never ripen to the full ear. The people shall be wasted by deadly slaughter, and the walls of cities shall be made desolate. Then shall the city of Gloucester be given for the healing and she shall interpose the foster-daughter of the Scourger. For she shall hold the balance whereby the medicine of healing is meted out, and in a brief space shall the island be renewed. Then shall two follow the sceptre, unto whom shall the horned Dragon minister. The one shall come in iron, and upon a flying serpent shall he ride. With his body naked shall he sit upon his back, and with his right hand shall he lay hold upon his tail. The seas shall be troubled at the noise of his crying, and fear shall fall upon the other because of him. Therefore shall the second take the Lion into his company, but a strife shall arise betwixt them, and they shall fight together. With mutual wounds shall the one be stricken of the other, but the fellness of the beast shall prevail. Then shall one come with harp and tabor, and shall appease the fierceness of the Lion. Wherefore the nations of the realm shall be at peace, and shall call upon the Lion to be holder of the balance. In the seat assigned him he shall pay heed unto the weights, but his palms shall he stretch forth into Scotland. They of the Northern province shall thereby be aggrieved and shall throw open the gates of the temples. The Wolf that beareth the ensign shall be captain of the companies, and Cornwall shall he encompass round about with his tail. A knight in a chariot shall withstand him, and that people shall he change into a boar. Wherefore the Boar shall lay waste the provinces, but his head shall he hide in the depths of the Severn sea.

"A man shall hug a lion in wine, and the dazzling of the gold shall blind the eyes of them that look thereon. Silver shall wax white in the circuit thereof, and shall be a vexation unto the wine-presses. Mortals shall be drunken with the wine that is set before them, and turning their back upon heaven, shall fix their eyes upon the earth. The stars shall turn their face away from them, and their wonted course shall be confounded. In the wrath of the stars shall the standing corn be withered and the dews of heaven shall be forbidden to fall. Root and branch shall change places, and the newness of the thing shall be as a miracle. The shining of the sun shall be dimmed by the amber of Mercury, and shall be a dread unto them that behold it. Stilbon of Arcady shall change his shield, and the helmet of Mars shall call unto Venus. The helmet of Mars shall cast a shadow, and the rage of Mercury shall overpass all bounds. Iron Orion shall bare his sword. Phœbus of the ocean shall torment his clouds. Jupiter shall trespass beyond his appointed bounds, and Venus forsake the way that hath been ordained unto her. The malignity of Saturn the star shall fall upon earth with the rain of heaven, and shall slay mankind as it were with a crooked sickle. The twice six houses of the stars shall mourn over the wayward wandering of their guests. The Twins shall surcease from their wonted embrace, and shall call the Urn unto the fountains. The scales of the Balance shall hang awry until the Ram shall set his crooked horns beneath them. The tail of the Scorpion shall breed lightnings, and the Crab fall at strife with the Sun. The Virgin shall forget her maiden shame, and climb up on the back of the Sagittary. The chariot of the Moon shall disturb the Zodiac, and the Pleiades shall burst into tears and lamentation. None hereafter shall return unto his wonted duty, but Ariadne shall lie hidden within the closed gateways of her sea-beaten headland. In the twinkling of an eye shall the seas lift them up, and the dust of them of old again begin to live. With a baleful blast shall the winds do battle together, and the sound thereof shall be heard amongst the stars."

# BOOK VIII

## [1]

When Merlin had delivered these and many other prophecies, all they that stood by were stricken with amazement at his words, albeit that they could not apprehend the full meaning thereof. Vortigern himself, marvelling above all other, did applaud the young man's wit no less than the predictions themselves. For none had the then present age produced that had on any such wise opened his lips in his presence. Accordingly, being fain to learn what should be the ending of his own life, he besought the youth to tell him what he knew thereof. Unto this said Merlin:

"Flee thou from the fire of the sons of Constantine, if flee it thou mayst! Even now are they fitting forth their ships—even now are they leaving the coasts of Brittany behind and spreading their sails upon the deep. They will make for the island of Britain and invade the Saxon race. That accursed people will they subdue, but first will they shut up thyself in a tower and burn thee! Unto thine own bane didst thou betray their father and invite the Saxons into the island. Thou didst invite them as thy bodyguard, they have come over as thy headsmen. Two deaths await thee, nor is it clear which one of the twain thou mayst first escape. For upon the one side, the Saxons will lay waste thy kingdom and will seek to compass thy death. Upon the other, the two brethren Aurelius and Uther Pendragon will enter into thy land seeking to revenge their father's death upon thee. Seek out refuge if thou mayst. Tomorrow will they make haven in Totnes. The faces of

the Saxons shall be red with blood: Hengist shall be
slain, and thereafter shall Aurelius Ambrosius be
crowned King. He shall give peace unto the nations: he
shall restore the churches, yet shall he die of poison.
Unto him shall succeed his brother Uther Pendragon,
whose days shall likewise be cut short by poison. At this
so black betrayal shall thine own descendants be present, whom the Boar of Cornwall shall thereafter devour!"

Straightway, when the morrow dawned, came Aurelius Ambrosius unto land.

## [2]

WHEN the tidings of their coming were bruited abroad,
the Britons who had been scattered with such slaughter
gathered them together again, and strengthened by the
comradeship of their fellow-countrymen, are fuller of
cheer than of late they have been wont. They called the
clergy together, anointed Aurelius as King, and did
homage to him according to custom. But when they
counselled falling upon the Saxons, the King dissuaded
them, being minded first of all to follow up Vortigern,
for so grievously did he take to heart the treachery that
had been wrought against his father, that nought him
seemed to do save first of all he might avenge him.
Accordingly, desirous of fulfilling his purpose, he
marcheth his army into Wales and maketh toward the
castle of Ganarew whither Vortigern had fled for refuge.
This castle was in the country of Archenfield, upon the
river Wye on the mountain that is called Doward.
When Ambrosius had come thereunto, remembering
the treason wrought against his father and brother, he
speaketh unto Eldol, Duke of Gloucester, saying: "See
now, noble Duke, the walls of this city, whether they
be strong enow to protect Vortigern, that I sheathe not
the point of my sword in his bowels. For violent death

hath he deserved, nor deem I that thou knowest not
how well he hath deserved it. O, most impious of men,
worthy to die in torment unspeakable! First, he betrayed
my father Constantine, who had delivered him and his
country from the ravages of the Picts; then Constans,
my brother, whom he raised to be King, only to destroy
him; then, when he had branded himself by his own
treacheries, he thrust his heathens in amongst the freemen of the land that he might exterminate all them
that loyally abided by their fealty unto me. Yet by God's
permission hath he now fallen unawares into the snare
that he had laid for His faithful. For when the Saxons
found him out in his iniquities they thrust him forth
of the kingdom, for the which ought none to be sorry.
Yet, methinketh, all men may well be sore grieved that
this accursed people whom this accursed man hath invited hither have slaughtered my noble freemen, have
laid waste my fruitful country, have destroyed the holy
churches and well-nigh done away all Christianity from
sea to sea. Now, therefore, my fellow-countrymen, quit
ye like men, and wreak your vengeance first of all upon
him that hath wrought all these evil deeds! Then let
us turn our arms against the enemies that compass us
around, and save the country from being swallowed up
in their insatiable maw!"

Forthwith they brought their engines of all kinds into
play and strove their best to breach the walls, but when
all else failed, they set the place on fire, and the fire,
finding fuel, spread blazing up till it had burned up the
tower and Vortigern therein.

[3]

WHEN the report of this reached Hengist and his Saxons
he was smitten with dread, for he was afeard of the
prowess of Aurelius. For such valour and hardihood was
in the man, that when he was in the parts of Gaul was

none other that durst meet him in combat man to man. For when he ran a tilt at any, either he would thrust down his enemy from his horse or frush his spear to flinders. Moreover he was freehanded of his bounties, diligent in observances of religion, moderate in all things, and above all things did he eschew a lie. Valiant afoot, more valiant yet a-horseback, and right well-skilled in conduct of an army. These prowesses of his whilst he was still sojourning in Brittany, had fame, in her busy flights abroad, brought report of into the island, insomuch as that the Saxons were adread thereof, and drew them unto the further side of Humber, where they garrisoned the cities and castles in those parts, for that the country had ever been open unto them as a land of refuge. For the nighness thereof unto Scotland gave them protection, seeing that Scotland had ever been wont to watch for occasion to do hurt unto the people of the country. Wherefore this tract of land, fearsome to dwell in, and void of native folk, had ever offered safe resort unto strangers, insomuch as on account of the nature no less than the situation of the land it had ever lain open unto the Picts and Scots, Danskers and Norwegians and others that landed therein with intent to lay waste the island. Knowing, therefore, that in that part of the country they were safe from their next neighbours, they fled thitherward, so that should need be they could take refuge as readily as in their own castles. So when this was told unto Aurelius, he took fresh hardihood and had good hope of a victory. Wherefore, calling the men of the country together as swiftly as might be, he reinforced his own army and started on his march towards the North. As he passed through the divers countries sore grieved was he to behold the desolation thereof, but most of all to see the churches all thrown down even to the ground, and the restoration thereof did he vow, so he might obtain the victory.

## [4]

HOWBEIT Hengist, when he learnt of his arrival, took courage again, and made choice among his fellow-soldiers of them that did most need encouragement, and gave them heart, exhorting each of them to stand their ground like men and to be nowise in dread in fighting against Aurelius. For he told them that he had but a few Armorican Britons with him, whose number was at most not more than ten thousand men. But as for the Island Britons, he held them as nought, for that he had so often defeated them in battle. Hence, therefore, he promised his men victory, and safety withal by reason of their greater numbers, for there were then some two hundred thousand men in arms. And when he had thus spirited up all of them and put them in stomach to fight, he advanced towards Aurelius as far as a field that was called Maesbeli, through the which Aurelius would have to pass, for he was minded to make a sudden and stealthy onslaught and to fall upon the Britons at unawares. Howbeit Aurelius got wind of the design, but so far from delaying on that account to approach the field, he rather marched forward with the greater speed. When he came in sight of the enemy, he formed his troops in order. Three thousand Bretons he told off to attend upon the knights, and the rest he set in line mixed-medley-wise along with the islanders. The South Welsh he stationed on the hills, the North Welsh in the forest hard by, to the end that in case the Saxons should flee thither they should find those there that would stop them.

## [5]

MEANWHILE Eldol, Duke of Gloucester, came unto the King, saying:

"This one day would be enow for all the days of my life, so God would grant me to do battle with Hengist man to man. For one of us twain should die or ever our swords should be still. For well do I mind me of the day that we came together as if we were to have peace. And when we were talking over the agreement, he did betray all of us that were there, and slew them all with knives save me alone, who found a stake and did thereby escape. Upon that same day fell four hundred and sixty barons and earls that had come thither all unarmed. It was in this sore jeopardy that God did convey unto me that stake, whereby I did defend me and made shift to get me away." Thus spake Eldol, and Aurelius did exhort all his comrades to set their hopes only in the Son of God, and then to fall right hardily upon the enemy and fight with one mind for their country. Upon the other part, Hengist set his troops in fighting order, and as he set them, instructed them how they should bear them in the battle, walking to and fro betwixt the battalions and giving orders unto each so as to inspirit them all with hardihood to fight. Then, when all the companies on both sides were drawn forth in battle-array, the foremost ranks engage, dealing blow upon blow and shedding no little blood. On the one side the Britons, on the other the Saxons, drop down to die of their wounds. Aurelius cheereth on his Christians, Hengist giveth the word unto his Paynims; and as the conflict thus was raging, ever among did Eldol seek occasion to get at handgrips with Hengist, but none such offered; for Hengist, when he saw his own men fall, and that the Britons by God's grace were gaining ground, straightway fled away and made for the Castle of Kaerconan, that is now called Conisbrough. Aurelius pursueth him, and whomsoever he overtook upon his way he either slew or made captive as bondsman. When, therefore, Hengist perceived that he was being hunted down of Aurelius, he was not minded to enter into the castle, but commanding his troops again to

form in rank, decided to renew the battle, for he knew
that the castle could in no wise withstand Aurelius, and
that all his defence lay in his own sword and spear. At
last, when Aurelius had overtaken him, he also ranked
his comrades in companies, and charged right hardily
upon him. Natheless, the Saxons hold their ground as
one man, and many on both sides are wounded to the
death. Blood floweth everywhere, and the cries of the
dying rouse the living to a fiercer wrath. At last the
Saxons would have prevailed, had not a company of
knights of the Bretons come down upon them. For
Aurelius had stationed them apart as he had done in
the first battle. When these charged down upon them,
the Saxons were forced to give ground, and after being
broken, albeit in nowise cut to pieces, were scarce able
to form in rank again. Then the Britons advance more
hardily and harass the enemy with one accord. Nor did
Aurelius stint to cheer on his men to smite down them
that came in his way, to give chase to them that fled,
and do all that man might do to comfort his comrades.
In like manner did Eldol; hurrying to and fro in all
parts of the field, and dealing deadly wounds upon the
foe, yet ever, whatsoever he did, was his heart set upon
having but one chance of foregathering with Hengist
man to man.

[6]

AND whilst the divers companies were thus charging
and cutting and thrusting in divers parts, it so fell out
that the twain did encounter one another at an even
advantage, and began to smite and smite yet again
either upon other, stroke upon stroke. O, but those
champions thirsted for the fight, and when one let
drive at other and their swords clashed together the
sparks flew at each blow as though they made lightning
flash amidst thunder. Long time was it doubtful which

of the twain had the more stalwart thews, for at one time would Eldol prevail and Hengist give ground; at another would Hengist prevail and Eldol give ground. And whilst they were still battling on this wise came up Gorlois, Duke of Cornwall, with the battalion he commanded and began to harass the enemy's companies. Thereupon, when Eldol espied him, he took fresh hardihood, and gripping Hengist by the nosepiece of his helmet, put forth all his force and dragged him forth into the midst of his own people. Rejoicing thereat with exceeding great gladness, he cried aloud: "God hath fulfilled my desire! Up, men! and down with these marauders before ye! In your hands is the victory, for in conquering Hengist we have conquered them!" In the midst of all this the Britons failed not to bear down upon the Paynims, charging again and again, and when they fell back, advancing with redoubled hardihood, giving not a moment's respite until the victory was won. At last the Saxons fled, whithersoever each man's sudden thought might lead. Some betook them to the cities; others to the forest mountains, others to their ships. But Octa, Hengist's son, with the greater part of the residue, made his way to York, while Eosa his kinsman garrisoned the city with a numberless host of armed men.

## [ 7 ]

AFTER that Aurelius had thus won the day, he took Conisbrough, whereof I have before made mention, and there sojourned three days. Meanwhile he bade the dead be buried, the wounded be attended, and the weary given rest, besides supplying them with comforts of all kinds. After this he called together his Dukes and bade them say what should be done with Hengist. Eldad, Bishop of Gloucester and brother of Eldol, was present, a man of the highest wisdom and piety. He,

when he beheld Hengist standing before the King,
bade the rest keep silence and spake unto him on this
wise: "Were all here to try to set this man free, yet
would I myself hew him in pieces; for therein should
I follow the ensample of Samuel the prophet when he
had Agag, King of the Amalekites, in his power; for he
hewed him to pieces, saying, 'As thy sword hath made
mothers childless, so shall I today make thy mother
childless among women.' Wherefore do ye the same
unto Hengist, for that he is another Agag." Eldol
thereupon took his sword, led Hengist without the city
and sent him unto hell with his head smitten off. But
Aurelius, that was ever sober in all things, bade him be
buried, and a mound of earth be heaped above his
body after the manner of the Paynims.

### [8]

THEN Aurelius led his army unto York to beleaguer
Octa, Hengist's son. And when he laid siege unto the
city, Octa misdoubted whether he might withstand him
and hold the city against so huge a host. After taking
counsel thereupon, he issued forth along with the more
noble of them that were with him, bearing a chain in
his hand and with dust upon his head, and presented
him before the King with these words: "My gods be
vanquished, nor do I falter to acknowledge that it is
thy God which reigneth and hath compelled so many
nobles to come unto thee on this wise. Wherefore do
thou accept of us and of this chain, and, save thou
have mercy upon us, have us bound and doom us unto
any punishment thou wilt." Aurelius was thereby
moved to pity, and taking counsel, bade declare what
should be done unto them. And when divers of them
had delivered divers counsel, Eldad the Bishop rose up
and spake his mind after this fashion: "The Gibeonites
of their own will did come unto the children of Israel,

and beseeching mercy did obtain mercy. Shall we Christians, therefore, be worse than Jews and deny mercy unto these? Mercy is that they beseech, mercy let them have! Broad is this island of Britain, and in many places void of inhabitants. Let us therefore make covenant with them that, so we suffer them to dwell at least in our desert places, they shall be vassal unto us for ever." The King thereupon agreed unto Eldad's proposal, and had mercy upon them. Moreover, moved thereto by the ensample of Octa, came Eosa and the rest of them that had fled and begged for mercy. He assigned unto them, therefore, the country upon the borders of Scotland, and confirmed a covenant with them.

## [9]

HAVING now triumphed over all his enemies, the King called together the earls and princes of the realm to meet him at York, and gave ordinance unto them to restore the churches which the Saxon people had destroyed. Howbeit, he himself began to rebuild the Metropolitan church of that city and the rest of the cathedral churches of the province. After a space of fifteen days, when he had stablished a gang of workmen in the several places, he repaired unto London, which the ravages of the enemy had not spared, and sore grieved at the destruction that had been wrought, recalled the residue of the citizens from all parts and set him to bring about their restoration. There also he made ordinance for the government of the kingdom, renewing the laws that had dropped on sleep, and allotting unto the grandchildren the possessions that their grandsires had lost. Whatsoever estates had lost all heirs he shared amongst his fellow-soldiers. For all his thought and intention was turned upon the restitution of the realm, the reformation of the churches, the renewal of

peace and law, and the administering of justice. He
next went on to Winchester to restore it the same as
the other cities, and when he had there established all
that had to be stablished toward the restoration
thereof, by advice of Bishop Eldad, he went unto the
monastery nigh Kaercaradoc, that is now called Salisbury, where the earls and princes lay buried whom the
accursed Hengist had betrayed. There was there a convent of three hundred brethren upon the Mount of
Amesbury, who, as is said, was the founder thereof in
days of old. When he looked around upon the place
where they lay dead, he was moved to pity and tears
began to flow. At last he fell to pondering within himself in what wise he might best make the place memorable, for worthy of remembrance did he deem the
green turf that covered so many noble warriors that had
died for their country.

## [ 10 ]

ACCORDINGLY he called together from all quarters the
master craftsmen in stone and wood, and bade them
put forth their utmost skill to contrive some new kind
of building that should stand for ever in memory of
men so worthy. But all of them, mistrusting their own
mastery in such a matter, were only able to meet him
with a "Nay." Whereupon Tremorinus, Archbishop of
Caerleon, came unto the King and saith he: "If man
there be anywhere strong enow to carry out this ordinance into effect, let Merlin, Vortigern's prophet, set
hand thereunto. For well I wot that never another
man in thy kingdom is there that is brighter of wit
than he, whether it be in foretelling that which shall
be or in devising engines of artifice. Bid him come
hither and set his wits to work, and I warrant he shall
build thee a memorial to last!" Accordingly, when Aurelius had asked many questions about him, he sent

divers messengers through the divers countries of the
kingdom to find and fetch him; and after they had
journeyed throughout the provinces they found him in
the country of Gwent, at the fountain of Galabes that
he wont to haunt, and, telling him what it was they
wanted, brought him unto the King. The King received him gladly, and bade him declare the future,
being fain to hear marvellous things. Unto whom Merlin: "Mysteries of such kind be in no wise to be
revealed save only in sore need. For, and I were to utter
them lightly or to make laughter, the spirit that teach-
eth me would be dumb and would forsake me in the
hour of need." At last, when he had in like manner
denied them all, the King was not minded to ask him
further about the future, but spake unto him of the
work he did propose to construct. Unto whom Merlin:

"If thou be fain to grace the burial-place of these
men with a work that shall endure for ever, send for
the Dance of the Giants that is in Killare, a mountain
in Ireland. For a structure of stones is there that none
of this age could arise save his wit were strong enough
to carry his art. For the stones be big, nor is there
stone anywhere of more virtue, and, so they be set up
round this plot in a circle, even as they be now there
set up, here shall they stand for ever."

## [11]

AT these words of Merlin, Aurelius burst out laughing,
and quoth he: "But how may this be, that stones of
such bigness and in a country so far away may be
brought hither, as if Britain were lacking in stones
enow for the job?" Whereunto Merlin made answer:
"Laugh not so lightly, King, for not lightly are these
words spoken. For in these stones is a mystery, and a
healing virtue against many ailments. Giants of old
did carry them from the furthest ends of Africa and

did set them up in Ireland what time they did inhabit
therein. And unto this end they did it, that they
might make them baths therein whensoever they ailed
of any malady, for they did wash the stones and pour
forth the water into the baths, whereby they that were
sick were made whole. Moreover, they did mix confec-
tions of herbs with the water, whereby they that were
wounded had healing, for not a stone is there that
lacketh in virtue of leechcraft." When the Britons
heard these things, they bethought them that it were
well to send for the stones, and to harry the Irish folk
by force of arms if they should be minded to withhold
them. At last they made choice of Uther Pendragon,
the King's brother, with fifteen thousand men, to attend to this business. They made choice also of Merlin,
so that whatsoever might have to be done should be
dealt with according his wit and counsel. Then, as soon
as the ships are ready, they put to sea and make for Ireland with a prosperous gale.

## [12]

AT that time was Gilloman King in Ireland, a youth of
marvellous prowess, who, so soon as ever he heard of
the Britons having landed in Ireland, got together a
huge army and started forth to meet them. And when
he had learned the reason wherefore they had come, he
laughed, and saith he unto them that stood by:

"No wonder the craven Saxon folk were strong
enough to lay waste the island of Britain when the
Britons themselves are such gross-witted wiseacres. Who
hath ever heard of such folly? Are the stones of Ireland
any better than those of Britain that our kingdom
should thus be challenged to fight for them? Arm yourselves, men, and defend your country, for never while
life is in me shall they carry off from us the very small-
est stone of the Dance."

Uther accordingly, seeing that they were ready to fight, fell upon them straightway at the double-quick. Forthwith the Britons prevailed, and, his Irishmen all cut up and slain, forced Gilloman to flee for his life. When they had won the day they pressed forward to Mount Killare, and when they reached the structure of stones rejoiced and marvelled greatly. Whilst they were all standing around, Merlin came unto them and said: "Now, my men, try what ye can do to fetch me down these stones! Then may ye know whether strength avail more than skill, or skill than strength." Thereupon at his bidding they all with one accord set to work with all manner devices, and did their utmost to fetch down the Dance. Some rigged up huge hawsers, some set to with ropes, some planted scaling ladders, all eager to get done with the work, yet natheless was none of them never a whit the forwarder. And when they were all weary and spent, Merlin burst out on laughing and put together his own engines. At last, when he had set in place everything whatsoever that was needed, he laid the stones down so lightly as none would believe, and when he had laid them down, bade carry them to the ships and place them inboard, and on this wise did they again set sail and returned unto Britain with joy, presently with a fair wind making land, and fetching the stones to the burial-place ready to set up. When this was reported unto Aurelius, he sent messengers throughout the countries of Britain, bidding summon clergy and laity, and enjoining them when summoned to assemble at the Mount of Amesbury with rejoicing and honour to set up the stones again round the foresaid burial-place. Accordingly, in obedience to the edict, came pontiffs and abbots and folk of every single order that were his subjects, and when all were met together on the day appointed, Ambrosius set the crown upon his own head and celebrated the Whitsuntide festival right royally, giving up the three following days running to the holiday. Meanwhile such honours as lacked a holder he distributed as bounties unto them of his household as rewards for their toil in his service. At that time two of the Metropolitan Sees, York, to wit, and Caerleon, were vacant without their shepherds. Wherefore, being minded to consult the common wish of his peoples, he gave York unto Samson, a man of high dignity and illustrious by the depth of his piety; and Caerleon unto Dubric, whom the providence of God had before singled out as like to be right serviceable in that same place. And when he had settled these and other matters in his realm, he bade Merlin set up the stones that he had brought from Ireland around the burial-place. Merlin accordingly obeyed his ordinance, and set them up about the compass of the burial-ground in such wise as they had stood upon Mount Killare in Ireland, and proved yet once again how skill surpasseth strength.

## [13]

AT that same time Pascentius, Vortigern's son, who had fled away to Germany, called out every knight in arms of that kingdom against Aurelius Ambrosius, being minded to avenge his father, and promised them exceeding plenty of gold and silver so he were able to subdue Britain unto himself with their assistance. And when he had bribed the whole youth of the country by his promises, he fitted out a passing great fleet, and, landing in the Northern parts of the island, began to lay them waste. And when message of this was brought unto the King, he assembled his host and marched forth to meet them, challenging his cruel foemen to do battle with him. They as willingly accepted the challenge, but coming into conflict with the Britons, were by the grace of God defeated and forced to take to flight.

[ 14 ]

PASCENTIUS, therefore, being thus compelled to flee
away, durst not return into Germany, but backing sail,
betook him unto Gilloman in Ireland, and was received
by him. And when he had made known the disaster
that had befallen him, Gilloman had compassion upon
him and made complaint of the injury that Uther, the
brother of Aurelius, had done him when he came in
quest of the Giants' Dance. At last they confirmed a
covenant of alliance betwixt them, and fitting out their
ships, embarked therein and made for the city of St.
Davids. This being bruited abroad, Uther Pendragon
levied an army and marched into Wales to do battle
with them, for his brother Aurelius lay sick at Winchester and could not go himself, greatly to the joy of
Pascentius, Gilloman and the Saxons that were with
them when they heard it, for they deemed that by reason of his malady they would easily be able to subdue
the kingdom of Britain. And whilst all the folk were
talking thereupon, came one of the Saxons named
Eopa, unto Pascentius, saying: "What boon wilt thou
bestow upon the man that shall slay Aurelius for thee?"
Saith Pascentius: "O, might I but find the man that
durst go through with such a resolve, I would give him
a thousand pounds of silver, and my good-will as long
as I live, and if that it be my luck to wear the crown
of the kingdom, I will make him a general of mine
army; and so much am I ready to confirm by oath."
Saith Eopa: "The British tongue have I learnt, and the
manners of the men I know well. Some cunning, moreover, have I in leechcraft. So, therefore, that thou fulfil
unto me this that thou dost promise, I will feign me
to be a Christian and a Briton, and when I shall have
obtained access unto the King as a leech, such a
draught will I compound for him as that he shall die

thereof. And that I may the more readily come unto
him, I will feign me to be a monk right passing devout
and right learned in all doctrine withal." And when
Eopa thus promised what he would do, Pascentius
struck the bargain with him and confirmed by oath the
conditions of the pledge. Eopa accordingly shaved his
beard, tonsured his head, took upon him the habit of
a monk, and, laden with his gallipots of drugs, started
on his way towards Winchester. As soon as he arrived
in that city he proffered his services unto them of the
King's household and found favour in their eyes, for
none at that time could have been more welcome unto
them than a leech. They therefore received him gladly,
and when he was led into the King's presence he promised to restore him his health, so he were treated with
his potions. Forthwith, accordingly, he was bidden to
prepare a drink, and privily mixing a poison therewithal, he offered the same unto the King. When Aurelius had taken and drunk it, the accursed malefactor
straightway bade him cover him up under the coverlid
and go to sleep, to the end that his detestable potion
might work the more strongly. The King at once
obeyed the traitor's bidding and went to sleep as if
upon the way to a speedy recovery. Presently, when the
poison had crept into the pores and veins of his body,
death, that wont to spare no man, ensued upon his
sleep. Meanwhile that accursed traitor made shift betwixt one and another to slip forth and took heed
never to show him in court again. Whilst these things
were being enacted at Winchester, there appeared a
star of marvellous bigness and brightness, stretching
forth one ray whereon was a ball of fire spreading forth
in the likeness of a dragon, and from the mouth of the
dragon issued forth two rays, whereof the one was of
such length as that it did seem to reach beyond the
regions of Gaul, and the other, verging toward the
Irish sea, did end in seven lesser rays.

## [ 15 ]

AT the appearance of this star all that did behold it
were stricken with wonder and fear. Uther, also, the
King's brother, who was leading a hostile army into
Wales, was smitten with no small dread, insomuch as
that he betook him unto sundry wizards to make
known unto him what the star might portend. Amongst
the rest, he bade call Merlin, for he also had come
along with the army so that the business of the fighting
might be dealt with according to his counsel. And
when he was brought unto the King and stood before
him, he was bidden declare what the star did betoken.
Whereupon, bursting into tears and drawing a long
breath, he cried aloud, saying:

"O, loss irreparable! O, orphaned people of Britain!
Dead is the renowned King of the Britons, Aurelius
Ambrosius, in whose death shall we all also be dead,
save God deign to be our helper! Wherefore hasten,
most noble Duke Uther, hasten and tarry not to do
battle upon thine enemies! The victory shall be thine,
and King thou shalt be of the whole of Britain! For
yon star doth betoken thee, and the fiery dragon that
is under the star! The ray, moreover, that stretcheth
forth toward the regions of Gaul, doth portend that a
son shall be born unto thee that shall be of surpassing
mighty dominion, whose power shall extend over all
the realms that lie beneath the ray; and the other ray
signifieth a daughter whose sons and grandsons shall
hold the kingdom of Britain in succession."

## [ 16 ]

BUT Uther, albeit misdoubting whether Merlin spake
true, continued the advance against the enemy, that

he had already begun, for he was so nigh unto St. Davids as that not more than half a day's march had to be covered. And when his advance was reported unto Gilloman, Pascentius and the Saxons that were with them, they issued forth to meet him and do battle with him. So soon as the armies came in sight of one another, they both set them in fighting array, and coming to close quarters, began a hand to hand engagement, soldiers being slain on the one side and the other as is wont in such cases. At last, when the day was far spent, Uther in the end prevailed and obtained the victory after Gilloman and Pascentius had been slain. The barbarians thereupon took to flight, and scampered off to their ships, pursued by the Britons who slew a number of them in their flight. The Duke's victory being thus by Christ's favour complete, he returned the swiftest he might after so sore travail unto Winchester. For messengers had arrived announcing the death of the King and bringing word that he was presently to be buried by the bishops of the land within the Giants' Dance, nigh the convent of Amesbury, according to the instructions he had given when alive. When they heard of his departure, the pontiffs and abbots and all the clergy of the province assembled in the city of Winchester, and honoured him with a funeral such as was befitting a King so mighty. And, for that in his lifetime he had commanded he should be buried in the graveyard he had enclosed, thither they bare his body and laid it in the ground with right royal ceremony.

[17]

BUT his brother Uther, calling together the clergy of the country, took upon him the crown of the island, and with universal assent was raised to be King. And, remembering in what wise Merlin had interpreted the meaning of the star aforementioned, bade two dragons be wrought in gold in the likeness of the dragon he had seen upon the ray of the star. And when that they had been wrought in marvellous cunning craftsmanship, he made offering of the one unto the chief church of the See of Winchester, but the other did he keep himself to carry about with him in the wars. From that day forth was he called Uther Pendragon, for thus do we call a dragon's head in the British tongue. And the reason wherefore this name was given unto him was that Merlin had prophesied he should be King by means of the dragon.

## [18]

IN the meantime, Octa, Hengist's son, and Eosa, his kinsman, now that they were quit of the covenant they had made with Aurelius Ambrosius, set them to work to harass the King and ravage his dominions. For they were now taking into their fellowship the Saxons that Pascentius had brought with him, and were sending their messengers into Germany for the rest. Octa, accordingly, having surrounded him with a passing great army, did invade the Northern provinces, nor did he stint to give his cruelty free course until he had destroyed all the cities and strong places from Scotland as far as York. At last, when he had begun to beleaguer that city, Uther Pendragon came upon him with the whole force of the kingdom and gave him battle. The Saxons stood their ground like men, remaining unbroken by the assaults of the Britons, who were forced at last to flee. The Saxons followed up the victory they had won, and pursued the Britons as far as Mount Damen, when the daylight failed them. Now this hill was steep, and at the top was a hazel coppice, but halfway up were tall broken rocks amongst which wild beasts might well make their lairs. Howbeit, the Britons took possession thereof and abode all that night amongst the rocks and hazel bushes. But when the Bear began to turn her chariot as it drew toward dawn, Uther bade call the earls and princes to treat with him in counsel how they might best fall upon the enemy. All accordingly came as quickly as might be into the King's presence, who bade them declare their counsel thereupon. They accordingly enjoined Gorlois, Duke of Cornwall, to speak his opinion first, for that he was a man of much counsel and ripe of age. "No need," saith he, "of beating about the bush and making long speeches, for we must make the best use of what remains of the night. What is most wanted just now is valour and hardihood if ye would fain enjoy your lives and liberties. The multitude of Paynims is huge and hungry for fight, while we are but a handful. If we wait until daylight overtaketh us, better, I ween, not fight them at all. Up, then, while the darkness lasteth, and coming down upon them in close order, let us rush their camp by a sudden surprise. For, whilst they have no suspicion and never dream of our falling upon them in such wise, if we make the rush with one accord and put forth our hardihood, I doubt not but we shall win the day."

This counsel pleased the King and all his men, and all obeyed his injunctions. Doing on their armour, they ranked them in companies and made towards the enemy's camp, intending to make a general onset upon them all at once. But when they drew nigh the scouts became aware of their approach, and woke up their sleepy comrades with the braying of their trumpets. In sore disorder and amazement the enemy leap up, some to arm them, some overcome with terror to flee whithersoever chance might lead them. But the Britons, marching in close rank, quickly approaching and reaching the camp, and, finding an entrance, rush in upon the enemy with drawn swords. The enemy thus surprised of a sudden could make no effectual resistance, while the Britons took courage from knowing all about what they were doing, rushing in hardily with a will and laying about them in deadly fashion. The Paynims were slain by thousands; Octa and Eosa were taken prisoners, and the Saxons utterly put to the rout.

## [19]

AFTER this victory Uther marched unto the city of Dumbarton and made ordinance for settling that province, as well as for restoring peace everywhere. He also went round all the nations of the Scots, and made that rebellious people lay aside their savage ways, for such justice did he execute throughout the lands as never another of his predecessors had ever done before him. In his days did misdoers tremble, for they were dealt punishment without mercy. At last, when he had stablished his peace in the parts of the North, he went to London and bade that Octa and Eosa should be kept in prison there. And when the Easter festival drew nigh, he bade the barons of the realm assemble in that city that he might celebrate so high holiday with honour by assuming the crown thereon. All obeyed accordingly, and repairing thither from the several cities, assembled together on the eve of the festival. The King, accordingly, celebrated the ceremony as he had proposed, and made merry along with his barons, all of whom did make great cheer for that the King had received them in such joyful wise. For all the nobles that were there had come with their wives and daughters as was meet on so glad a festival. Among the rest, Gorlois, Duke of Cornwall, was there, with his wife Igerna, that in beauty did surpass all the other dames of the whole of Britain. And when the King espied her amidst the others, he did suddenly wax so fain of her love that, paying no heed unto none of the others, he turned all his attention only upon her. Only unto her did he send dainty tit-bits from his own dish; only unto her did he send the golden cups with messages through his familiars. Many a time did he smile upon her and spake merrily unto her withal. But when her husband did perceive all this, straightway he waxed wroth and retired from the court without leave taken. Nor was any that might recall him thither, for that he feared to lose the one thing that he loved better than all other. Uther, waxing wroth hereat, commanded him to return and appear in his court that he might take lawful satisfaction for the affront he had put upon him. And when Gorlois was not minded to obey the summons, the King was enraged beyond all measure and sware with an oath that he would ravage his demesnes so he hastened not to make him satisfaction. Forthwith, the quarrel betwixt the two abiding unsettled, the King gathered a mighty army together and went his way into the province of Cornwall and set fire to the cities and castles therein. But Gorlois, not daring to meet him in the field for that he had not so many armed men, chose rather to garrison his own strong places until such time as he obtained the succour he had besought from Ireland. And, for that he was more troubled upon his wife's account than upon his own, he placed her in the Castle of Tintagel on the seacoast, as holding it to be the safer refuge. Howbeit, he himself betook him into the Castle of Dimilioc, being afeard that in case disaster should befall him both might be caught in one trap. And when message of this was brought unto the King, he went unto the castle wherein Gorlois had ensconced him, and beleaguered him and cut off all access unto him. At length, at the end of a week, mindful of his love for Igerna, he spake unto one of his familiars named Ulfin of Rescraddeck: "I am consumed of love for Igerna, nor can I have no joy, nor do I look to escape peril of my body save I may have possession of her. Do thou therefore give me counsel in what wise I may fulfil my desire, for, and I do not, of mine inward sorrow shall I die." Unto whom Ulfin: "And who shall give thee any counsel that may avail, seeing that there is no force that may prevail whereby to come unto her in the Castle of Tintagel? For it is situate on the sea, and is on every side encompassed thereby, nor none other entrance is there save such as a narrow rock doth furnish, the which three armed knights could hold against thee, albeit thou wert standing there with the whole realm of Britain beside thee. But, and if Merlin the prophet would take the matter in hand, I do verily believe that by his counsel thou mightest compass thy heart's desire."

The King, therefore, believing him, bade Merlin be called, for he, too, had come unto the leaguer. Merlin came forthwith accordingly, and when he stood in presence of the King, was bidden give counsel how the King's desire might be fulfilled. When he found how sore tribulation of mind the King was suffering, he was moved at beholding the effect of a love so exceeding great, and saith he: "The fulfilment of thy desire doth demand the practice of arts new and unheard of in this thy day. Yet know I how to give thee the semblance of Gorlois by my leechcrafts in such sort as that thou shalt seem in all things to be his very self. If, therefore, thou art minded to obey me, I will make thee like unto him utterly, and Ulfin will I make like unto Jordan of Tintagel his familiar. I also will take upon me another figure and will be with ye as a third, and in such wise we may go safely unto the castle and have access unto Igerna." The King obeyed accordingly, and gave heed strictly unto that which Merlin enjoined him. At last, committing the siege into charge of his familiars, he did entrust himself unto the arts and medicaments of Merlin, and was transformed into the semblance of Gorlois. Ulfin was changed into Jordan, and Merlin into Brithael in such sort as that none could have told the one from the other. They then went their way toward Tintagel, and at dusk hour ar-

rived at the castle. The porter, weening that the Duke
had arrived, swiftly unmade the doors, and the three
were admitted. For what other than Gorlois could it
be, seeing that in all things it seemed as if Gorlois himself were there? So the King lay that night with Igerna
and enjoyed the love for which he had yearned, for as
he had beguiled her by the false likeness he had taken
upon him, so he beguiled her also by the feigned dis-
courses wherewith he did full artfully entertain her.
For he told her he had issued forth of the besieged city
for naught save to see to the safety of her dear self and
the castle wherein she lay, in such sort that she believed
him every word, and had no thought to deny him in
aught he might desire. And upon that same night was
the most renowned Arthur conceived, that was not only
famous in after years, but was well worthy of all the
fame he did achieve by his surpassing prowess.

[ 20 ]

IN the meantime, when the beleaguering army found
that the King was not amongst them, they did unadvisedly make endeavour to breach the walls and challenge the besieged Duke to battle. Who, himself also
acting unadvisedly, did straightway sally forth with his
comrades in arms, weening that his handful of men
were strong enow to make head against so huge a host
of armed warriors. But when they met face to face in
battle, Gorlois was amongst the first that were slain,
and all his companies were scattered. The castle, moreover, that they had besieged was taken, and the treasure that was found therein divided, albeit not by fair
casting of lots, for whatsoever his luck or hardihood
might throw in his way did each man greedily clutch
in his claws for his own. But by the time that this outrageous plundering had at last come to an end messengers had come unto Igerna to tell her of the Duke's

death and the issue of the siege. But when they beheld
the King in the likeness of the Duke sitting beside her,
they blushed scarlet, and stared in amazement at finding that he whom they had just left dead at the
leaguer had thus arrived hither safe and sound, for
little they knew what the medicaments of Merlin had
accomplished. The King therefore, smiling at the tidings, and embracing the countess, spake saying: "Not
slain, verily, am I, for lo, here thou seest me alive, yet,
natheless, sore it irketh me of the destruction of my
castle and the slaughter of my comrades, for that which
next is to dread is lest the King should overtake us
here and make us prisoners in this castle. First of all,
therefore, will I go meet him and make my peace with
him, lest a worst thing befall us." Issuing forth accordingly, he made his way unto his own army, and putting
off the semblance of Gorlois again became Uther Pendragon. And when he understood how everything had
fallen out, albeit that he was sore grieved at the death
of Gorlois, yet could he not but be glad that Igerna
was released from the bond of matrimony. Returning,
therefore, to Tintagel, he took the castle, and not the
castle only, but Igerna also therein, and on this wise
fulfilled he his desire. Thereafter were they linked together in no little mutual love, and two children were
born unto them, a son and a daughter, whereof the son
was named Arthur and the daughter Anna.

[ 21 ]

And as the days and seasons passed by, the King was
overtaken by a malady that did of a long time afflict
him. In the meantime, the keepers of the prison
wherein Octa and Eosa, of whom I have spoken above,
were leading a life full wearisome, fled away with
them unto Germany and struck terror throughout the
kingdom. For the rumour ran that they had roused the

whole of Germany, and had fitted out a passing mighty
fleet, intending to return unto the island and destroy
it, as, indeed, was the fact, for they did so return with
such a fleet and a numberless host of companions, and,
entering into the parts of Scotland, did visit the cities
and the people of the land with fire and sword. Whereupon the army of Britain is given in charge unto Loth
of Lothian to keep the enemy at a distance. For he was
also Earl of Carlisle, a right valiant knight and ripe
as well in years as in counsel, and, his prowess approving him worthy thereof, the King had given unto him
his daughter Anna and the charge of the kingdom
whilst his malady lay upon him. He in his campaign
against the enemy was oftentimes repulsed by them,
and had to betake him into his cities, but yet more
often did he put them to flight and scatter them, forc-
ing them to flee at one time unto the forests and at another unto their ships. For the issue of the battles
betwixt them was so doubtful that none could tell unto
which of the twain the victory should be accorded.
That which did most hurt unto the Britons was their
own pride, for that they did disdain to obey the Earl's
summons unto arms, whereby coming the fewer into
the field, they were unable to overpower the greater
numbers of the enemy.

[ 22 ]

THE island being thus well-nigh all laid waste, when
the reason thereof was reported unto the King, he
waxed wroth beyond what his infirmity was able to
bear, and bade all his barons come together before him
that he might rebuke them for their pride and luke-
warmness. And when he beheld them all in his presence, he chided them with words of chastisement, and
sware that he himself would lead them against the enemy. Accordingly he bade make a litter wherein he

might be carried, seeing that his malady did hinder
him of moving otherwise from place to place. And all
of them he bade be ready, so that, should occasion befall, they might march against the enemy. Forthwith
the litter is made ready, and all likewise are ready to
start when the day and occasion arrived.


[ 23 ]


SETTING the King within the litter, they started for St.
Albans, where the Saxons were sore distressing all the
people. And when Octa and Eosa learnt how the Britons had arrived and had brought with them the King
in a litter, they did disdain to fight him withal for that
he had to be carried about and could not even go
alone. Such an one, they said, was half-dead already,
and it would ill become so great men as were they to
fight him. They withdrew them accordingly into the
city, leaving the gates open as if to show how little they
were afeard. But when this was reported unto Uther,
he bade leaguer the city as swiftly as might be, and
made assault upon the walls on every side. The Britons obeyed, laid siege to the city and stormed the walls.
Carrying slaughter amongst the Saxons, they were just
entering by the breaches they had made, when the Saxons began to bethink them of withstanding them in
earnest, and seeing the advantage they had already
gained, repented them of their former arrogance, and
set to work to defend them as best they might, climb-
ing upon the walls and driving back the Britons with
all manner weapons of offence. At last, whilst the fight
was still raging betwixt them, the night drew on that
doth invite all men unto repose. Many thereupon
would fain have rested from the toil of arms, but more
were of counsel that it were better to keep on fighting
until they had made an end of their enemies. Howbeit, the Saxons, when they understood how grievously

they had erred in their pride, and that they had
thereby given away the victory unto the Britons, made
resolve to sally forth at dawn and challenge the Britons to a pitched battle in the field, and this was done
accordingly. For so soon as Titan had brought back
the light of day, they marched forth in orderly array
in pursuance of their design. The Britons perceiving
the same, divided their force into companies, and coming to meet them were the first to begin the attack.
The Saxons straightway stand their ground; the Britons press forward, and much blood is shed on both
sides. Not until the day was far spent did victory declare for the Britons, and the Saxons turned tail, leaving Octa and Eosa dead upon the field. So overjoyed
was the King at the issue of the battle, that whereas
afore he was too weak to lift him up without help of
another, he now raised him with a light effort and sate
him upright in the litter as though he were of a sudden restored unto health. Then, with a laugh, he cried
out in a merry voice: "These marauders called me the
half-dead King, for that I was lying sick of my malady
in the litter, and so in truth I was. Yet would I rather
conquer them half-dead, than be conquered by them
safe and sound and have to go on living thereafter. For
better is death with honour than life with shame."

[ 24 ]

HOWBEIT, although the Saxons were defeated, never a
whit the more for that did they abate their malice, but
marching off into the provinces of the North did harass the people of those parts without respite. King
Uther, as he had proposed, was eager to pursue them,
but his princes did dissuade him therefrom for that
after the victory his malady lay yet more grievously
upon him. Wherefore the enemy did with the greater
hardihood press forward against him and put forth all

their strength by every means to subdue the kingdom unto themselves. Giving loose, moreover, unto their wonted treachery, they devise plots for making away with the King by secret practices. And, for that they might get at him none other way, they resolved to get rid of him by poison, which they did. For whilst he was still lying in the city of St. Albans, they sent messengers in the habit of poor men to spy out the state of the court, and when they had learnt exactly how matters stood, they found out one device, whereof they made choice above all other for carrying out their treachery against him. For nigh the court was a spring of passing bright clear water, whereof the King was wont to drink when by reason of his malady other liquors did go against his stomach. Unto this spring accordingly these accursed traitors did obtain access, and did so infect the same with poison all round about as that the water flowing therefrom was all corrupted. When, therefore, the King did next drink of the water he was seized of a sudden by death, as were also a hundred others after him unto such time as the treason was discovered, when the spring was covered over with a mound of earth. And when the King's death was bruited abroad the bishops assembled with all the clergy of the realm and bare his body unto the convent of Amesbury, and laid it in the ground after kingly wise by the side of Aurelius Ambrosius within the Giants' Dance.

# BOOK IX

## [ 1 ]

AFTER the death of Uther Pendragon, the barons of Britain did come together from the divers provinces unto the city of Silchester, and did bear on hand Dubric, Archbishop of Caerleon, that he should crown as king, Arthur, the late King's son. For sore was need upon them; seeing that when the Saxons heard of Uther's death they had invited their fellow-countrymen from Germany, and under their Duke Colgrin were bent upon exterminating the Britons. They had, moreover, entirely subdued all that part of the island which stretcheth from the river Humber, as far as the sea of Caithness. Dubric, therefore, sorrowing over the calamities of the country, assembled the other prelates, and did invest Arthur with the crown of the realm. At that time Arthur was a youth of fifteen years, of a courage and generosity beyond compare, whereunto his inborn goodness did lend such grace as that he was beloved of well-nigh all the peoples in the land. After he had been invested with the ensigns of royalty, he abided by his ancient wont, and was so prodigal of his bounties as that he began to run short of wherewithal to distribute amongst the huge multitude of knights that made repair unto him. But he that hath within him a bountiful nature along with prowess, albeit that he be lacking for a time, natheless in no wise shall poverty be his bane for ever. Wherefore did Arthur, for that in him did valour keep company with largesse, make resolve to harry the Saxons, to the end that with their treasure he might make rich the retainers that

were of his own household. And herein was he mon-
ished of his own lawful right, seeing that of right ought
he to hold the sovereignty of the whole island in virtue of his claim hereditary. Assembling, therefore, all
the youth that were of his allegiance, he made first for
York. And when Colgrin was ware of this, he got together his Saxons, Scots, and Picts, and came with a
mighty multitude to meet him nigh the river Douglas,
where, by the time the battle came to an end, the more
part of both armies had been put to the sword. Natheless, Arthur won the day, and after pursuing Colgrin's
flight as far as York, did beleaguer him within that
city. Thereupon, Baldulf, hearing of his brother's
flight, made for the besieged city with six thousand
men to relieve him. For, at the time his brother had
fought the battle, he himself was upon the seacoast
awaiting the arrival of Duke Cheldric, who was just
coming from Germany to their assistance. And when
he had come within ten miles of the city, he was resolved to make a night march and fall upon them by
surprise. Howbeit, Arthur was ware of his purpose, and
bade Cador, Duke of Cornwall, go meet him that same
night with six hundred horse and three thousand foot.
He, choosing a position on the road whereby the enemy were bound to march, surprised them by an
assault on the sudden, and cutting up and slaying the
Saxons, drave Baldulf off in flight. Baldulf, distressed
beyond measure that he could convey no succour to his
brother, took counsel with himself in what wise he
might have speech of him, for he weened that so he
might get at him, they might together devise some shift
for the safety of them both. Failing all other means of
access unto him, he shaved off his hair and his beard,
and did upon him the habit of a jongleur with a ghittern, and walking to and fro within the camp, made
show as had he been a minstrel singing unto the tunes
that he thrummed the while upon his ghittern. And,
for that none suspected him, by little and little he

drew nigh unto the walls of the city, ever keeping up the disguise he had taken upon him. At last he was found out by some of the besieged, who thereupon drew him up with cords over the wall into the city and brought him unto his brother, who, overjoyed at the sight of him, greeted him with kisses and embraces. At last, after talking over every kind of shift, when they had fallen utterly into despair of ever issuing forth, the messengers they had sent into Germany returned, bringing with them unto Scotland six hundred ships full of stout warriors under Duke Cheldric; and when Arthur's counsellors heard tell of their coming, they advised him to hold the leaguer no longer, for that sore hazard would it be to do battle with so mighty a multitude of enemies as had now arrived.

[2]

ARTHUR, therefore, in obedience to the counsel of his retainers, retired him into the city of London. Hither he summoned all the clergy and chief men of his allegiance and bade them declare their counsel as to what were best and safest for him to do against this inroad of the Paynim. At last, by common consent of them all, messengers are sent unto King Hoel in Brittany with tidings of the calamitous estate of Britain. For Hoel was sister's son unto Arthur, born unto Budicius, King of the Bretons. Where, so soon as he heard of the invasion wherewith his uncle was threatened he bade fit out his fleet, and mustering fifteen thousand men-at-arms, made for Southampton with the first fair wind. Arthur received him with all honour due, and the twain embraced the one the other over and over again.

## [3]

A few days later they set forth for the city of Kaerliud-coit, then besieged by the Paynim already mentioned, the which city lieth upon a hill betwixt two rivers in the province of Lindsey, and is otherwise called Lincoln. Accordingly, when they had come thither with their whole host, they did battle with the Saxons and routed them with no common slaughter, for upon that day fell six thousand of them, some part drowned in the rivers and some part smitten of deadly weapons. The residue, in dismay, forsook the siege and fled, but Arthur stinted not in pursuit until they had reached the forest of Caledon, wherein they assembled again after the fight and did their best to make a stand against him. When the battle began, they wrought sore havoc amongst the Britons, defending themselves like men, and avoiding the arrows of the Britons in the shelter afforded by the trees. When Arthur espied this he bade the trees about that part of the forest be felled, and the trunks set in a compass around them in such wise as that all ways of issuing forth were shut against them, for he was minded to beleaguer them therein until they should be starven to death of hunger. This done, he bade his companies patrol the forest, and abode in that same place three days. Whereupon the Saxons, lacking all victual and famishing to death, besought leave to issue forth upon covenant that they would leave all their gold and silver behind them so they might return unto Germany with nought but their ships only. They promised further to give them tribute from Germany and to leave hostages for the payment thereof. Arthur, taking counsel thereupon, agreed unto their petition, retaining all their treasure and the hostages for payment of the tribute, and granting only unto them bare permission to depart. Natheless, whilst that they were ploughing the seas as they returned homeward, it repented them of the covenant they had made, and tacking about, they returned into Britain, making the shore at Totnes. Taking possession of the country, they devastated the land as far as the Severn sea, slaying the husbandmen with deadly wounds. Marching forth from thence they made for the country about Bath and besieged that city. When word of this was brought unto the King, astonied beyond measure at their wicked daring, he bade judgment be done upon their hostages and hanged them out of hand, and, abandoning the expedition whereby he intended to repress the Picts and Scots, hurried away to disperse the leaguer. Howbeit, that which did most sorely grieve him in this strait was that he was compelled to leave his nephew Hoel behind him lying sick in the city of Dumbarton. When at last he arrived in the province of Somerset, and beheld the leaguer nigh at hand, he spake in these words: "For that these Saxons, of most impious and hateful name, have disdained to keep faith with me, I, keeping my faith unto my God, will endeavour me this day to revenge upon them the blood of my countrymen. To arms, therefore, ye warriors, to arms, and fall upon yonder traitors like men, for, of a certainty, by Christ's succour, we cannot fail of victory!"

[4]

WHEN he had thus spoken, the holy Dubric, Archbishop of Caerleon, went up on to the top of a certain mount and cried out with a loud voice:

"Ye men that be known from these others by your Christian profession, take heed ye bear in mind the piety ye owe unto your country and unto your fellow-countrymen, whose slaughter by the treachery of the Paynim shall be unto ye a disgrace everlasting save ye press hardily forward to defend them. Fight ye therefore for your country, and if it be that death overtake ye, suffer it willingly for your country's sake, for death itself is victory and a healing unto the soul, inasmuch as he that shall have died for his brethren doth offer himself a living sacrifice unto God, nor is it doubtful that herein he doth follow in the footsteps of Christ who disdained not to lay down His own soul for His brethren. Whosoever, therefore, amongst ye shall be slain in this battle, unto him shall that death be as full penance and absolution of all his sins, if so be he receive it willingly on this wise."

Forthwith, thus cheered by the benison of the blessed man, each one hastened to arm him to do his bidding, and Arthur himself doing upon him a habergeon worthy of a king so noble, did set upon his head a helm of gold graven with the semblance of a dragon. Upon his shoulders, moreover, did he bear the shield that was named Pridwen, wherein, upon the inner side, was painted the image of holy Mary, Mother of God, that many a time and oft did call her back unto his memory. Girt was he also with Caliburn, best of swords, that was forged within the Isle of Avallon; and the lance that did grace his right hand was called by the name Ron, a tall lance and a stout, full meet to do slaughter withal. Then, stationing his companies, he made hardy assault upon the Saxons that after their wont were ranked wedge-wise in battalions. Natheless, all day long did they stand their ground manfully maugre the Britons that did deliver assault upon assault against them. At last, just verging upon sundown, the Saxons occupied a hill close by that might serve them for a camp, for, secure in their numbers, the hill alone seemed all the camp they needed. But when the morrow's sun brought back the day, Arthur with his army clomb up to the top of the hill, albeit that in the ascent he lost many of his men. For the Saxons, dashing down from the height, had the better advantage in dealing their wounds, whilst they could also run far

more swiftly down the hill than he could struggle up.
Howbeit, putting forth their utmost strength, the
Britons did at last reach the top, and forthwith close
with the enemy hand to hand. The Saxons, fronting
them with their broad chests, strive with all their endeavour to stand their ground. And when much of the
day had been spent on this wise, Arthur waxed wroth
at the stubbornness of their resistance, and the slow-
ness of his own advance, and drawing forth Caliburn,
his sword, crieth aloud the name of Holy Mary, and
thrusteth him forward with a swift onset into the
thickest press of the enemy's ranks. Whomsoever he
touched, calling upon God, he slew at a single blow,
nor did he once slacken in his onslaught until that he
had slain four hundred and seventy men single-handed
with his sword Caliburn. This when the Britons beheld,
they followed him up in close rank dealing slaughter
on every side. Colgrin and Baldulf his brother fell
amongst the first, and many thousands fell besides.
Howbeit, as soon as Cheldric saw the jeopardy of his
fellows, he turned to flee away.

## [5]

THE King having won the victory, bade Cador, Duke
of Cornwall, pursue the enemy, while he himself hastened his march into Scotland, for word had thence
been brought him that the Scots and Picts were besieging Hoel in the city of Dumbarton, wherein, as I have
said, he was lying afflicted of grievous sickness, and sore
need it was he should come swiftly to his succour lest
he should be taken by the barbarians along with the
city. The Duke of Cornwall, accordingly, accompanied
by ten thousand men, was not minded, in the first place,
to pursue the fleeing Saxons, deeming it better to make
all speed to get hold of their ships and thus forbid their
embarking therein. As soon as he had taken possession

of the ships, he manned them with his best soldiers, who could be trusted to take heed that no Paynim came aboard, in case they should flee unto them to escape. Then he made best haste to obey Arthur's orders by following up ,the enemy and slaying all he overtook without mercy. Whereupon they, who but just now had fallen upon the Britons with the all fury of a thunder-bolt, straightway sneak off, faint of heart, some into the depths of the forest, others into the mountains and caves, anywhither so only they may live yet a little longer. At last, when they found all shelter failing, they march their shattered companies into the Isle of Thanet. Thither the Duke of Cornwall follows hard upon their heels, smiting them down without mercy as was his wont; nor did he stay his hand until after Chel-dric had been slain. He compelled them to give hostages for the surrender of the whole residue.

[6]

HAVING thus established peace, he marched towards Dumbarton, which Arthur had already delivered from the oppression of the barbarians. He next led his army into Moray, where the Scots and Picts were beleaguered, for after they had thrice been defeated in battle by Arthur and his nephew they had fled into that province. When they had reached Loch Lomond, they occupied the islands that be therein, thinking to find safe refuge: for this lake doth contain sixty islands and receiveth sixty rivers, albeit that but a single stream doth flow from thence unto the sea. Upon these islands are sixty rocks plain to be seen, whereof each one doth bear an eyrie of eagles that there congregating year by year do notify any prodigy that is to come to pass in the king-dom by uttering a shrill scream all together in concert. Unto these islands accordingly the enemy had fled in order to avail them of the protection of the lake. But

small profit reaped they thereby, for Arthur collected a
fleet and went round about the inlets of the rivers for
fifteen days together, and did so beleaguer them as that
they were famished to death of hunger by thousands.
And whilst that he was serving them out on this wise
arrived Gillamaur, King of Ireland, with a mighty host
of barbarians in a fleet, to bring succour unto the
wretched islanders. Whereupon Arthur left off the leaguer and began to turn his arms against the Irish,
whom he forced to return unto their own country, cut
to pieces without mercy. When he had won the victory,
he again gave all his thoughts to doing away utterly
the race of the Scots and Picts, and yielded him to treating them with a cruelty beyond compare. Not a single
one that he could lay hands on did he spare, insomuch
as that at last all the bishops of the miserable country
assembled together with all the clergy of their obedience, and came unto him barefoot, bearing relics of
the saints and the sacred objects of the church, imploring the King's mercy for the safety of their people. As
soon as they came into his presence, they prayed him
on their bended knees to have pity on the down-trod-
den folk, for that he had visited them with pains and
penalties enow, nor was any need to cut off the scanty
few that still survived to the last man. Some petty portion of the country he might allot unto them whereon
they might be allowed to bear the yoke of perpetual
bondage, for this were they willing to do. And when
they had besought the King on this wise, he was moved
unto tears for very pity, and, agreeing unto the petition
of the holy men, granted them his pardon.

[7]

THESE matters ended, Hoel did explore the site of the
foresaid lake, and marvelled greatly to behold how so
many rivers, so many islands, so many rocks and so

many eyries of eagles did all so exactly agree in number.
And while he thus marvelled, holding the same for a
miracle, Arthur came unto him and told him there was
another lake in the same province even yet more marvellous. "It lieth," saith he, "not far hence, and it hath
twenty foot in breadth and the same measure in length,
with but five foot of depth. Howbeit, within this
square, whether it be by artifice of man or by ordinance
of nature, do breed four manner fishes in the four corners thereof; nor never is a fish of one quarter found
in any of the others. Moreover," saith he, "another lake
is there in the parts of Wales nigh the Severn, which
the men of that country do call Linligwan, whereinto
when the sea floweth it is received as into a whirlpool
or swallow, in suchwise as that the lake is never the
fuller for the waters it doth ingulf so as to cover the
margent of the banks thereof. Natheless, when the sea
ebbeth again, it doth spout forth the waters it hath
sucked in as it were a mountain, and overplasheth and
covereth the banks. At such a time, were the folk of all
that country to stand anigh with their faces toward the
lake and should be sprinkled of the spray of the waves
upon their garments, they should scarce escape, if indeed they did at all escape, being swallowed up of the
lake. Natheless, should they turn their back to the lake,
they need have no fear of being sprinkled, even though
they should stand upon the very brink."

[8]

PARDON granted unto the Scottish people, the King
made for York, there to celebrate the forthcoming
Christmas festival. And when he was entered into the
city and beheld the desolation of the holy churches, he
was sore grieved and moved unto compassion. For Samson the Archbishop had been driven forth along with
all the other holy men of religion, and the half-burnt

churches had ceased from the offices of God, so fiercely had the fury of the Paynim prevailed. Forthwith he summoned a convocation of the clergy and people, and appointed Pyramus his chaplain unto the Metropolitan See; restored the churches that were cast down even to the ground, and did grace them with convents of religious both men and women. The barons also that had been driven out by the incursions of the Saxons did he restore unto their former honours.

## [9]

IN that city were three brethren born of blood royal, Loth, to wit, and Urian and Angusel, that had held the principality of those parts before the Saxons had prevailed. Being minded, therefore, to grant unto them as unto the others their hereditary rights, he restored unto Angusel the kingly power of the Scots, and conferred the sceptre of the people of Moray upon Urian. Howbeit, Loth, who in the days of Aurelius Ambrosius had married Arthur's own sister, who had borne unto him Gawain and Modred, he did reinstate in the Dukedom of Lothian and of the other provinces thereby that had appertained unto him aforetime. At last, when he had re-established the state of the whole country in its ancient dignity, he took unto him a wife born of a noble Roman family, Guenevere, who, brought up and nurtured in the household of Duke Cador, did surpass in beauty all the other dames of the island.

## [10]

WHEN the next summer came on he fitted out his fleet and sailed unto the island of Ireland, that he desired to subdue unto himself. No sooner had he landed than Gillamaur, beforementioned, came to meet him with

a host past numbering, purposing to do battle with him.
But as soon as the fight began, his folk, naked and
utterly unarmed, fled whithersoever they might find a
place of refuge. Gillamaur was forthwith taken prisoner
and compelled to surrender, and the rest of the princes
of the country, smitten with dismay, likewise surrendered them after their King's ensample. All parts of
Ireland thus subdued, he made with his fleet for Iceland, and there also defeated the people and subjugated
the island. Next, for far and wide amongst the other
islands it was rumoured that no country could stand
against him, Doldavius, King of Gothland, and Gunvasius, King of the Orkneys, came of their own accord,
and promising a tribute, did homage unto him. At the
end of winter he returned into Britain, and re-estab-
lishing his peace firmly throughout the realm, did abide
therein for the next twelve years.


[ 11 ]


AT the end of this time he invited unto him all soever
of most prowess from far-off kingdoms and began to
multiply his household retinue, and to hold such
courtly fashion in his household as begat rivalry
amongst peoples at a distance, insomuch as the noblest
in the land, fain to vie with him, would hold himself as
nought, save in the cut of his clothes and the manner
of his arms he followed the pattern of Arthur's knights.
At last the fame of his bounty and his prowess was
upon every man's tongue, even unto the uttermost ends
of the earth, and a fear fell upon the Kings of realms
oversea lest he might fall upon them in arms and they
might lose the nations under their dominion. Grievously tormented of these devouring cares, they set them
to repairing their cities and the towers of their cities,
and built them strongholds in places meet for defence, to the end that in case Arthur should lead an

expedition against them they might find refuge therein
should need be. And when this was notified unto
Arthur, his heart was uplifted for that he was a terror
unto them all, and he set his desire upon subduing the
whole of Europe unto himself. Fitting forth his fleets
accordingly, he made first of all for Norway, being
minded to set the crown thereof upon the head of
Loth, his sister's son. For Loth was grandson of Sichelm,
King of Norway, who at that time had died leaving the
kingdom unto him. But the Norwegians disdained to
receive him, and had raised one Riculf to the kingly
power, deeming that, so they garrisoned their cities, he
would be able to withstand Arthur himself. At that
time Gawain, the son of Loth, was a youth of twelve
years, and had been sent by his uncle to be brought up
as a page in the service of Pope Sulpicius, from whom
he had received arms. Accordingly, when Arthur, as I
had begun to tell, landed upon the coast of Norway,
King Riculf met him with the whole people of the
Kingdom and did battle; but after much blood had
been shed upon both sides, the Britons at last prevailed,
and making an onset, slew Riculf with a number of his
men. When they had won this victory they overran and
set fire to the cities, scattering the country folk, nor did
they cease to give full loose to their cruelty until they
had submitted the whole of Norway as well as Denmark unto the dominion of Arthur. These countries
thus conquered, as soon as Arthur had raised Loth to
be King of Norway Arthur sailed for Gaul, and dividing his force into companies began everywhere to lay
the country waste. The province of Gaul at that time
had been committed to the charge of Flollo, tribune of
Rome, who ruled it under the Emperor Leo. He, when
he was aware of Arthur's arrival, summoned every soldier in arms that owned his allegiance and fought
against Arthur, but in no wise might he stand against
him. For the youth of all the islands he had conquered were in Arthur's company, whence it was

of common report that his army was so great that scarce
of any the greatest might he be overcome. In his retinue, moreover, was the better part of the knighthood
of Gaul, whom by his much largesse he had bound unto
himself. Flollo, therefore, when he saw that he had
been worsted in the battle, forthwith forsaking the
field, fled with a few of his men unto Paris. There, reassembling his straggling army, he put the city in estate
of defence and again was fain to do battle with Arthur.
But whilst he was thinking of strengthening his army
by auxiliaries from the neighbouring countries, Arthur
came upon him at unawares and besieged him in the
city. At the end of a month, Flollo, taking it grievously
to heart that his people should be famished to death,
sent unto Arthur challenging him to single combat on
condition that whichsoever of the twain should be conqueror should have the kingdom of the other. For he
was of great stature, hardihood, and valour, and of his
overweening confidence herein had sent this challenge
hoping that it might open unto him a door of safety.
When the message was brought unto Arthur, mightily
was he rejoiced at Flollo's proposal, and sent back word
that he was ready and willing to abide by the conditions thereof. Thereupon each did duly enter into covenant with the other, and the twain met in an island
that is without the city, all the folk watching to see what
might be the issue. Both were armed full seemly, and
each bestrode a destrier of marvellous swiftness; nor
was it easy to forecast which of the twain were most
like to win the day. Taking their stand opposite each
other, and couching lance in rest, they forthwith set
spur to their steeds and smote together with a right
mighty shock. But Arthur, who bare his spear the more
heedfully, thrusted the same into the top of Flollo's
breast, and shielding off the other's blow with all the
force he might, bare him to the ground. Then, unsheathing his sword, he was hastening to smite him,
when Flollo, on his legs again in an instant, ran upon

him with his spear levelled, and with a deadly thrust
into his destrier's chest brought both horse and rider
to the ground. When the Britons saw their King lying
his length on the field, they thought he was slain and
could scarce be withholden from breaking the covenant and setting on the Gauls with one accord. But before they had resolved to transgress the bounds of peace
Arthur was quickly on his legs again, and, covering him
with his shield, was hastily stepping up to meet Flollo,
who was bearing down upon him. And now, standing
up to each other man to man, they redouble buffet on
buffet, each bent upon fighting it out to the death. At
last Flollo found an opening and smote Arthur on the
forehead, and, had not the crash of the stroke on the
helmet blunted the edge of his sword, the wound might
well have been Arthur's death. But when the blood
welled forth, and Arthur saw his habergeon and shield
all red therewithal, his wrath waxed yet more burning
hot, and raising Caliburn aloft, with all his force he
brought it down through the helmet on to the head of
Flollo and clove it sheer in twain. With this stroke,
Flollo fell, and beating the ground with his heels, gave
up his ghost to the winds.

When the tidings was known throughout the army,
the citizens all ran together, and, opening the gates,
delivered themselves up unto Arthur. He, after thus
achieving the victory, divided his army into two com-
mands, giving one into commission unto Duke Hoel,
and bidding him go conquer Guitard, Duke of the
Poitevins, whilst he himself with the other command
busied him with subduing the other provinces. Thereupon Hoel marched into Aquitaine, invaded the cities
of the country, and after harassing Guitard in a number of battles, compelled him to surrender. He next laid
waste Gascony with fire and sword, and subjugated the
princes thereof. After a space of nine years, when he
had subdued all the parts of Gaul unto his dominion,
Arthur again came unto Paris and there held his court.

He there also summoned a convocation of the clergy
and people, and did confirm the stablishment of the
realm in peace and law. At that time, moreover, he
made grant of Neustria, which is now called Normandy,
unto Bedevere his butler, and the province of Anjou
unto Kay his seneschal. Many other provinces also did
he grant unto the noblemen that did him service in his
household. At last, when all the states and peoples were
stablished in his peace, he returned into Britain at the
beginning of spring.

[ 12 ]

WHEN the high festival of Whitsuntide began to draw
nigh, Arthur, filled with exceeding great joy at having
achieved so great success, was fain to hold high court,
and to set the crown of the kingdom upon his head, to
convene the Kings and Dukes that were his vassals to
the festival so that he might the more worshipfully celebrate the same, and renew his peace more firmly
amongst his barons. Howbeit, when he made known
his desire unto his familiars, he, by their counsel, made
choice of Caerleon wherein to fulfil his design. For, situate in a passing pleasant position on the river Usk in
Glamorgan, not far from the Severn sea, and abound-
ing in wealth above all other cities, it was the place
most meet for so high a solemnity. For on the one side
thereof flowed the noble river aforesaid whereby the
Kings and Princes that should come from oversea might
be borne thither in their ships; and on the other side,
girdled about with meadows and woods, passing fair
was the magnificence of the kingly palaces thereof with
the gilded verges of the roofs that imitated Rome. Howbeit, the chiefest glories thereof were the two churches,
one raised in honour of the Martyr Julius, that was
right fair graced by a convent of virgins that had dedicated them unto God, and the second, founded in the

name of the blessed Aaron, his companion, the main
pillars whereof were a brotherhood of canons regular,
and this was the cathedral church of the third Metropolitan See of Britain. It had, moreover, a school of two
hundred philosophers learned in astronomy and in the
other arts, that did diligently observe the courses of the
stars, and did by true inferences foretell the prodigies
which at that time were about to befall unto King
Arthur. Such was the city, famed for such abundance
of things delightsome, that was now busking her for
the festival that had been proclaimed. Messengers were
sent forth into the divers kingdoms, and all that owed
allegiance throughout the Gauls and the neighbour islands were invited unto the court. Came accordingly
Angusel, King of Albany, that is now called Scotland;
Urian, King of them of Moray; Cadwallo Lawirh, King
of the Venedotians, that now be called the North
Welsh; Stater, King of the Demeti, that is, of the South
Welsh; Cador, King of Cornwall; the Archbishops of
the three Metropolitan Sees, to wit, of London and
York, and Dubric of Caerleon. He, Primate of Britain
and Legate of the Apostolic See, was of so meritorious
a piety that he could make whole by his prayers any
that lay oppressed of any malady. Came also the Earls
of noble cities; Morvid, Earl of Gloucester; Mauron of
Worcester; Anaraut of Salisbury; Arthgal of Cargueir,
that is now called Warwick; Jugein from Leicester;
Cursalem from Caichester; Kimmarc, Duke of Canterbury; Galluc of Salisbury; Urbgennius from Bath;
Jonathal of Dorset; Boso of Rhydychen, that is Oxford.
Besides the Earls came champions of no lesser dignity,
Donaut map Papo; Cheneus map Coil; Peredur map
Eridur; Grifuz map Nogoid; Regin map Claud; Edde-
lein map Cledauc; Kincar map Bangan; Kimmarc;
Gorbonian map Goit; Clofaut; Run map Neton; Kim-
belin map Trunat; Cathleus map Catel; Kinlith map
Neton, and many another beside, the names whereof
be too long to tell. From the neighbour islands came

likewise Gillamaur, King of Ireland; Malvasius, King of Iceland; Doldavius, King of Gothland; Gunvasius, King of the Orkneys; Loth, King of Norway; Aschil, King of the Danes. From the parts oversea came also Holdin, King of Flanders; Leodegar, Earl of Boulogne; Bedevere the Butler, Duke of Normandy; Borel of Maine; Kay the Seneschal, Duke of Anjou; Guitard of Poitou; the Twelve Peers of the Gauls whom Guerin of Chartres brought with him; Hoel, Duke of Brittany, with the Barons of his allegiance, who marched along with such magnificence of equipment in trappings and mules and horses as may not easily be told. Besides all these, not a single Prince of any price on this side Spain remained at home and came not upon the proclamation. And no marvel, for Arthur's bounty was of common report throughout the whole wide world, and all men for his sake were fain to come.

[13]

WHEN all at last were assembled in the city on the high day of the festival, the archbishops were conducted unto the palace to crown the King with the royal diadem. Dubric, therefore, upon whom the charge fell, for that the court was held within his diocese, was ready to celebrate the service. As soon as the King had been invested with the ensigns of kingship, he was led in right comely wise to the church of the Metropolitan See, two archbishops supporting him, the one upon his right hand side the other upon his left. Four Kings, moreover, to wit, those of Scotland, Cornwall, and North and South Wales, went before him, bearing before him, as was their right, four golden swords. A company of clerics in holy orders of every degree went chanting music marvellous sweet in front. Of the other party, the archbishops and pontiffs led the Queen, crowned with laurel and wearing her own ensigns, unto the church

of the virgins dedicate. The four Queens, moreover, of
the four Kings already mentioned, did bear before her
according to wont and custom four white doves, and
the ladies that were present did follow after her rejoicing greatly. At last, when the procession was over, so
manifold was the music of the organs and so many were
the hymns that were chanted in both churches, that the
knights who were there scarce knew which church they
should enter first for the exceeding sweetness of the
harmonies in both. First into the one and then into the
other they flocked in crowds, nor, had the whole day
been given up to the celebration, would any have felt
a moment's weariness thereof. And when the divine
services had been celebrated in both churches, the King
and Queen put off their crowns, and doing on lighter
robes of state, went to meat, he to his palace with the
men, she to another palace with the women. For the
Britons did observe the ancient custom of the Trojans,
and were wont to celebrate their high festival days, the
men with the men and the women with the women
severally. And when all were set at table according as
the rank of each did demand, Kay the Seneschal, in a
doublet furred of ermines, and a thousand youths of
full high degree in his company, all likewise clad in
ermines, did serve the meats along with him. Of the
other part, as many in doublets furred of vair did follow Bedevere the Butler, and along with him did serve
the drinks from the divers ewers into the manifold-
fashioned cups. In the palace of the Queen no less did
numberless pages, clad in divers brave liveries, offer
their service each after his office, the which were I to go
about to describe I might draw out my history into an
endless prolixity. For at that time was Britain exalted
unto so high a pitch of dignity as that it did surpass all
other kingdoms in plenty of riches, in luxury of adornment, and in the courteous wit of them that dwelt
therein. Whatsoever knight in the land was of renown
for his prowess did wear his clothes and his arms all of

one same colour. And the dames, no less witty, would apparel them in like manner in a single colour, nor would they deign have the love of none save he had thrice approved him in the wars. Wherefore at that time did dames wax chaste and knights the nobler for their love.

## [14]

REFRESHED by their banqueting, they go forth into the fields without the city, and sundry among them fall to playing at sundry manner games. Presently the knights engage in a game on horseback, making show of fighting a battle whilst the dames and damsels looking on from the top of the walls, for whose sake the courtly knights make believe to be fighting, do cheer them on for the sake of seeing the better sport. Others elsewhere spend the rest of the day in shooting arrows, some in tilting with spears, some in flinging heavy stones, some in putting the weight; others again in playing chess or at the dice or in a diversity of other games, but all without wrangling; and whosoever had done best in his own game was presented by Arthur with a boon of price. And after the first three days had been spent on this wise, upon the fourth day all they that had done service in virtue of the office they held were summoned, and unto each was made grant of the honour of the office he held, in possession, earldom, to wit, of city or castle, archbishopric, bishopric, abbacy, or whatsoever else it might be.

## [15]

Now the blessed Dubric, piously yearning after the life of a hermit, did depose himself from the archiepiscopal See, and David, the King's uncle, was consecrated in his place, whose life was an ensample of all goodness unto them whom he had instructed in his doctrine. In the place, moreover, of the holy Samson, Archbishop of Dol, was appointed Teliau, an illustrious priest of Llandaff, with the consent of Hoel, King of Brittany, unto whom the good life and conditions of the man had commended him. The Bishopric of Silchester also was assigned to Maugan, and that of Winton unto Durian, and the pontifical mitre of Dumbarton unto Eleden. And whilst Arthur was allotting these benefices amongst them, behold, twelve men of ripe age and worshipful aspect, bearing branches of olive in their right hands in token of embassy, approach anigh the King with quiet step and words as quiet, and after saluting him, present unto him a letter on behalf of Lucius Hiberius conceived in these words:

"Lucius, Procurator of the Republic, unto Arthur, King of Britain, wisheth that which he hath deserved.

"With much marvel do I marvel at the insolence of thy tyranny. I do marvel, I say, thereat, and at the injury that thou hast done unto Rome. When I recall it to remembrance, I am moved unto wrath for that thou art so far beside thyself as not to acknowledge it, and art in no hurry to perceive what it is to have offended the Senate by thy wrongful deeds, albeit none better knoweth than thou that the whole world oweth vassalage thereunto. For the tribute of Britain that the Senate hath commanded thee to pay, and that hath been paid these many ages unto Gaius Julius, and unto his successors in the dignity of Rome, thou hast presumed to hold back in contempt of an empire of so lofty rank. Thou hast, moreover, seized from them Gaul, seized from them the province of the Burgundians, seized from them all the islands of the Ocean sea, the Kings whereof have paid tribute unto our forefathers from the time that the Roman power did in those parts prevail. Now, therefore, seeing that the Senate hath decreed to demand lawful redress of thee for heaping so huge a pile of injuries upon them, I do command thee that thou appear in Rome, and do appoint the middle day of August in the year next coming as the term of thine appearance, there to make satisfaction unto thy lords, and to abide by such sentence as their justice shall decree. Wherein if thou dost make default, I myself will enter into thy dominions and will take heed by means of the sword to restore unto the Republic all those lands whereof thy mad presumption hath plundered her."

When this letter was read in presence of the King and his earls, Arthur went apart with them into the Giants' Tower, that is at the entrance of the palace, to treat with them as to what ordinance they ought to make as against a mandate of the kind. But, just as they had begun to mount the stair, Cador, Duke of Cornwall, that was ever a merry man, burst out on laughing before the King, and spake unto him on this wise:

"Until now it hath been my fear that the easy life the Britons have led this long time they have been at peace might make them wax craven, and utterly do away in them their renown in knighthood wherein they have ever been held to excel all other nations. For where use of arms is none, and nought is there to do but to toy with women and play at the dice and such like follies, none need doubt but that cowardice will tarnish all they once had of valour and honour and hardihood and renown. For nigh upon five year is it since we took to junketings of the kind for lack of the sports of Mars. Wherefore, methinks, God Himself hath put the Romans upon this hankering, that so He may deliver us from our cowardize and restore us to our prowess as it wont to be in the old days."

And whilst he was saying this and more to the same purpose, they were come to their seats, and when they were all set, Arthur spake unto them thus:

## [16]

"COMRADES," saith he, "alike in adversity and in prosperity, whose prowess I have made proof of in giving of counsel no less than in deeds of arms, now earnestly bethink ye all in common, and make ye wise provision as to what ye deem best for us to do in face of such mandate as is this, for that which is diligently provided for by a wise man aforehand is the more easily borne withal when it cometh to the act. The more easily therefore shall we be able to withstand the attack of Lucius, if we shall first with one accord have applied us to weighing heedfully the means whereby we may best enfeeble the effect thereof. Which, verily, I deem not greatly to be dreaded of us, seeing that he doth with so unreasonable cause demand the tribute that he desireth to have from Britain. For he saith that we ought of right to give it unto him, for that it was paid unto Julius Cæsar and the other his successors, who, invited by the discords of the ancient Britons, did of old invade Britain by force of arms, and did thus by violence subdue unto their power the country tottering as it then was with evil dissensions. But, forasmuch as it was on this wise that they possessed them of the country, it hath been only by an injustice that they have taken tribute thereof. For nought that is taken by force and violence can be justly possessed by him that did the violence. Wherefore a cause without reason is this that he pretendeth whereby he assumeth that we are of right his tributaries. Howbeit, sith that he thus presumeth to demand of us that which is unjust, let us also, by like reasoning, ask tribute of Rome from him, and let him that is the better man of the twain carry off that which he hath demanded to have. For, if it be that because Julius Cæsar and the rest of the Roman Kings did conquer Britain in old days, he doth therefore decree that tribute ought now to be paid unto him there-from, in like manner do I now decree that Rome ought of right to pay tribute unto me, forasmuch as mine ancestors did of yore obtain possession of Rome. For Belinus, that most high and mighty King, did, with the assistance of his brother, Brennius, to wit, Duke of the Burgundians, take the city, and in the midmost of the market-place thereof did hang a score of the most noble Romans; and moreover, after they had taken it, did for many a year possess the same. Constantine, also, the son of Helena, no less than Maximian, both of them nigh of kindred unto myself, and both of whom, the one after the other, wore the crown of Britain, did also obtain the throne of the Roman empire. Bethink ye, therefore, whether we should ask tribute of Rome? But as to Gaul or the neighbour islands of the Ocean, no need is there of answer, inasmuch as he shrank from defending them at the time we took them out of his dominion."

And when he had thus spoken with more to the same effect, Hoel, King of Brittany, rising up in precedence of all the rest, made answer unto him on this wise:

[17]

"WERE each one of us to take thought within himself, and were he able to turn over in his mind all the arguments upon every point in question, I deem that no better counsel could he find than this which the wise discretion of thy policy hath thus proposed unto our acceptance. For so exactly hath thy provident forethought anticipated our desire, and with such Tullian dew of eloquence hast thou besprinkled it withal, that we ought all of us to praise without ceasing the affection of a man so constant, the power of a mind so wise, the profit of counsel so exceeding apt to the occasion.

For if, in accordance with thine argument, thou art minded to go to Rome, I doubt not that the victory shall be ours, seeing that what we do justly demand of our enemies they did first begin to demand of us. For whosoever doth seek to snatch away from another those things that be his own doth deserve to lose his own through him whom he seeketh to wrong. Wherefore, sith that the Romans do desire to take from us that which is our own, beyond all doubt we shall take their own from them, so only we be allowed to meet them in the field. Behold, this is the battle most to be desired by all Britons. Behold the prophecies of the Sibyl that are witnessed by tokens true, that for the third time shall one of British race be born that shall obtain the empire of Rome. Already are the oracles fulfilled as to the two, sith that manifestly, as thou hast said, the two illustrious princes, Belinus and Constantine have worn the imperial crown of the Roman empire. And now in thee have we the third unto whom is promised that highest height of honour. Hasten thou, therefore, to receive that which God tarrieth not to grant. Hasten to subjugate that which doth desire to be subjugated! Hasten to exalt us all, who, in order that thou thyself mayst be exalted, will shrink not from receiving wounds, nay, nor from losing our very lives. And that thou mayst carry this matter through I will accompany thy presence with ten thousand men-at-arms."

[18]

WHEN Hoel had made an end of his speech, Angusel also, King of Scotland, went on to declare what was his mind in the matter on this wise:

"From the moment that I understood my lord to be so minded as he hath said, such gladness hath entered into my heart that I know not how to utter it at this present. For in all our past campaigns that we have fought against kings so many and so mighty, all that we have done meseemeth as nought so long as the Romans and the Germans remain unharmed, and we revenge not like men the slaughter they have formerly inflicted upon our fellow-countrymen. But now that leave is granted us to meet them in battle, I rejoice with exceeding great joy, and do yearn with desire for the day to come when we shall meet. I am athirst for their blood, even as for a well-spring when I had for three days been forbidden to drink. O, may I see that morrow! How sweet will be the wounds whether I give them or receive! when the right hand dealeth with right hand. Yea, death itself will be sweet, so I may suffer it in revenging our fathers, in safeguarding our freedom, in exalting our King! Let us fall upon these half men, and falling upon them, tread them under foot, so that when we have conquered them we may spoil them of their honours and enjoy the victory we have won. I will add two thousand horsemen to our army besides those on foot."

[19]

THEREAFTER the rest said what there was left to say. Each promised the knight's service that was due from him, so that besides those that the Duke of Brittany had promised, sixty thousand were reckoned from the island of Britain alone of armed men with all arms. But the Kings of the other islands, inasmuch as they had not yet taken up with the custom of having knights, promised foot soldiers as many as were due from them, so that out of the six islands, to wit, Ireland, Iceland, Gothland, the Orkneys, Norway, and Denmark, were numbered six score thousand. From the duchies of the Gauls, Flanders, Ponthieu, Normandy, Maine, Anjou, and Poitou, eighty thousand; from the twelve earldoms of those who came along with Guerin of Chartres, twelve hundred. Altogether they made one hundred and eighty-three thousand two hundred besides those on foot, who were not so easy to reckon.

## [ 20 ]

KING ARTHUR, seeing that all those of his allegiance were ready with one accord, bade them return quickly unto their own countries and call out the armies they had promised; so that in the Kalends of August they might hasten unto the haven of Barfleur, and from thence advance with him to the frontiers of the Burgundians to meet the Romans. Howbeit, he sent word unto the Emperors through their ambassadors that in no wise would he pay the tribute, nor would go to Rome for the sake of obeying their decree, but rather for the sake of demanding from them what they had by judicial sentence decreed to demand from him. Thereupon the ambassadors depart, the Kings depart, the barons depart, nor are they slow to perform what they had been bidden to do.

# BOOK X

## [1]

LUCIUS HIBERIUS, when he learnt that such answer had
been decreed, by command of the Senate called forth
the Kings of the Orient to make ready their armies and
come with him to the conquest of Britain. In haste accordingly came Epistrophus, King of the Greeks; Mus-
tensar, King of the Africans; Alifatima, King of Spain;
Hirtacius, King of the Parthians; Boccus of the Medes;
Sertorius of Libya; Serses, King of the Ituraeans; Pandrasus, King of Egypt; Micipsa, King of Babylon; Politetes, Duke of Bithynia; Teucer, King of Phrygia;
Evander of Syria; Echion of Bœotia; Hippolytus of
Crete, with the dukes and barons of their allegiance.
Of the senatorial order, moreover, Lucius Catellus,
Marius Lepidus, Gaius Metellus Cotta, Quintus Milvius Catulus, Quintus Carucius, and so many others as
were reckoned to make up a total of forty thousand one
hundred and sixty.

## [2]

ALL needful ordinance made, they started on their expedition Britainwards at the beginning of the Kalends
of August. When Arthur learned that they were upon
the march, he made over the charge of defending
Britain unto his nephew Mordred and his Queen
Guenevere, he himself with his army making for
Southampton, where he embarked with a fair breeze of
wind. And whilst that he was thronged about with his

numberless ships, and was cleaving the deep with a prosperous course and much rejoicing, a passing deep sleep as about the middle of the night did overtake him, and in his sleep he saw in dream a certain bear flying in the air, at the growling whereof all the shores did tremble. He saw, moreover, a dreadful dragon come flying from the West that did enlumine the whole country with the flashing of his eyes. And when the one did meet the other there was a marvellous fight betwixt them, and presently the dragon leaping again and again upon the bear, did scorch him up with his fiery breath and cast down his shrivelled carcass to the earth. And thereby awakened, Arthur did relate his dream unto them that stood by, who expounded the same unto him saying that the dragon did betoken himself, but the bear some giant with whom he should encounter; that the fight did foretoken a battle that should be betwixt them, and that the dragon's victory should be his own. Natheless, Arthur did conjecture otherwise thereof, weening that such vision as had befallen him was more like to have to do with himself and the Emperor. At last, when the night had finished her course and the dawn waxed red, they came to in the haven of Barfleur, and pitching their tents thereby, did await the coming of the Kings of the islands and the Dukes of the neighbour provinces.

[3]

MEANWHILE tidings are brought unto Arthur that a certain giant of marvellous bigness hath arrived out of the parts of Spain, and, moreover, that he hath seized Helena, niece of Duke Hoel, out of the hands of them that had charge of her, and hath fled with her unto the top of the mount that is now called of Michael, whither the knights of the country had pursued him. Howbeit, nought might they prevail against him, neither by sea nor by land, for when they would attack him, either he would sink their ships with hugeous rocks, or slay the men with javelins or other weapons, and, moreover, devour many half-alive. Accordingly, in the following night at the second hour, he took with him Kay the Seneschal and Bedevere the Butler, and issuing forth of the tents, unknown to the others, started on his way towards the mount. For of such puissance was his own valour that he deigned not lead an army against such monsters, as holding himself singly enow for their destruction, and being minded to spirit up his men to follow his ensample. Now, when they came anigh the mount, they espied a great fire of wood a-blazing thereupon, and another smaller fire upon a smaller mount not far away from the first. So, being in doubt which were the one whereupon the giant had his wone, they sent Bedevere to spy out the certainty of the matter. He, therefore, finding a little boat, oared him first unto the smaller mount, for none otherwise might he attain thereunto, seeing that it was set in the sea. And when he began to climb up towards the top he heard above him the ullaloo of a woman wailing above him, and at first shuddered, for he misdoubted him the monster might be there. But quickly recovering his hardihood, he drew his sword from the scabbard and mounted to the very top, whereon nought found he save the fire of wood they had espied. But close thereby he saw a newly-made grave-mound, and beside it an old woman weeping and lamenting, who, so soon as she beheld him, stinted her tears forthwith and spake unto him on this wise: "O, unhappy man, what evil doom hath brought thee unto this place? O, thou that must endure the pangs unspeakable of death, woe is me for thee! Woe is me that a monster so accurst must this night consume the flower of thine youth! For that most foul and impious giant of execrable name shall presently be here, that did carry hither unto this mount the niece of our Duke, whom I have but just now sithence buried in this grave, and me, her nurse, along with her. On what unheard of wise will he slay thee and tarry not? Alas for the sorrow and the doom! This most queenly foster-child of mine own, swooning with terror when this abhorred monster would fain have embraced her, breathed forth the life that now can never know the longer day that it deserved! But, as he could not with his foul lechery despoil her who was mine other soul, mine other life, mine other sweetness of gladness, so now inflamed with a detestable lust, he has pressed his force and violence upon me, all unwilling, as may God and mine eld bear witness! Flee thou, my beloved, flee lest he return to use me after his wont and find thee here, and rend thee limb from limb by a pitiable death!" But Bedevere, moved to the heart deeply as heart of man may be moved, soothed her with words of comfort, and promising her such cheer as speedy suc-cour might bring, returned unto Arthur and told him the story of what he had found. Howbeit, Arthur, grieving over the damsel's hapless fate, bade them that they should allow him to attack the monster singly, but if need were should come unto his rescue and fall upon the giant like men. They made their way from thence unto the greater mount, and giving their horses in charge to their squires, began to climb the mount, Ar-thur going first. Just then that unnatural monster was by the fire, his chops all besmeared with the clotted blood of half-eaten swine, the residue whereof he was toasting on spits over the live embers. The moment he espied them, when nought was less in his thought, he hastened him to get hold of his club, which two young men could scarce have lifted from the ground. The King forthwith unsheathed his sword, and covering him with his shield, hurried as swiftly as hurry he might to be beforehand with him, and prevent his get-ting hold of the club. But the giant, not unaware of his intention, had already clutched it and smote the King upon the cover of his shield with such a buffet as that

the sound of the stroke filled the whole shore, and did
utterly deafen his ears. But Arthur, thereupon blazing
out into bitter wrath, lifted his sword and dealt him
a wound upon his forehead, from whence the blood
gushed forth over his face and eyes in such sort as well-
nigh blinded his sight. Howbeit, the blow was not
deadly, for he had warded his forehead with his club
in such wise as to scape being killed outright. Natheless, blinded as he was with the blood welling forth,
again he cometh on more fiercely than ever, and as a
wild boar rusheth from his lay upon a huntsman, so
thrust he in within the sweep of Arthur's sword,
gripped him by the loins, and forced him to his knees
upon the ground. Howbeit, Arthur, nothing daunted,
soon slipped from out his clutches, and swiftly bestir-
ring him with his sword, hacked the accursed monster
first in one place and then in another, and gave him
no respite until at last he smote him a deadly buffet on
the head, and buried the whole breadth of his sword
in his brain-pan. The abhorred beast roared aloud and
dropped with a mighty crash like an oak torn up by
the roots in the fury of the winds. Thereupon the King
brake out on laughing, bidding Bedevere strike off his
head and give it to one of the squires to carry to the
camp as a rare show for sightseers. Natheless, said he,
never had he forgathered with none other of so puissant hardihood since he slew the giant Ritho upon
Mount Aravius, that had challenged him to fight with
him. For this Ritho had fashioned him a furred cloak
of the beards of the kings he had slain, and he had bidden Arthur heedfully to flay off his beard and send it
unto him with the skin, in which case, seeing that Arthur did excel other kings, he would sew it in his honour above the other beards on his cloak. Howbeit, in
case he refused, he challenged him to fight upon such
covenant, that he which should prove the better man
of the twain should have the other's beard as well as
the furred cloak. So when it came to the scratch Arthur

had the best of it and carried off Ritho's beard and his
cloak, and sithence that time had never had to do with
none so strong until he lighted upon this one, as he
is above reported as asserting. After he had won this
victory as I have said, they returned just after daybreak
to their tents with the head; crowds coming running
up to look upon it and praising the valour of the man
that had delivered the country from so insatiable a
man. But Hoel, grieving over the loss of his niece, bade
build a church above her body upon the mount where
she lay, the which was named after the damsel's grave,
and is called the Tomb of Helena unto this day.

## [4]

WHEN all were come together that Arthur had expected, he marched from thence to Autun, where he
thought the Emperor was. But when he had come as
far as the river Aube, tidings were brought him that
he had pitched his camp not far away, and was marching with an army so huge that it was impossible, so
they said, to withstand him. Howbeit, so little was Arthur affrighted thereat, that no change made he in his
plans, but pitched his camp upon the river bank, from
whence he could freely lead forth his army, and
whither in case of need he could as easily repair. He
then sent two of his earls, Boso of Oxford and Guerin
of Chartres, together with his nephew Gawain, unto
Lucius Hiberius, to intimate unto him that either he
must retire forthwith beyond the frontier of Gaul or
come next day to try conclusions with him as to which
of the twain had the better right to the country. Thereupon the young men of the court, rejoicing exceedingly at the prospect, began to egg on Gawain to start
the quarrel before leaving the Emperor's camp, so that
they might have occasion to come to blows with the
Romans forthwith. Away went the envoys accordingly

to Lucius, and bade him retreat from Gaul at once or come out next day to fight. And when he made them answer that he had not come thither to retreat, but on the contrary to command, a nephew of his that was there, one Gaius Quintillianus, took occasion to say that the Britons were better men at bragging and threatening than in deeds of hardihood and prowess. Gawain thereat waxing wroth, drew his sword wherewith he was girt, and running upon him smote off his head, coming swiftly away with his companions to their horses. The Romans, some on foot and some on horse, start in hot pursuit, straining their utmost to wreak revenge for their fellow-countryman upon the fleeing legates. But Guerin of Chartres, when one of them was almost nigh enow to touch him, wheeled round of a sudden and couching his spear thrust him through the armour and right through the middle of the body, and stretched him out as flat as he might upon the ground. Boso of Oxford, waxing jealous at seeing Guerin do so daring a deed, turned back his own destrier and thrust his spear into the gullet of the first man he met, and forced him, mortally wounded, to part company with the hackney whereon he was pursuing him. Meanwhile, Marcellus Mucius, burning to be first to avenge Quintillianus, was hard upon the back of Gawain and had begun to lay hold upon him, when Gawain suddenly turning round, clove him with the sword he still held in his hand sheer through helmet and skull down to the breast. Gawain, moreover, bade him when he should meet Quintillianus, whom he had slain in the camp, in hell, to tell him that in such manner of bragging and threatening were none better men than the Britons.

Gawain then, reassembling his comrades, counselled that all should turn back, and that in charging all together each should do his best to slay his man. All agreed accordingly; all turned back; and each killed his man. Howbeit, the Romans kept on pursuing them and now and again with spear or sword made shift to wound some few of them, but were unable either to hold or to unhorse any. But whilst they were following up the pursuit nigh a certain wood, straightway forth issue therefrom about six thousand Britons, who having intelligence of the flight of the earls, had hidden them therein for the purpose of bringing them succour. Sallying forth, they set spur to their horses, and rending the air with their shouts and covering them with their shields, attack the Romans on the sudden, and presently drive them in flight before them. Pursuing them with one accord, they smite some from their horses with their spears, some they take prisoner, some they slay. When word of this was brought to the Senator Petreius, he took with him a company of ten thousand men, and hastened to succour his comrades, and compelled the Britons to hasten back to the wood from whence they had made the sally, not without some loss of his own men. For in their flight the Britons turned back, and knowing the ground well, did inflict passing heavy slaughter upon their pursuers. Whilst the Britons were thus giving ground, Hider, the son of Nun, with five thousand men, hurried to their assistance. They now make a stand, and whereas they had afore shown their back to the Romans, they now show their front and set to work to lay about them like men as stoutly as they might. The Romans also stand up to them stiffly, and one while it is Briton that gets stricken down and another while Roman. But the Britons were yearning with all their soul for a fight, and cared not greatly whether they won or lost in the first bout so long as the fighting were really begun, whereas the Romans went to work more heedfully, and Petreius Cotta, like a good captain as he was, skilfully instructed them how and when to advance or retreat, and thus did the greater damage to the Britons. Now, when Boso took note of this, he called a number of them that he knew to be the hardiest aside from the others, and spake unto them on this wise: "Seeing that we began this battle without Arthur's knowledge, we must take right good heed that we get not the worst of it in our adventure. For and if it be that we come to grief herein, we shall not only do heavy damage to our men, but we shall have the King cursing us for our fool-hardiness. Wherefore, pluck up your courage, and follow me into the Roman ranks, and if that we have any luck we will either slay Petreius or take him prisoner." So they all set spur to their horses, and charging with one accord into the enemies' ranks, came to where Petreius was giving orders to his men. Boso rushed in upon him as swiftly as he might, grasped him round the neck, and, as he had made up his mind to do afore-hand, dropped down with him to the ground. There-upon the Romans come running up to rescue him from the enemy, and the Britons as quickly run up to succour Boso. A mighty slaughter is made betwixt them, with mighty shouting and uproar as the Romans struggle to deliver the duke and the Britons to hold him. On both sides were wounders and wounded, strik-ers and stricken to the ground. There, moreover, could it be seen which was the better man at thrust of spear and stroke of swords and fling of javelin. At last the Britons falling upon them in close rank, unbroken by the Roman charge, move off into the safety of their own lines along with Petreius. From thence forthwith they again charge upon the Romans, now bereft of their captain and for the most part enfeebled and dis-pirited and beginning to turn tail. They press forward and strike at them in the rear, cut down them they strike, plunder them they cut down, and pass by them they have plundered to pursue the rest. Howbeit, a number of them they take prisoner whom they are minded to present unto the King. In the end, when they had inflicted mischief enow upon them, they made their way back to the camp with their spoil and their captives, and, relating all that had befallen them pre-

sented Petreius Cotta and the rest of the prisoners unto
Arthur and wished him joy of the victory. He, in return, did bid them joy, and promised them honours
and increase of honours seeing that they had done
deeds of such prowess in his absence. Being minded,
moreover, to thrust the captives into prison, he called
unto him certain of his sergeants to bring them on the
morrow unto Paris, and deliver them unto the charge
of the reeves of the city until further ordinance should
be made on their behalf. He further commanded Duke
Cador, Bedevere the Butler and the two Earls Borel
and Richer, with their retinues, to convoy them so far
on their way as that they need be under no fear of
molestation by the Romans.


[5]


BUT the Romans happening to get wind of this ar-
rangement, by command of the Emperor made choice
of fifteen thousand of their men to march that very
night so as to be beforehand, and to rescue the prisoners after defeating the convoy. These were to be under
the command of the Senators Vulteius Catellus and
Quintus Carucius, besides Evander, King of Syria, and
Sertorius, King of Libya, who started on the appointed
march with the said soldiers at night, and hid them in
a position convenient for an ambuscade upon the road
they weened that the party would travel by. On the
morrow the Britons begin their march with the prisoners, and had well-nigh reached the place, not knowing
what snares the crafty enemy had set for them. Howbeit, no sooner had they entered that part of the road
than the Romans sallied forth of a sudden and surprised and broke the ranks of the British who were
quite unprepared for an attack of the kind. Natheless,
albeit they were thus taken aback, they soon drew together again and made a stout defence, setting some to

guard the prisoners whilst the rest divided into companies to do battle with the enemy. Richer and Bedevere were in command of the company that kept guard over the prisoners, Cador, Duke of Cornwall, with Borel, taking command of the rest. But the Romans had all burst in upon them disorderly, and took no heed to dispose their men in companies, their one care, indeed, being which should be first to slaughter the Britons before they could form their ranks and marshal them so as to defend themselves. By reason of this the Britons were reduced to so sore straits that they would shamefully have lost the prisoners they were convoying had not good luck swiftly brought them the succour they needed. For Guitard, Duke of the Poitevins, who had discovered the stratagem, had arrived with three thousand men, by whose timely assistance the Britons did at last prevail and pay back the evil turn of the slaughter upon the insolent brigands that had assaulted them. But many of their own men did they lose in the first onset, for among others they lost Borel, the renowned Earl of Maine, who, while battling with Evander, King of Syria, was pierced through the throat with his spear, and poured forth his life with his blood. They lost, moreover, four barons, Hirelglas, of Periron, Maurice of Cahors, Aliduc of Tintagel, and Her, the son of Hider, than whom none hardier were easy to be found. Natheless, the Britons stinted nought of their hardihood nor gave them up to despair, but straining every endeavour determined to keep safe their prisoners and cut down their enemies to the last. In the end the Romans, unable to stand up against them, hastily retreated from the field and began to make for their camp. But the Britons, still pursuing them, slew many and took more prisoners, nor did they rest until Vulteius Catellus and Evander, King of Syria, were slain and the rest utterly scattered. When they had won the victory, they sent the prisoners they were convoying on to Paris, and marching back unto their King with them that they had lately taken, promised him hope of supreme victory, seeing that so few had won the day against so many enemies that had come against them.

## [6]

LUCIUS HIBERIUS, meanwhile, taking these disasters sorely to heart, was mightily perplexed and distressed to make resolve whether it were better for him to hazard a general engagement with Arthur, or to throw himself into Autun and there await assistance from the Emperor Leo. In the end he took counsel of his fears, and on the night following marched his armies into Langres on his way to Autun. As soon as Arthur discovered this scheme, he determined to be beforehand with him on the march, and that same night, leaving the city on his left, he took up a position in a certain valley called Soissie, through which Lucius would have to pass. Disposing his men in companies as he thought best, he posted one legion close by under the command of Morvid, Earl of Gloucester, so that, if need were, he would know whither to betake him to rally his broken companies and again give battle to the enemy. The rest of his force he divided into seven battalions, and in each battalion placed five thousand five hundred and fifty-five men, all fully armed. One division of each consisted of horse and the remainder of foot, and order was passed amongst them that when the infantry advanced to the attack, the cavalry advancing in close line slantwise on their flanks should do their best to scatter the enemy. The infantry divisions, British fashion, were drawn up in a square with a right and left wing. One of these was commanded by Angusel, King of Scotland, and Cador, Duke of Cornwall, the one in the right wing and the other in the left. Another was in command of two earls of renown, to wit, Guerin of Chartres, and Boso of Rhydychen.

which in the tongue of the Saxons is called Oxford. A third was commanded by Aschil, King of the Danskers, and Loth, King of the Norwegians. The fourth by Hoel, Duke of Brittany, and Gawain, the King's nephew. After these four were four others stationed in the rear, one of which was in the command of Kay the Seneschal and Bedevere the Butler. Holdin, Duke of the Flemings, and Guitard, Duke of the Poitevins, commanded the second; Jugein of Leicester, Jonathal of Dorset, and Cursalem of Caichester the third, and Urbgenius of Bath the fourth. To the rear of all these he made choice of a position for himself and one legion that he designed to be his bodyguard, and here he set up the golden dragon he had for standard, whereunto, if need should be, the wounded and weary might repair as unto a camp. In that legion which was in attendance upon himself were six thousand six hundred and sixty-six men.

## [7]

WHEN all these dispositions were made, Arthur spake unto his fellow-soldiers on this wise:—

"Lieges mine, ye that have made Britain Lady of thirty realms, I do bid ye joy of your prowess, that meseemeth hath in nowise failed ye, but rather hath waxed the stronger albeit that for five years no occasion have ye had to put it to the proof, and hitherto have given more thought unto the disports of an easy life than unto the practice of arms. Natheless, in no wise have ye degenerated from the inborn valour of your race, but staunch as ever, have scattered in flight before ye these Romans that pricked by the spur of their own pride would fain curtail ye of your freedom. Already, marching with a host larger than your own, have they ventured to begin the attack, and failing to withstand your advance, have taken refuge with shame

in yonder city. At this moment they are ready to issue
forth from thence upon their march towards Autun.
Through this valley must they pass, and here falling
upon them when they least expect it, may you meet
and slaughter them like sheep. Surely they deemed that
the cowardize of the nations of the East was in ye when
they were minded to make your country tributary and
yourselves bond-slaves! What! have they heard not of
the battles ye fought with the Danskers and Norwegians and the Dukes of the Gauls, when ye delivered
them from their shameful yoke and gave them into
my allegiance? We, therefore, that were strong enow
to subdue the mightier, shall doubtless prove stronger
yet against this feebler foe, so we only take the same
pains in the same spirit to crush these emasculate cravens. Only obey my will and command as loyal comrades of mine own, and what honours, what treasures
await each one of ye! For so soon as we have put these
to the rout, forthwith we start for Rome. For us to
march upon Rome is to take it and possess. Yours shall
be the gold and silver, the palaces and castles, the
towns and cities and all the riches of the vanquished!"

Whilst he yet spake thus all unite in a mighty cheer,
ready to meet death rather than flee from the field leaving him there alive.

[8]

Now Lucius Hiberius, who had been warned of their
design and the trap that was laid for him, was not
minded to flee as he had at first proposed, but plucking
up his courage to march to the valley and meet them.
With this design he called his Dukes together and spake
unto them thus:—

"Venerable Fathers, unto whose empire the realms
of the East and of the West do owe their allegiance,
call ye now your fathers unto remembrance, how they

shrank not from shedding their blood to vanquish the enemies of the Commonweal, but leaving unto their children an ensample of prowess and knightly hardihood, did so bear them in the field as though God had decreed that none of them should die in battle. Wherefore full oft did they achieve the triumph, and in the triumph avoidance of death, for that unto none might aught else befall than was ordained by the providence of God. Hence sprang the increase of the Commonweal; hence the increase of their own prowess; hence, moreover, came it that the uprightness, the honour, and the bounty that are wont to be in them of gentle blood, ever flourishing amongst them from age to age, have exalted them and their descendants unto the dominion of the whole world. This is the spirit I would fain arouse within ye. I do appeal unto ye that ye be mindful of your ancient valour, and be staunch thereunto. Let us seek out our foemen in the valley wherein they now lurk in ambush for us, and fight to win from them that which is our own of right! Nor deem ye that I have made repair unto this city for refuge as though I would shrink from them or their invasions. On the contrary, I reckoned upon their foolishly pursuing us, and believed that we might surprise them by suddenly falling upon them when they were scattered in pursuit so as to put them to the rout with a decisive slaughter. But now that they have done otherwise than we expected, let us also do otherwise. Let us seek them out and fall upon them hardily, or, if so be that they are strong enow to fall upon us first, let us stand our ground with one accord and abide their first onset. On this wise, without doubt, we shall win the day, for in most battles he that hath been able to withstand the first charge hath most often come off the conqueror."

So when he had made an end of speaking thus, with much more to the same effect, all with one assent agreeing and pledging them by oath with joining of hands, they all hastened to do on their armour, and

when they were armed at last, sally forth from Langres
and march to the valley where Arthur had stationed
his men. They, likewise, had marshalled their men
in twelve wedge-shaped battalions, all infantry, and
formed, Roman fashion, in the shape of a wedge, so
that when the army was in full array each division contained six thousand six hundred and sixty-six soldiers.
Unto each, moreover, they appointed captains to give
orders when to advance and when to stand their
ground against the enemy's onset. Unto one they appointed Lucius Catellus, the senator, and Alifatima,
King of Spain, commanders. Unto the second, Hirtacius, King of the Parthians, and Marius Lepidus, the
senator; upon the third, Boccus, King of the Medes,
and Gaius Metellus, the senator; unto the fourth, Sertorius, King of Libya, and Quintus Milvius, senator.
These four divisions were placed in the vanguard of
the army. In their rear came another four, whereof
one was under the command of Serses, King of the
Ituraeans; the second under Pandrasus, King of Egypt;
the third under Politetes, Duke of Bithynia; the fourth
under Teucer, Duke of Phrygia. Behind these again
were other four battalions, one captained by Quintus
Carucius, senator; the second by Lellius of Hostia; the
third by Sulpicius Subuculus; the fourth by Mauricius
Silvanus. Lucius himself was moving hither and thither
amongst them giving orders and instructions how they
should behave them. In their midst he bade set up
firmly the golden eagle that he had brought with him
for standard, and warned the men that should any by
misadventure be separated from the ranks, he should
endeavour to return thereunto.

[9]

AFTER that they were arrayed the one against the other,
Britons on this side and Romans on that, javelins up-

right, forthwith upon hearing the blare of the trumpets the battalion under the command of the King of
Spain and Lucius Catellus fell hardily upon the division led by the King of Scotland and the Duke of Cornwall, but could in no wise make any breach in the close
ranks of them that opposed them. And whilst they were
still struggling most fiercely to make head against them,
up came the division captained by Guerin and Boso,
who, spurring their horses to a gallop, charged against
the assailants, and breaking right through and beyond
them came face to face with the battalion that the King
of the Parthians was leading against Aschil, King of
the Danes. Straight, the battalions fling them the one
upon another, burst through each other's ranks and
batter together in a general melly. Pitiable is the
slaughter wrought betwixt them amidst the din as one
after another droppeth on both sides, beating the
ground with head or heels and retching forth his life
with his blood. But the first grave disaster fell upon
the Britons, for Bedevere the Butler was slain and Kay
the Seneschal wounded unto the death. For Bedevere
when he met Boccus, King of the Medes, fell dead,
smitten through by his spear amidst the ranks of the
enemy, and Kay the Seneschal, in attempting to avenge
him, was surrounded by the Median troops and received a deadly hurt. Natheless, after the wont of good
knight, opening a way with the wing that he led, he
slew and scattered the Medes, and would have brought
off his company unharmed and returned with them to
their own ranks had he not been met by the division
of the King of Libya, the assault whereof dispersed all
his men. Natheless, still retreating, albeit with but four
of his followers, he made shift to flee unto the Golden
Dragon, bearing with him the corpse of Bedevere. Alas!
what lamentation was there amongst the Normans
when they beheld the body of their Duke rent by so
many wounds! Alas, what wailing was there amongst
the Angevins when they searched with all the arts of

leechcraft the wounds of Kay their earl! But no time
was that for sorrowing when the blood-bespattered
ranks rushing one upon another scarce allowed space
for a sigh ere they were forced to turn to defend their
own lives. And now Hirelglas, the nephew of Bedevere,
wroth beyond measure at his death, took with him a
company of three hundred men of his own, and like
a wild boar amidst a pack of hounds dashed with a
sudden gallop of their steeds right through the ranks
of the enemy towards the place where he had espied
the standard of the King of the Medes, little reckon-
ing of aught that might befall himself so only he might
avenge his uncle. Gaining the place he desired, he slew
the King and carried him off to his comrades, and laying the corpse by the side of that of the Butler, hewed
it utterly to pieces. Then, with a mighty shout cheering on the troops of his fellow-countrymen, he called
upon them to fall upon the enemy and harass them
with charge after charge now, whilst their courage was
still hot, whilst the hearts of their foes were still quaking with terror; whilst they had the advantage in bearing down upon them hand to hand through their companies being more skilfully ordered than those of the
enemy, and being thus able to renew the attack more
often and to inflict a deadlier damage. Thus cheered
by his counsel, they made a general charge upon the
enemy from every quarter, and the slaughter on both
sides waxed exceeding heavy. For on the side of the
Romans, besides numberless others, fell Alifatima, King
of Spain, and Micipsa of Babylon, as well as the senators Quintus Milvius and Marius Lepidus. On the side
of the Britons fell Holdin, King of Flanders, and
Leodegar of Boulogne, besides three Earls of Britain,
Cursalem of Caichester, Galluc of Salisbury, and Urbgennius of Bath. The troops they led thus, sore enfeebled, retreated until they came upon the battalion of
the Bretons commanded by Hoel and Gawain. But the
Bretons thereupon, like a fire bursting into a blaze,

made a charge upon the enemy, and rallying them that
had retreated, soon compelled those that but just before
had been the pursuers to flee in their turn, and ever
followed them up, slaying some and stretching others
on the ground, nor ceased from their slaughter until
they reached the bodyguard of the Emperor, who, when
he saw the disaster that had overtaken his comrades,
had hastened to bring them succour.

[10]

In the first onset the Bretons suffered great loss. For
Kimmarcoch, Earl of Tréguier, fell, and with him two
thousand men. Fell also three barons of renown, Ri-
chomarch, Bloccovius, and Iaguvius of Ballon, who,
had they been princes of kingdoms, would have been
celebrated by fame to all after-ages for the passing
great prowess that was in them. For when they were
charging along with Hoel and Gawain, as hath been
said, not an enemy escaped that came within their
reach, but either with sword or with spear they sent
the life out of him. But when they fell in with the
bodyguard of Lucius, they were surrounded on all
sides by the Romans, and fell along with Kimmarcoch
and his followers. But Hoel and Gawain, than whom
have no better knights been born in later ages, were
only spurred to keener endeavour by the death of their
comrades, and rode hither and thither, one in one direction and the other in another searching the companies of the Emperor's guards for occasion to do them
a hurt. And now Gawain, still glowing with the fire
kindled by his former exploits, endeavoured to cleave
an opening, whereby he might come at the Emperor
himself and forgather with him. Like a right hardy
knight as he was, he made a dash upon the enemy,
bearing some to the ground and slaying them in the
fall, while Hoel, in no wise less hardy than he, fell like

a thunderbolt upon another company, cheering on his
men, and smiting the enemy undaunted by their blows,
not a moment passing but either he struck or was
stricken. None that beheld them could have said which
of the twain was the doughtier knight or quitted him
better that day.

[ 11 ]

HOWBEIT, Gawain thus dashing amidst the companies,
found at last the opening he longed for, and rushing
upon the Emperor forgathered with him man to man.
Lucius, then in the flower and prime of youth, had
plenty of hardihood, plenty of strength and plenty of
prowess, nor was there nought he did more desire than
to encounter such a knight as would compel him to
prove what he was worth in feats of arms. Wherefore,
standing up to Gawain, he rejoiceth to begin the encounter and prideth him therein for that he hath heard
such renown of him. Long while did the battle last betwixt them, and mighty were the blows they dealt one
upon other or warded with the shields that covered
them as each strove for vantage to strike the death-
blow on the other. But whilst that they were thus in
the very hottest of the fight, behold the Romans, suddenly recovering their vigour, make a charge upon the
Bretons and come to their Emperor's rescue. Hoel and
Gawain and their companies are driven off and sore
cut up, until all of a sudden they came up over against
Arthur and his company. For Arthur, hearing of the
slaughter just inflicted upon his men, had hurried forward with his guard, and drawing forth Caliburn, best
of swords, had cheered on his comrades, crying out in
a loud voice and hot words: "What be ye men doing?
Will ye let these womanish knaves slip forth of your
hands unharmed? Let not a soul of them escape alive!
Remember your own right hands that have fought in

so many battles and subdued thirty realms to my dominion! Remember your grandsires whom the Romans stronger than themselves made tributaries! Remember your freedom that these half men feebler than yourselves would fain reave away from ye! Let not a single one escape alive—not a single one escape! What be ye doing?" Shouting out these reproaches and many more besides, he dashed forward upon the enemy, flung them down, smote them—never a one did he meet but he slew either him or his horse at a single buffet. They fled from him like sheep from a fierce lion madly famishing to devour aught that chance may throw in his way. Nought might armour avail them but that Caliburn would carve their souls from out them with their blood. Two Kings, Sertorius of Libya, and Politetes of Bithynia did their evil hap bring in front of him, whom he despatched to hell with their heads hewn off. And when the Britons beheld in what wise their King did battle, they took heart and hardihood again, and fell with one accord upon the Romans, pressing forward in close rank, so that whilst they afoot cut them down on this wise, they a-horseback did their best to fling them down and thrust them through. Natheless, the Romans made stout resistance, and, urged on by Lucius, strove hard to pay back the Britons for the slaughter inflicted on the guard of their renowned King. On both sides the battle rageth as though it had been but just begun. On this side, as hath been said, Arthur many a time and oft smiting the enemies, exhorted the Britons to stand firm; on the other, Lucius Hiberius exhorted his Romans, and gave them counsel, and led them in many a daring exploit of prowess. Nor did he himself cease to fight with his own hand, but going round from one to another amongst his companies slew every single enemy that chance threw in his way, either with his spear or his sword. Thus a most unconscionable slaughter took place on either side, for at one time the Britons and at another the Romans

would have the upper hand. In the end, while the
battle was still going on thus, lo and behold, Morvid,
Earl of Gloucester, with the legion which as I have said
above was posted betwixt the hills, came up full speed
and fell heavily on the enemy's rear just at a moment
they least expected it, broke through their lines, scattering them in all directions, with exceeding great
slaughter. Many thousand Romans fell in this onslaught, and amongst them even the Emperor himself,
slain in the midst of his companies by a spear-thrust
from a hand unknown. And thus, ever following up
their advantage, the Britons, albeit with sore travail,
won the victory that day.

## [ 12 ]

THE Romans, thus scattered, betook them, some to the
waste-lands and forests, some to the cities and towns,
each fleeing to the refuge he deemed safest. The Britons pursue them, take them prisoner, plunder them,
put them miserably to the sword, insomuch as that the
more part of them stretch forth their hands womanish-
wise to be bound so only they might have yet a little
space longer to live. The which, verily, might seem to
have been ordained by providence divine, seeing that
whereas in days of yore the Romans had persecuted the
grandsires of the Britons with their unjust oppressions,
so now did the Britons in defence of the freedom
whereof they would have bereft them, and refusing the
tribute that they did unrighteously demand, take vengeance on the grandchildren of the Romans.

## [ 13 ]

THE victory complete, Arthur bade the bodies of his
barons be separated from the carcasses of the enemy,

and embalmed in kingly wise, and borne when embalmed into the abbeys of the province. Bedevere the Butler was carried unto Bayeux, his own city that was builded by Bedevere the first, his great-grandfather, and loud was the lamentation that the Normans made over him. There, in a certain churchyard in the southern part of the city, was he worshipfully laid next the wall. But Kay, grievously wounded, was borne in a litter unto Chinon, a town he himself had builded, and dying a brief space after of the same wound, was buried, as became a Duke of Anjou, in a certain forest in a convent of brethren hermit that dwelt there no great way from the city. Holdin, likewise, Duke of the Flemings, was borne into Flanders and buried in his own city of Thérouanne. Howbeit, the rest of the earls and barons were carried, as Arthur had enjoined, unto the abbeys in the neighbourhood. Having pity, moreover, upon his enemies, he bade the folk of the country bury them. But the body of Lucius he bade bear unto the Senate with a message to say that none other tribute was due from Britain. Then he abode in those parts until after the following winter, and busied him with bringing the cities of the Burgundians into his allegiance. But the summer coming on, at which time he designed to march unto Rome, he had begun to climb the passes of the mountains, when message was brought him that his nephew Modred, unto whom he had committed the charge of Britain, had tyrannously and traitorously set the crown of the kingdom upon his own head, and had linked him in unhallowed union with Guenevere the Queen in despite of her former marriage.

# BOOK XI

## [1]

HEREOF, verily, most noble Earl, will Geoffrey of Monmouth say nought. Natheless, according as he hath found it in the British discourse aforementioned, and hath heard from Walter of Oxford, a man of passing deep lore in many histories, in his own mean style will he briefly treat of the battles which that renowned King upon his return to Britain after this victory did fight with his nephew. So soon therefore as the infamy of the aforesaid crime did reach his ears, he forthwith deferred the expedition he had emprised against Leo, the King of the Romans, and sending Hoel, Duke of Brittany, with the Gaulish army to restore peace in those parts, he straightway hastened back to Britain with none save the island Kings and their armies. Now, that most detestable traitor Modred had despatched Cheldric, the Duke of the Saxons, into Germany, there to enlist any soever that would join him, and hurry back again with them, such as they might be, the quickest sail he could make. He pledged himself, moreover, by covenant to give him that part of the island which stretcheth from the river Humber as far as Scotland, and whatsoever Horsus and Hengist had possessed in Kent in the time of Vortigern. Cheldric, accordingly, obeying his injunctions, had landed with eight hundred ships full of armed Paynims, and doing homage unto this traitor did acknowledge him as his liege lord and king. He had likewise gathered into his company the Scots, Picts, and Irish, and whomsoever else he knew bare hatred unto his uncle. All told, they numbered some eight hundred thousand Paynims and Christians, and in their company and relying on their assistance he came to meet Arthur on his arrival at Richborough haven, and in the battle that ensued did inflict sore slaughter on his men when they were landed. For upon that day fell Angusel, King of Scotland, and Gawain, the King's nephew, along with numberless other. Iwen, son of Urian his brother, succeeded Angusel in the kingdom, and did afterward win great renown for his prowesses in those wars. At last, when with sore travail they had gained possession of the coast, they revenged them on Modred for this slaughter, and drove him flee-ing before them. For inured to arms as they had been in so many battles, they disposed their companies right skilfully, distributing horse and foot in parties, in such wise that in the fight itself, when the infantry were en-gaged in the attack or defence, the horse charging slant-wise at full speed would strain every endeavour to break the enemies' ranks and compel them to take to flight. Howbeit, the Perjurer again collected his men together from all parts, and on the night following marched into Winchester. When this was reported unto Queen Guenevere, she was forthwith smitten with de-spair, and fled from York unto Caerleon, where she pur-posed thenceforth to lead a chaste life amongst the nuns, and did take the veil of their order in the church of Julius the Martyr.

[2]

But Arthur, burning with yet hotter wrath for the loss of so many hundred comrades-in-arms, after first giving Christian burial to the slain, upon the third day marched upon that city and beleaguered the miscreant that had ensconced him therein. Natheless, he was not minded to renounce his design, but encouraging his ad-herents by all the devices he could, marched forth with his troops and arrayed them to meet his uncle. At the first onset was exceeding great slaughter on either side, the which at last waxed heavier upon his side and compelled him to quit the field with shame. Then, little caring what burial were given unto his slain, "borne by the swift-oared ferryman of flight," he started in all haste on his march toward Cornwall. Arthur, torn by inward anxiety for that he had so often escaped him, pursued him into that country as far as the river Camel, where Modred was awaiting his arrival. For Modred, being, as he was, of all men the boldest and ever the swiftest to begin the attack, straightway marshalled his men in companies, preferring rather to conquer or to die than to be any longer continually on the flight in this wise. There still remained unto him out of the number of allies I have mentioned sixty thousand men, and these he divided into six battalions, in each of which were six thousand six hundred and sixty-six men-at-arms. Besides these, he made out of the rest that were over a single battalion, and appointing captains to each of the others, took command of this himself. When these were all posted in position, he spake words of encouragement unto each in turn, promising them the lands and goods of their adversaries in case they fought out the battle to a victory. Arthur also marshalled his army over against them, which he divided into nine battalions of infantry formed in square with a right and left wing, and having appointed captains to each, exhorted them to make an end utterly of these perjurers and thieves, who, brought from foreign lands into the island at the bidding of a traitor, were minded to reave them of their holdings and their honours. He told them, moreover, that these motley barbarians from divers kingdoms were a pack of raw recruits that knew nought of the usages of war, and were in no wise able to make stand against valiant men like themselves, seasoned in so many battles, if they fell upon them hardily and fought like men. And whilst the twain were still exhorting their men on the one side and the other, the battalions made a sudden rush each at other and began the battle, struggling as if to try which should deal their blows the quicker. Straight, such havoc is wrought upon both sides, such groaning is there of the dying, such fury in the onset, as it would be grievous and burdensome to describe. Everywhere are wounders and wounded, slayers and slain. And after much of the day had been spent on this wise, Arthur at last, with one battalion wherein were six thousand six hundred and sixty-six men, made a charge upon the company wherein he knew Modred to be, and hewing a path with their swords, cut clean through it and inflicted a most grievous slaughter. For therein fell that accursed traitor and many thousands along with him. Natheless not for the loss of him did his troops take to flight, but rallying together from all parts of the field, struggle to stand their ground with the best hardihood they might. Right passing deadly is the strife betwixt the foes, for well-nigh all the captains that were in command on both sides rushed into the press with their companies and fell. On Modred's side fell Cheldric, Elaf, Egbricht, Bruning, that were Saxons, Gillapatric, Gillamor, Gillasel, Gillarn, Irish. The Scots and Picts, with well-nigh all that they commanded, were cut off to a man. On Arthur's side, Odbricht, King of Norway, Aschil, King of Denmark, Cador Limenic, Cassibelaunus, with many thousands of his lieges as well Britons as others that he had brought with him. Even the renowned King Arthur himself was wounded deadly, and was borne thence unto the Isle of Avallon for the healing of his wounds, where he gave up the crown of Britain unto his kinsman, Constantine, son of Cador, Duke of Cornwall, in the year of the Incarnation of Our Lord five hundred and forty-two.

## [3]

WHEN Constantine was crowned King, the Saxons and
the two sons of Modred raised an insurrection against
him, but could nought prevail, and after fighting many
battles, the one fled to London and the other to Winchester, and did enter and take possession of those cities. At that time died the holy Daniel, that most devout
prelate of the church of Bangor, and Theon, Bishop of
Gloucester, was elected unto the archbishopric of London. At that time also died David, that most holy Archbishop of Caerleon, in the city of St. Davids, within his
own abbey, which he loved above all the other monas-
teries of his diocese, for that it was founded by the
blessed Patrick who had foretold his nativity. For whilst
he was there sojourning for a while with his fellow-
brethren he was smitten of a sudden lethargy and died
there, being buried in the same church by command of
Malgo, King of North Wales. In his place, Kinoc, priest
of the church of Llanbadarn, was appointed to the Metropolitan See, and was thus promoted unto the higher
dignity.

## [4]

BUT Constantine pursued the Saxons and subdued
them unto his allegiance; and took the two sons of Modred. The one youth, who had fled into the church of
St. Amphibalus at Winchester, he slew before the altar;
but the other, who was in hiding in the monastery of
certain brethren in London, he did there find beside
the altar and slew by a cruel death. In the third year
thereafter he was himself slain by Conan, smitten by
God's judgment, and was buried by the side of Uther
Pendragon within the structure of stones set together

with marvellous art not far from Salisbury which in the
English tongue is called Stonehenge.


### [5]

UNTO him succeeded Aurelius Conan, a youth of wondrous prowess, his nephew, who, as he held the monarchy of the whole island, so might he have been
worthy the crown thereof had he not been a lover of
civil war. For he raised disturbance against his uncle,
who of right ought to have reigned after Constantine,
and thrust him into prison, and after slaying both his
sons, did himself obtain the kingdom, and died in the
second year of his reign.


### [6]

UNTO Conan succeeded Vortipore, against whom the
Saxons raised an insurrection, bringing over their fellow-countrymen from Germany in a passing mighty
fleet. But he did battle with them and overcame them,
and after that he had obtained the monarchy of the
whole kingdom did govern the people thereof for four
years in diligence and in peace.


### [7]

UNTO him succeeded Malgo, one of the comeliest men
in the whole of Britain, the driver-out of many tyrants,
redoubted in arms, more bountiful than others and renowned for prowess beyond compare, yet hateful in the
sight of God, for his sodomitic vice. He obtained the
sovereignty of the whole island, and after many exceeding deadly battles did add unto his dominions the six

neighbour islands of the Ocean, to wit, Ireland, Iceland, Gothland, the Orkneys, Norway, and Denmark.

## [8]

UNTO Malgo succeeded Careticus, a lover of civil wars, hateful unto God and unto the Britons. The Saxons, having had experience of his shiftiness, went unto Gormund, King of the Africans, in Ireland, wherein, adventuring thither with a vast fleet, he had conquered the folk of the country. Thereupon, by the treachery of the Saxons, he sailed across with a hundred and sixty thousand Africans into Britain, which in one province the Saxons by perjuring their oath of fealty, and in another the Britons by continually carrying on civil wars amongst themselves, were utterly laying waste. Entering into covenant, therefore, with the Saxons, Gormund made war upon Careticus, and after many battles betwixt them, drove him fleeing from city unto city until he forced him into Cirencester and did there beleaguer him. Here Isembard, nephew of Lewis, King of the Franks, came unto him and entered into a league of friendship with him and forsook his Christianity for his sake upon condition that he would grant him his assistance in seizing the kingdom of Gaul away from his uncle, by whom, as he said, he had been driven forth by violence and wrong. When Gormund at last had taken and burnt the said city, he did battle with Careticus and drove him fleeing beyond the Severn into Wales. Then he desolated the fields, set fire to all the neighbouring cities, nor did he stint his fury until he had burnt up well-nigh the whole face of the country from sea to sea; in such sort that all the colonies were battered to the ground by rams, and all they that dwelt therein along with the priests of the churches delivered up to the flashing of their swords or the crackling of the flames. The residue of them that were slaughtered in

these dreadful visitations had no choice but to flee unto
whatsoever shelter might seem to promise safety.

## [9]

WHEREFORE, O thou neglectful nation, borne down by
the weight of thine outrageous iniquities, wherefore,
ever thirsting after civil wars, hast thou thus enfeebled
thee by these discords within thine own household?
Thou that of old didst subdue the kingdoms that lie
afar off unto thy might, thou that wast planted a noble
vine, wholly a right seed, how art thou now turned into
the degenerate plant of a bitter vine, that thus thou
canst no longer protect thine own country, thine own
wives and children from thine enemies. Yea, onward!
On with thine inward discords, little understanding that
word of the Gospel, "Every kingdom divided against
itself shall be made desolate and the house shall fall
upon the house!" For that thy kingdom hath been divided against itself, for that the rage of civil war and
the smoke of envy have darkened thy mind, for that
thy pride hath forbidden thee to pay thine allegiance
unto one only King, therefore now dost thou behold
thy country made desolate by these most sacrilegious
heathen and the houses thereof falling upon the houses,
that thy children yet unborn shall mourn. For they
shall see the whelps of the barbarian lioness lords over
their strong places and their cities and over all else
that is now their own. Forth of all these shall they be
driven, and scarce again if ever shall they recover the
glories of their ancient estate!

## [10]

HOWBEIT, after that the tyrant of evil omen had laid
waste, as hath been said, well-nigh the whole island

with his countless thousands of Africans, the more part
thereof which was called England did he make over
unto the Saxons through whose treachery he had come
into the land. The remnant of the Britons did therefore withdraw them into the western parts of the kingdom, Cornwall, to wit, and Wales, from whence they
ceased not to harry their enemies with frequent and
deadly forays. Then the archbishops, to wit, Theon of
London, and Thadioceus of York, when they beheld
all the churches within their obedience destroyed even
to the ground, fled away with all the clergy that had
survived so dreadful a calamity unto the shelter of the
forests of Wales, bearing with them the relics of the
saints, fearing lest so many holy bones of such pious
men of old might be scattered and lost in the invasion
of the barbarians were they to stay and offer themselves
to instant martyrdom, thus leaving the relics in such
imminent peril. Many of them betook them in a mighty
fleet unto Brittany, so that the whole church of the two
provinces, England, to wit, and Northumbria, was left
desolate of all the convents of religious therein. But of
this will I tell the story elsewhere, when I come to
translate the Book of their Exile.

## [ 11 ]

THEREAFTER for many ages did the Britons lose the
crown of the kingdom and the sovereignty of the island,
nor made they any endeavour to recover their former
dignity. On the contrary, they did many a time and oft
lay waste that part of the country which did still remain unto them, subject now not unto one king only,
but unto three tyrants. But neither did the Saxons as
yet obtain the crown of the island, for they also were
subject unto three kings, and did at one time send
forth their forays against themselves, and at another
against the Britons.

## [12]

IN the meantime was Augustine sent by the blessed
Pope Gregory into Britain to preach the Word of God
unto the English, who, blinded by heathen superstition,
had wholly done away with Christianity in that part of
the island which they held. Howbeit, in the part belonging to the Britons the Christianity still flourished
which had been held there from the days of Pope Eleutherius and had never failed amongst them. But after
Augustine came, he found in their province seven
bishoprics and an archbishopric provided with most
godly prelates besides a number of abbacies wherein
the Lord's flock held right order. Amongst others there
was in the city of Bangor a certain most noble church
wherein was said to be such a number of monks that
when the monastery was divided into seven portions
with a prior set over each, not one of them had less
than three hundred monks, who did all live by the labour of their own hands. Their abbot was called
Dinoot, and was in marvellous wise learned in the liberal arts. He, when Augustine did demand subjection
from the British bishops, in order that they might undertake in common the task of preaching the Gospel
unto the English people, made answer with divers ar-
guings, that they owed no subjection unto him as of
right, nor were they minded to bestow their preaching
upon their enemies, seeing that they had an archbishop
of their own, and that the nations of the Saxons did
persist in withholding their own country from them;
whence they did ever hold them in the deepest abhor-
rence, and recked nought of their faith and religion,
and in nought had more in common with the Saxons
than with dogs.

## [13]

ETHELBERT, therefore, King of the men of Kent, when he saw that the Britons did disdain to make subjection unto Augustine, and did despise his preaching, took the same in grievous dudgeon and stirred up Ethelfrid, King of the Northumbrians, and the other Saxon knights to collect a mighty army and go unto the city of Bangor to make away utterly with the Abbot Dinoot and the rest of the clerics that did hold them in scorn. Agreeably therefore unto his counsel, they mustered a marvellous great army, and upon their way unto the province of the Britons came unto Leicester, where Brocmail, Earl of that city, was expecting their arrival. There had come also unto the same city out of the divers provinces of Britain a numberless company of monks and hermits, and more especially from the city of Bangor, to pray for the safety of their people. Thereupon, assembling all his armies from every quarter, Ethelfrid, King of the Northumbrians, gave battle unto Brocmail, who, making such stand as he could against him with a lesser number of soldiers, quitted the city and fled, but not before he had inflicted exceeding great slaughter upon the enemy. But Ethelfrid, after he had taken the city, understanding the reason, wherefore the said monks had come unto the city, bade his men first turn their arms against them, and thus upon that very day one thousand two hundred of them, adorned with the palm of martyrdom, did obtain a seat in the kingdom of Heaven. These, when the said tyrant of the Saxons went forward on his march towards the city of Bangor, hearing of his mad outrage, the Dukes of the Britons, to wit, Blederic, Duke of Cornwall, Margadud, King of the South Welsh, and Cadvan, King of the North, came from all parts to meet him, and joining battle with him, drove him fleeing wounded before them, but so passing great was the number of his army slain, that it was reckoned not less than about ten thousand and sixty-six had fallen. On the side of the Britons likewise fell Blederic, Duke of Cornwall, who was their commander in those battles.

# BOOK XII

## [1]

THEREAFTER all the princes of the Britons did come together in the city of Leicester, and took common counsel that they would make Cadvan their King, and that
under his command they would pursue Ethelfrid beyond the Humber. When they had set the crown of the
kingdom upon his head, they all assembled together
from all parts and crossed the Humber. And when message of this was brought unto Ethelfrid he allied all
the Kings of the Saxons unto himself and marched to
meet Cadvan. But when they had marshalled their companies on both sides their friends came and made peace
betwixt them on these conditions, that they should possess Britain, Ethelfrid on the further side Humber, and
Cadvan on the hither side. And after that they had confirmed this covenant by oath and giving of hostages,
such a friendship sprang up betwixt them as that they
had all things in common. In the meanwhile it so fell
out that Ethelfrid did drive forth his own wife and took
unto himself another, and in such hatred did he hold
her that he had driven forth that he banished her from
the kingdom of Northumbria. Whereupon, for that
Ethelfrid was father of her child as yet unborn, she
went unto King Cadvan, beseeching his intervention
that she might be restored unto her husband. And
when he might in no wise persuade Ethelfrid to grant
her petition she abode in Cadvan's household until
such time as she was delivered of a son. Now a little
later, a son was born unto King Cadvan of the Queen
his wife, for she too at that time had been heavy with

child; and thereafter were the two boys, whereof the
one was called Cadwallo and the other Edwin, nurtured together as became princes of the blood royal.
And when in course of time their boyhood had grown
into youth, their parents sent them unto Solomon, King
of the Bretons, that in his household they might learn
the lessons of knighthood and the customs of courtly
manners. They accordingly were received of him kindly,
and diligently cared for, soon beginning to be admitted
to his familiarity, in such sort that none other was there
of their age in his court that could be more private
with the King or speak unto him more merrily withal.
At last they did often do battle before him in encounter
with his enemies, and did win much fame of their
valour in many exploits of prowess.

## [2]

In later days, after the death of their parents, they returned into Britain, and, taking over the helm of the
kingdom, renewed the friendship that had been betwixt their fathers. After two years had passed away,
Edwin besought Cadwallo that he might have a crown
of his own, and fulfil the constituted ceremonies of sovereignty in the parts of Northumbria in such wise as he
himself fulfilled them according to ancient wont upon
the hither side of the Humber. And when a conference
was being held upon the matter nigh the river Duglas,
and the wiser sort were taking counsel together what
were best to be done, Cadwallo chanced to be lying on
the other bank of the river with his head resting on the
bosom of a certain nephew of his whom they called
Brian. And whilst the messengers brought him word
what was being said upon both sides at the conference,
Brian wept, and the tears flowing from his eyes did so
fall as that they bedewed the King's face and his beard.
The King, weening that it was a shower of rain, lifted

up his head, and seeing that the youth was all melted in tears, asked him the cause of this sudden sorrow. Unto whom he made answer:

"Good cause have I to weep continually and the British people no less, for that ever since the country was visited by the invasion of these barbarians in the days of Malgo never hath she known a prince that might avail to restore her unto her ancient dignity. And now even the petty residue of her honour is being minished by thy sufferance, seeing that these Saxon adventurers, who have ever proved traitors unto her, must now begin to share with her the honours of the kingly crown. For, once let them be exalted by having a king of their own, they will be held of so much higher renown in the country from whence they came as that ready enow will their fellow-barbarians be to come at their call, when they bid them to our shores to assist them in the extermination of our race. For ever hath it been their wont to deal treacherously, nor never keep firm faith with none. Wherefore, say I, by us ought they ever more to be not exalted but cast down. When King Vortigern first took them into his service as retainers, they abode here as under a shadowy show of peace, as though they were ready to fight for our country, but as soon as ever they were strong enough openly to manifest their wickedness and to return evil for good they did betray him and wrought grievous slaughter upon the people of his kingdom. Next they did betray Aurelius Ambrosius, unto whom, after vowing the most awful sacraments of allegiance, they gave poison as he sat at meat with them at a banquet. Next, they betrayed Arthur, when, casting aside the allegiance they owed him, they fought against him with his nephew Modred. Last of all, belying their fealty unto King Careticus, they brought in upon him Gormund, King of the Africans, by whose invasion hath the country been reft from the people and the King himself driven forth with shame."

## [3]

WHEN he spake thus, Cadwallo repented him of having harboured the thought of such a covenant, and sent word unto Edwin that he could in no wise persuade his counsellors to agree upon his granting Edwin's petition, for that they said it was against right, and against the ancient traditions of the island that the single sovereignty of the crown should be divided betwixt two crowned heads. Thereat Edwin waxed wroth, and dismissing the conference, he retired into Northumbria, saying that he would wear Cadwallo's crown maugre his head, which, when Cadwallo understood, he sent back word that he would smite off his head under the crown if he durst presume to be crowned within the kingdom of Britain.

## [4]

DISCORD having thus arisen betwixt them, and the men of both having harried the lands of the other in a number of armed forays, both at last met on the further side of Humber, and in the battle that was fought Cadwallo lost many thousands of his men and was put to flight, making his way in such haste as he might through Scotland unto the island of Ireland. But Edwin, after he had won the victory, led his army through the provinces of Britain, and burning the cities, did grievously torment the citizens and husbandsmen. But whilst that he was thus giving a loose unto his cruelty, Cadwallo was ever endeavouring to return unto his country by ships, but could never make shift to do so, for that unto whatsoever haven he steered his course there was Edwin with his host to meet him and forbid his landing. Now there was come unto him a

certain right cunning wizard out of Spain, by name
Pellitus, who was learned in the flight of birds and the
courses of the stars, and did foretell unto him all disaster that might befall, and along of him it was that
Edwin had witting of Cadwallo's return so as thus he
was able to meet him, shatter his ships and drown their
crews, and close every port against him. Cadwallo,
therefore, not knowing what to do, and well-nigh falling into utter despair of ever returning, at last bethought him of going unto Solomon, King of the
Bretons, to ask for help and counsel, so that he might
be able to return unto his country. And as he was making sail for Brittany a wild gale arose of a sudden and
the ships of his companions were so scattered thereby,
as that in a short space no one of them remained by another. The pilot of the King's ship was smitten with
such terror that he let go the rudder and committed the
ship to the guidance of hazard, so that all that night
they lay in peril of death while she tossed hither and
thither upon the heaving of the billows. At dawn upon
the morrow they made a certain island that is called
Guernsey, where with sore travail they made shift to
come ashore. Howbeit, Cadwallo was seized of so sore
grief for the loss of his shipmates that for three days and
nights he loathed all food and lay sick abed. But upon
the fourth day early he was taken with a mighty longing for venison meat, and calling Brian unto him told
him what it was that he did most desire. Brian thereupon took his bow and quiver, and went throughout
the island, so that if good luck should bring any deer
in his way he might take back meat thereof unto Cadwallo. And when he had searched it from end to end
without finding that whereof he was in quest, he was
in grievous straits for that he might not fulfil his lord's
desire, and sore adread lest his sickness should end in
his death were he unable to satisfy his longing. He fell
therefore upon practising a new art. He cut open his
own thigh and took therefrom a slice of the flesh, and

making a spit ready did toast the same thereon and bore it unto the King for venison. Presently, he, weening it to be flesh of deer, began to eat thereof, and was mightily refreshed, much marvelling that never aforetime had he tasted meat so sweet in flavour. At last, when he had eaten his fill, he was of merrier and lighter cheer, insomuch as that after three days he was all sound and whole again. Then, for the wind stood fair, they make ready the ship's outfit, and hoisting sail embark on their deep-sea voyage and make for the city of Kidalet. Then, coming unto King Solomon, they are of him received right kindly as was beseeming men so worshipful, and when he learnt the reason of their coming thither he promised them his help in these words:

[5]

"SORE grief is it unto us, most noble youths, that the land of your grandsires should be thus oppressed of a barbarous folk, and that ye have been ignominiously driven forth from thence. Yet, natheless, seeing that others be able to defend their realms, a marvel is it, meseemeth, that your people should have lost an island so fruitful, and are unable to make stand against this nation of the Angles, whom our own men here do count as nought. For whilst the folk of this my Britain did dwell along with your own folk in your own Britain they did hold dominion over all kingdoms of the provinces, nor was there a people anywhere, save only the Roman people, strong enow to subjugate them. Nor were the Romans themselves able to do this that I have said of their own might, but through the strife that had arisen amongst the nobles of the island. But the Romans, albeit that they held it subject for a time, yet after their rulers were either lost to the island or slain, did either themselves retire therefrom, or else were driven out with shame. But after the Britons came into

the province under their Dukes Maximian and Conan,
the residue that remained behind have never thereafter
enjoyed such privilege as to hold possession of the
crown of the kingdom in unbroken succession. For albeit that many of their princes have maintained the
ancient dignity of their forefathers, yet a still greater
number of feebler heirs have succeeded them who have
lost it utterly when their enemies did invade them.
Hence do I grieve over the weakness of your country,
for that ye be come of the same blood as ourselves, and
are therefore called Britons no less than are our own
folk, who, as ye see, do hold our own against all our
neighbours in arms."

[6]

WHEN he had made an end of speaking thus, with more
to like purpose, Cadwallo, some little shamed, made
answer on this wise:

"Manifold thanks do I render unto thee, O King,
'sprung of grandsires whose great-grandsires were kings,'
for that thou hast promised to help me to recover my
kingdom. Howbeit, this which thou saidst, that it is
marvellous my people have not maintained their ances-
tral dignity sithence the Britons did come into those
provinces meseemeth is in no wise a marvel. For the
more noble of the whole realm did follow the Dukes
thou hast named, and only the ignoble did remain behind and did possess them of their lands and honours.
These, thus suddenly raised to noble rank, were puffed
up by their new dignities far beyond their predecessors.
They were purse-proud by reason of the abundance of
their riches; they waxed wanton for that no sense of
honour did restrain their lust. Amongst them, moreover, as the historian Gildas bears witness, did prevail
that which is the overthrow of all that is good, the hatred of truth and of them that assert the truth—the

love of a lie and of them that do forge lies, the acceptance of the evil for the good, the reverence of iniquity
rather than of charity, the acknowledgment of Satan as
an angel of light. Kings were anointed not for God's
sake, but for that they were more cruel than others;
and were murdered but a brief while thereafter by
them that did anoint them, not by examination of the
truth of any charge against them, but for that they had
chosen others yet more cruel in their stead. If any of
them were more merciful or did seem, even were it but
a little, to show favour unto truth, against him as the
subverter of Britain were hurled all the weapons of
their hatred. Lastly, all things whatsoever that were
pleasing or displeasing unto God they weighed as of
equal account in the balance, if indeed the things that
were hateful did not turn the scale. Therefore did they
all things that were contrary to the safety of the people,
as though the True Physician of all men were unwilling
to bestow healing upon them. And all this was done not
only by worldly laymen, but even by the Lord's own
flock and the shepherd's thereof without distinction.
No cause for marvel, therefore, is it that such degenerate ones, hated of God for sins so grievous, should
have lost the country they had on this wise polluted.
For God was minded to take vengeance upon them
when He suffered a nation of strangers to overrun them
and drive us out of the fields that our fathers did possess. Natheless, a worthy deed it were, so God allow, to
restore our people unto their ancient dignity, but it
should be a lasting reproach unto our race, that we
were feeble rulers, who in this our time laboured
nought to maintain our rights. Moreover, I do with the
more confidence beseech thy help for that we had both
one great-grandfather's grandfather. For Malgo, that
mighty King of Britain who reigned fourth after
Arthur, begat two sons, whereof the one was called
Ennian and the other Run. Ennian was father of Beli,
Beli of Iago, Iago of Cadvan, my father. But Run, who

after his brother's death was driven forth by the invasion of the Saxons, did come hither into this province,
and gave his daughter unto Duke Hoel, the son of Hoel
the Great, who conquered so many kingdoms with
Arthur. Unto him was born Alan, the father of thine
own father Hoel, who, so long as he lived, was no small
terror unto the Gauls."

[7]

In the meantime, while he was spending the winter
with Solomon, they made resolve that Brian should
cross over into Britain and by some means or other
make away with King Edwin's wizard lest by his wonted
craft he should forewarn him of Cadwallo's coming.
Accordingly, after he had landed at Southampton, he
did upon him the garments of a certain poor man,
feigning him to be the poor man himself. He wrought
him a staff of iron sharp at the end wherewith to slay
the wizard in case he should chance to fall in with him,
and then made his way to York, in the which city Edwin was at that time sojourning. And when he was
come thither he joined him with a company of poor
men that waited for alms before the King's door. And
whilst that he was pacing to and fro, behold, his sister
came forth of the great hall, with an ewer in her hand
wherein she was carrying water unto the Queen. She
had been carried off by Edwin from the city of Worcester what time he was wreaking havoc in the provinces
of the Britons after the flight of Cadwallo. When, therefore, she passed in front of Brian, he knew her at once,
and with eyes overflowing with tears called unto her in
a low voice. The damsel, turning her head at his voice,
was at first in doubt who it might be, but when she
drew nigher and recognised her brother, she was like
to have fallen in a swoon for dread lest by any mishap
he should be known and taken by his enemies. Where-

fore, deferring kisses and familiar greetings for the
time, she spake with him as though she were talking of
some other indifferent matter, and told him briefly how
the buildings of the court lay, pointing them out, and
pointing out also the wizard of whom he was in search,
who chanced to be walking up and down amongst the
poor men whilst the alms was being distributed unto
them. Brian, therefore, when he had taken knowledge
of the man, bade his sister steal privily forth of her
chamber the next night and come unto him without
the city hard by a certain old church where he would
await her coming among the dark arches of the place.
He then joined him in amongst the throng of poor folk
in that part where Pellitus was setting them in place,
and the moment there was an opening to smite him, he
lifted up the pilgrim's staff I have already spoken of
and thrust it in under the wizard's chest, and slew him
with that same blow. Instantly he dropped the staff
amongst the throng, and passed on unnoticed, so that
none suspected him, and by God's grace made shift to
reach the hiding-place I have mentioned. But when
night came on, his sister, who tried every endeavour to
get forth and join him, found that get forth she could
not, for that Edwin, affrighted at the murder of Pellitus,
had set watchers round the court, who, spying into
every hidden corner, denied all means of issue. When
Brian made discovery of this, he betook him away from
that place and went unto Exeter, where he called the
Britons together and made known unto them what he
had done. Then, sending messengers unto Cadwallo, he
garrisoned that city and sent word unto all the barons
of the Britons to see to the defences of their castles and
cities, and await in gladness the coming of Cadwallo,
who, having secured the succour of Solomon, was
shortly about to undertake their defence. These tidings
being bruited throughout the whole island, Peanda,
King of the Mercians, with a mighty multitude of
Saxons, came to Exeter and beleaguered Brian therein.

## [ 8 ]

MEANWHILE Cadwallo landed in Britain with ten thousand men whom King Solomon had placed under his command, and soon made his way towards Exeter where King Peanda was holding the leaguer; and when he drew anigh, he divided his men into four companies and lost no time before he fell upon the enemy. And when he joined battle, Peanda was forthwith taken prisoner and his army utterly put to the rout. And when he saw that none other way of safety was open to him he made his submission unto Cadwallo, and gave hostages, pledging him to do battle along with him against the Saxons. Having thus won the victory over him, Cadwallo called his barons together, who for a long time past had slipped out of his hands, and made for Northumbria against Edwin, never ceasing to lay waste the country on his march. When this was reported unto Edwin, he summoned all the petty Kings of the Angles to join him, and, meeting Cadwallo in the field that is called Hatfield, did battle with the Britons. The fighting was quickly over. Edwin was slain and wellnigh all the folk he had with him, as also was his son Offrid, and Godbold, King of the Orkneys, who had come to help him.

## [ 9 ]

HAVING obtained this victory, Cadwallo marched through all the provinces of the Angles, and wrought such havoc upon the Saxons as that scarce would he spare the womankind or the tender years of their little ones, putting all that he found to most grievous torture, forasmuch as he was minded utterly to sweep the English race out of the bounds of Britain. Then next he fought a battle with Osric, who had succeeded **Edwin,** and slew him with his two nephews who ought of right to have reigned after him, as also slew he Aedan, **King** of the Scots, who had come to their assistance.


[ 10 ]


AFTER all these were slain, Oswald succeeded to the kingdom of Northumberland, whom, with the rest of them that had fought against him, Cadwallo drove fleeing before him as far as the wall in that province which Severus the Emperor had builded of old betwixt England and Scotland. Then, afterward, he sent Peanda, King of the Mercians, and the more part of his army unto that place to do battle with him. But Oswald, one night when he was beleaguered by the aforesaid Peanda in the place called Hevenfeld, that is the Field of Heaven, did there set up a Cross of the Lord, and gave orders unto his fellow-soldiers that they should cry aloud at the very topmost of their voices in these words: "Let us all bend our knees before the living and true God Almighty, beseeching Him with one accord that He deliver us from the proud army of the British King and of his accursed commander Peanda, for He himself knoweth that we have undertaken these just wars for the salvation of our country." All did according as they had been commanded, and, marching forth against the enemy at early dawn, they did achieve the victory which the merit of their faith had deserved. When word of this was brought unto Cadwallo, he, blazing out into fiery wrath, collected his army and followed in pursuit of the holy King Oswald, and in the midst of a battle that was fought at the place called Bourne, Peanda did fall upon him and slay him.

## [ 11 ]

OSWALD being thus slain along with many thousands of his men, his brother Oswi succeeded him in the kingdom of Northumbria, and by dint of heavy bribes of gold and silver given to Cadwallo, who now possessed the empire of all Britain, did obtain his peace and became his vassal. Thereupon his brother Alfrid, and Ordwald, his brother's son, raised an insurrection against him. But when they found that they could in no wise stand against him, they fled away unto Peanda, King of the Mercians, imploring him that he would collect an army and go with them to the further side Humber to reave Oswi of his kingdom. But Peanda, for that he was adread of breaking the peace which King Cadwallo had established throughout the realm of Britain, deferred starting any disturbance without his leave until such time as he could in some way or another work upon him either to march against King Oswi himself, or at least grant him licence to do battle with him. When, therefore, King Cadwallo held high court one Whitsuntide and celebrated the festival by wearing the crown of Britain in London, and all of the Kings of the Angles save Oswi alone, and all the Dukes of the Britons were present, Peanda went unto the King and asked him wherefore Oswi alone was absent when all the rest of the princes of the Saxons were there? And when Cadwallo made answer that it was by reason of a sickness that lay upon him, Peanda went on to tell him that Oswi had sent for Saxons into Germany that he might revenge the death of his brother Oswald upon them both. He added, moreover, that he had broken the King's peace, seeing that he alone had begun the war and contention betwixt them when he had driven Ethelfrid, King of Northumbria, and Ordwald, his brother's son, forth of their kingdom by levying war

against them. He did therefore further beseech leave
to be allowed either to slay him or to drive him forth
of his kingdom.


[12]


THE KING, therefore, whose own thoughts were somewhat divided betwixt the divers aspects of the matter,
called his familiars apart and bade them declare their
opinions upon a case of the kind. And after much counsel had been given, Margadud, King of the South
Welsh, spake amongst the rest:

"My Lord, seeing that it hath ever been thy purpose
to drive the race of the Angles forth of the frontiers of
Britain, wherefore shouldst thou now turn aside from
thy resolve and suffer them to live in peace in our
midst? Go to, now! Give them leave at least to fall out
amongst themselves and slaughter one another at will
until they shall have exterminated themselves from our
land! No faith is to be kept with one that is ever hatch-
ing of treason and laying of snares to catch him unto
whom of right he oweth fealty. These Saxons, in sooth,
ever since they did first set foot in our country have
never done naught but lurk in ambush to betray our
folk. What faith ought we to keep with them? Give
Peanda leave to make war upon Oswi the swiftest he
may, that thus they may kill one another in civil discord
to their hearts' content and our island be rid of the
whole pack of them!"


[13]


WITH these and many other words, Cadwallo was prevailed upon to grant Peanda leave to do battle with
Oswi. Peanda accordingly got together a huge army,
marched to the Humber, and laying waste that province

of the country, began to harass that King in bitter
earnest. Oswi, thereby reduced to his last shift, promised
him numberless right royal treasures and bribes beyond
all belief to put an end to the havoc he was wreaking,
abandon the invasion he had begun and go quietly
home. And when he found that he could in no wise prevail upon him to grant his entreaties, the King, relying
on divine succour, albeit that his army were the smaller,
gave him battle nigh the river Winwed, and won a victory wherein Peanda, together with thirty Dukes, was
slain. Peanda being thus killed, Wulfred his son, by
grant of Cadwallo, succeeded him in the kingdom. He,
leaguing himself with Ebba and Edbert, Dukes of the
Mercians, rebelled against Oswi, but at the command
of Cadwallo made peace with him. At last, at the end
of eight-and-forty years, Cadwallo, that most noble and
puissant King of the Britons, borne down by old age
and sickness, departed this life upon the fifteenth of the
Kalends of December. The Britons embalmed his body
with balsams and sweet-scented condiments, and set it
with marvellous art within a brazen image cast to the
measure of his stature. This image, moreover, in armour of wondrous beauty and craftsmanship, they set
upon a brazen horse above the West Gate of London
in token of the victory I have spoken of, and as a terror
unto the Saxons. They did likewise build beneath it a
church in honour of St. Martin, wherein are divine
services celebrated for him and the faithful departed.

[ 14 ]

CADWALLADER his son succeeded him in the government
of the kingdom, a youth whom Bede calleth Caedwald.
In the beginning he maintained him stoutly and made
good peace, but after he had worn the crown twelve
years he fell into feeble health and civil dissension
brake out amongst the Britons. His mother was the sis-

ter of Peanda but only on her father's side, Peanda being born of a different mother; she was sprung from a noble family of Gwent. It was after King Cadwallo had entered into the covenant of amity with her brother Peanda that he took her to wife and that she bare him Cadwallader.

## [ 15 ]

HE, therefore, as I began to tell ye, falling sick, the Britons begin to quarrel, and by their accursed discords destroy the wealth of the country. A second calamity, moreover, followeth on the first, for a deadly and memorable famine fell upon the foolish folk, insomuch as that every province was empty of all sustenance of food, save only such partial provision as the huntsman's art could supply. And upon the heels of this famine followed a pestilence of death so grievous as that in a brief space so great was the multitude of people laid low, the living were not enough to bury the dead. By reason whereof, the miserable remnant of the people forsaking their own country in flocks did make their way unto lands oversea, with mighty lamentation chanting under the folds of the sails: "Thou hast given us, O Lord, even as sheep unto the slaughter, and amongst the nations hast Thou scattered us." Yea, even King Cadwallader himself, voyaging with his wretched fleet for Brittany, did make addition unto the lamentation on this wise: "Woe unto us, miserable sinners, for our grievous iniquities, wherewith we have never ceased to offend against God so long as space was granted unto us for repentance! Wherefore the vengeance of His might lieth thus heavy upon us, and doth uproot us from our native soil, albeit that never were the Romans of old nor after them the Scots nor the Picts nor even the crafty treasons of the Saxons able to exterminate our people. In vain have we so oft recovered our country from them, seeing that it was not God's will we should reign therein for ever. He, the true Judge, when He saw that in no wise were we minded to cease from our iniquities and that no man could drive us forth of the kingdom, willed Himself to chastise our folly, and hath now directed against us this visitation of His wrath whereby we are compelled to forsake our own country by multitudes at a time. Now, therefore, return ye Romans; ye Scots and Picts return; return, ye marauding Saxons! Behold, Britain lieth open unto ye! She that never might ye avail to dispeople, hath by the wrath of God been now left desolate! Not your valour driveth us forth, but the might of Him that is over all, the God whom never hath our people been slow to offend."

### [ 16 ]

In the midst of these and other lamentations was Cadwallader borne forth unto the shore of Brittany, and upon his landing, came with all his multitude unto King Alan, nephew of Solomon, and by him was worthily received. Britain, therefore, deserted of all her people save some few whom death had spared in the parts of Wales for a space of eleven years together, became a place abhorred even of the Britons themselves; nor, in sooth, did the Saxons find it a home to be desired at that same time, for they, too, died therein without intermission. But when the deadly plague had ceased, the remnant of them, true unto their ancient wont, sent word unto their fellow-countrymen in Germany, telling them that now the island of Britain was deserted of her own people they might lightly take possession thereof, so only they would come together and dwell therein. So, when they understood these tidings, that accursed folk, collecting a countless host of men and women, landed in the parts of Northumbria and inhabited the desolated provinces from Scotland even

unto Cornwall. For none indweller was there to say
them nay, save only the few and needy little remnants
of the Britons that had survived and herded together
in the forest fastnesses of Wales. From that time the
power of the Britons ceased in the island, and the English began to reign.

# [17]

THEN, after some brief space of time had elapsed and
the Saxon people had thus been reinforced, Cadwallader, bethinking him that his kingdom was now
purged from the contagion of the plague, besought help
of Alan that he might be restored unto his former kingdom. But when the King had granted his petition, behold, even as he was fitting out his fleet, the Voice of an
Angel spake unto him in thunder, forbidding him to
emprise the adventure, for that God had willed the
Britons should no longer reign in Britain before that
time should come whereof Merlin had prophesied unto
Arthur. The Voice bade him, moreover, that he should
go unto Pope Sergius at Rome, where, after due penance done, he should be numbered amongst the blessed.
Yet, further, the Voice told him that the people of the
Britons should again possess the island by merit of their
faith when the appointed time should come, but that
this time should not be until the Britons had obtained
his relics and had translated them from Rome into
Britain. Then, when the relics had likewise been revealed of the other saints, which had been hidden away
by reason of the invasion of the Paynims, they should
recover the kingdom they had lost. And when this message had been spoken in the ears of the holy man, he
went straightway unto King Alan and made known
unto him that which had been revealed unto himself.

## [18]

THEN Alan took divers books, as that of the prophecies of the Eagle that did prophesy at Shaftesbury, and of the songs of Sibyl and Merlin, and began to search all things that were therein to see whether Cadwallader's revelation did agree with the written oracles. And when he found no discrepancy therein, he did counsel Cadwallader to be obedient unto the divine dispensation, and foregoing all thought of recovering Britain, to perform that which the angelic monition had bidden him. He counselled him, moreover, to send his son Ivor and his nephew Ini to rule over the remnant of the Britons in the island, lest the people born of their ancient race should lose their freedom by the invasion of the barbarians. Then Cadwallader, renouncing worldly things for the sake of God and His kingdom everlasting, came unto Rome, and was confirmed by Pope Sergius, and no long time after, being smitten of a sudden lethargy, upon the twelfth day of the Kalends of May in the year of Our Lord's incarnation, six hundred and eighty-nine, was released from the contagion of the flesh and did enter into the hall of the kingdom of Heaven.

## [19]

WHEN Ivor and Ini had got ships together, they raised all the men they could, and made for the island, where for nine-and-sixty years they harassed the English people, and did most cruelly raid their lands, but all to little avail. For the said pestilence and famine and customary dissensions had so caused this proud people to degenerate that they could no longer keep their foes at a distance. And, as barbarism crept in, they were no longer called Britons but Welsh, a word derived either from Gualo, one of their Dukes, or from Guales, their Queen, or else from their being barbarians. But the Saxons did wiselier, kept peace and concord amongst themselves, tilled their fields and builded anew their cities and castles, and thus throwing off the sovereignty of the Britons, held the empire of all England under their Duke Athelstan, who was the first to wear a crown amongst them. But the Welsh, degenerating from the nobility of the Britons, never afterwards recovered the sovereignty of the island, but on the contrary, quarrelling at one time amongst themselves, and at another with the Saxons, never ceased to have bloodshed on hand either in public or private feud.

## [20]

HOWBEIT, their Kings who from that time have succeeded in Wales I hand over in the matter of writing unto Caradoc of Llancarfan, my contemporary, as do I those of the Saxons unto William of Malmesbury and Henry of Huntingdon, whom I bid be silent as to the Kings of the Britons, seeing that they have not that book in the British speech which Walter, Archdeacon of Oxford, did convey hither out of Brittany, the which being truly issued in honour of the aforesaid princes, I have on this wise been at the pains of translating into the Latin speech.

## THE END

# SPECIAL DEDICATIONS

*(At the end of Book I, Chapter 1, in what was no doubt a special presentation copy of his book, Geoffrey added the following paragraph:)*

Do thou, also, Galeran, Count of Meulan, our other pillar of the realm, lend thine assistance that, under the combined direction of you both, the issue of my book now made public may shine forth in an even fairer light. For thee, sprung from the race of that most renowned King Charlemagne, hath thy mother, Philosophy, taken unto her bosom and indocrinated thee in the subtleties of her sciences and afterward directed thee unto the camps of kings that thou mightest achieve renown in knightly exercises, wherein, valiantly surpassing thy comrades-in-arms, thou hast learnt to stand forth as a terror unto thine enemies and as a protection unto thine own people. Being, therefore, as thou art, the trusty protection of them that are thine own, receive myself, thy prophet-bard, and this my book, issued for thine own delectation, under thy protection, so that lying at mine ease beneath the guardianship of so far-spreading a tree, I may be able to pipe my lays upon the reed of mine own muse in safe security even in the face of the envious and the wicked.

*(In another presentation copy Geoffrey changed the last paragraph of Book I, Chapter 1, to read as a dedication to "Stephen, King of England, . . . nephew of the illustrious Henry, King of the English . . ." This was followed by the paragraph translated above, which was reworded to read as a secondary dedication to "Robert, Earl of Gloucester, . . . sprung from that most renowned King Henry. . . .")*
*(See Bibliographical Note, p. xxv)*

# INDEX TO INDIVIDUAL CHAPTERS

*(Arabic figures refer to the Chapters, Italic figures to the Pages.)*

267

# INDEX OF PERSONAL NAMES

*(Roman figures refer to the Books, Arabic figures to the Chapters.)*

271

## INDEX OF PLACE NAMES

*(Roman figures refer to the Books, Arabic figures to the Chapters.)*

# INDEX OF FOLK-LORE AND LEGEND

*(Roman figures refer to the Books, Arabic figures to the Chapters.)*